Rekindling Commitment

DENNIS T. JAFFE
CYNTHIA D. SCOTT
GLENN R. TOBE

How to Revitalize
Yourself, Your Work, and
Your Organization

Rekindling
Commitment

Jossey-Bass Publishers · San Francisco

Substantial discounts on bulk quantities of Jossey-Bass books are available to corporations, professional associations, and other organizations. For details and discount information, contact the special sales department at Jossey-Bass Inc., Publishers. (415) 433-1740; Fax (415) 433-0499.

Library of Congress Cataloging-in-Publication Data

Jaffe, Dennis T.
    Rekindling commitment : how to revitalize yourself, your work, and your organization / Dennis Jaffe, Cynthia Scott, Glenn Tobe. —1st ed.
      p.   cm. — (The Jossey-Bass management series)
    Includes bibliographical references and index.
    ISBN 1-55542-704-9
    1. Organizational change. 2. Employee motivation. I. Scott, Cynthia D. II. Tobe, Glenn R. III. Title. IV. Series.
HD58.8.J34 1994   94-9266
658.4′06—dc20   CIP

FIRST EDITION
HB Printing 10 9 8 7 6 5 4 3 2 1   *Code 9471*

The Jossey-Bass Management Series

CONTENTS

PREFACE

This is an era of turmoil and transition for organizations and those who work in them. It is a time when we urgently need to renew and reinvigorate ourselves, our corporations, and all the institutions in our society. We believe that we are all responsible for helping our organizations make the changes they need, for if we don't, nobody else will.

In many ways, our organizations are failing us, and in failing us, they are losing our allegiance. More and more people are withdrawing from their companies, from their government, from the hope that our world can significantly improve. In the past decade, the economic strength of the United States and its ability to succeed have been questioned. The concerns go beyond whether we, as a nation, have the will to succeed in the competitive global marketplace. The question is whether organizations can develop employees who have the skills for the task and who want to contribute to making the organization work. In more personal terms, the question is "Why should I give to the organization?" This book is our attempt at an answer.

WHY REKINDLE COMMITMENT?

Commitment is the glue that binds us to our organization, whether that organization is a corporation, a public agency, a school, a service firm, or a partnership. The commonality among them all is that they are places where people give their personal service and invest their energy.

Our investment can be deep or shallow, broad or narrow, limited or comprehensive. If, as employees, our commitment is low, then our connection to the organization is weak and we offer less of our energy and skills in its service. High commitment leads to the opposite result: We *want* to give our energy and skills. We believe that people really want to make a difference and that they have more skills and abilities than organizations are using; in fact, what people want to give is what organizations need most.

The demands on organizations today are so great that they cannot operate without high commitment from their employees. But too many organizations have needlessly alienated their key resource—their employees. With downsizing, cost-cutting, mergers, and other changes, employees have been given the distinct feeling that they are simply costs to be trimmed. Those who are left are told to work harder to keep their jobs. They are asked to sacrifice and give up benefits. This atmosphere does not exactly inspire high morale, or a willingness to take responsibility. Instead, employees feel betrayed and have lost faith in their organizations. The effect of organizational upheaval has been increasing distrust and the employees' decision to look out for themselves.[1]

There is a crisis of the spirit in the workplace. As work demands more and more of people, they become more susceptible to burnout—unless they get something fair and meaningful from the organization in return. What people want is not just higher pay and more benefits. They want to work where they are able to give their best and where work is meaningful and rewarding in a personal sense. Unfortunately, organizations and their leaders don't always act on the fact that there is a growing convergence between what individuals want from their work and what organizations need from them.

Rekindling employee commitment is the primary challenge facing organizations today. Rebuilding trust may become the theme in the workplace as we move into the next century. Trust is the key to gain people's willingness to give.

We suggest that trust requires a very different kind of company: to regain trust, the organizations themselves have to change. New workplaces are emerging in every industry and in public institutions, as each copes with the dilemmas of how to get employees to meet new demands on the organization. From the changes taking place in today's forerunner organizations, we can see a preview of what the future organization will look like. The company that builds high commitment is less hierarchical than the traditional workplace. It is continually evolving, learning, and redefining in response to a vision of the future. It shows trust and respect for employees, and it sees the relationship between good business and this trust.

COMMITMENT AND EMPOWERMENT

We use the term *empowerment* to define the process that builds commitment in the workplace. Using this term was somewhat risky for us. It is out of favor with some managers because they associate it with chaos, selfishness, self-indulgence, and a workplace that is out of control. But empowering people does not mean telling them they can do what they wish and they aren't accountable for the results. Rather, it is allowing people to make decisions and do what they think is right in order to get the results for which they are held accountable. Empowerment is thus personal power released within the context of organizational needs.

Because empowerment begins with the individual's realization of his or her own power to make a difference, we begin with the role of the individual. The individual influences and helps the work group to grow, and the group does the same for the organization. This book will show you how to release the empowerment resource within yourself and use it to revitalize your work, your team, and your organization.

Empowerment is a contagious skill. When you use it, it spreads to other people. So empowerment solves several problems that come up in the high-pressure workplace:

- It resolves issues of commitment, by supporting people's desire for meaning, purpose, and community at work. Empowerment allows people to see the link between what they value and the work of the organization; it makes them feel important.

- It creates a workplace where people are healthier and able to continue high-pressure work over time. It provides people with the resources and tools to deal with stress and frustration by meeting challenges and building control.

- It develops the urge to make a difference and it harnesses all to the goal of moving the traditional organization toward the new organizational form.

Empowerment and change frequently start in the middle and move up the organization rather than from the top down. Many new ideas get to the top through the leadership of empowered people throughout the organization. Empowered employees look beyond the limited responsibilities of getting their own jobs done to see that they also need to be responsible for helping the organization to grow and change.

We propose a new basis for the work contract between individual and organization—*the empowerment contract*, a work agreement between two mature, responsible, honest adults. We suggest that it is through this kind of contract that we can re-build and renew our commitment to our organizations.

Organizations today need a particular form of empowered employees, whom we define as *change leaders*. We must help our organizations change by taking leadership and doing what has to be done. We may well be stretching ourselves or acting outside of the boundaries of expected behavior. But only by taking such risks will we really feel connected to the organization, and only if we risk doing what is right will the organization be likely to grow and meet the challenges it faces. The role is not always comfort-able. But organizations need employees who challenge them, and who "push the envelope" so that companies are not merely reacting but creating change.

It is true that when we begin to stand up for change, our jobs can be endangered. But, in fact, everyone's job is endan-gered all the time today. The choice is simply whether we want to plunge in with new methods or remain behind the wave.

Empowered individuals and groups begin to help the orga-nization redesign itself. The empowered organization is the one people envision when asked to picture their ideal workplace, where they could work to their highest capacity. Empowerment expands everyone's capacity to work, and thereby adds to the capability of the organization to respond to a difficult environ-ment. Even more important, empowerment has positive per-sonal effects. Empowered people stop feeling like victims and begin feeling a sense of mastery over their lives. Empowerment leads to action and to self-development. This in turn increases self-esteem and the ability to get what one wants in life.

THE PURPOSE AND PERSPECTIVE OF THIS BOOK

Our purpose in this book is not to tell people what they already know—that organizations with committed employees work bet-ter and feel better than others or that some individual work-places are great places to work. Our purpose is to help those individuals within organizations who are concerned about their own commitment to take steps to deepen their bond with their organizations. The old work contract has been shredded; people and companies need to find a new basis for working together. Employees are often waiting for senior management to change before they change. This is a costly waiting game for both the person and the organization. Valuable human and organizational capital is lost. Although responsibility is shared, the individual employee can take the first steps rather than wait in frustration for the company to act.

We offer a somewhat unusual perspective in this book, much needed in this time of continual change. Business books usually address top management—telling the CEO or management about what the company needs to do to be successful. They talk about the need for leadership during change and focus on how the top leadership needs to be on board. Other books focus on individual improvement strategies, telling individuals how to improve their own status and power or how to develop particular skills.

Neither of these perspectives is sufficient to solve the whole problem. We have encountered chief executives and senior managers who gripe about explaining their vision one more time and are frustrated in their attempts to help people change their behavior. We have also seen individuals re-create themselves and become active and empowered only to find the organizational structure and culture unable to change with them. Individuals reading more typical management books may see opportunities for their company and for themselves, but they may also respond by turning off or distancing. This gap can be bridged only through a combination of perspectives, which together form a holistic perspective of organizational renewal. With this perspective, we turn the traditional management book on its head.

In *Rekindling Commitment*, we write about the role of the individual in redesigning the organization. Our message is that organizational renewal is a task for everyone. The future of the organization (and therefore of continued employment for everyone) and of the competitiveness of our nation rests on developing a positive partnership between the individual and the organization. Individuals in organizations need to secure their futures by taking responsibility for the repair and redefinition of their workplace.

There is no magic cure. Renewal is not the sole responsibility of the executive and his or her team. It will require a more intensive involvement from many individuals and managers who all take on responsibility. Therefore, in focusing on the need for leadership, we emphasize that leadership is not restricted to the few at the top. Leadership is a general capacity that everyone in the company can develop. The new organization needs scores of leaders in order to succeed.

The old skills are not enough to build the new organization. To do so we must question ourselves deeply and make major changes. Similarly, organizations cannot successfully change without first helping people change. Yet a single focus on either the organization or the individual is not enough. The change to an empowered environment can only result from a partnership.

This book is our heartful attempt to explore how employees and their organizations can work together to renew their organizations. It is the result of over ten years of grappling with these issues. Our clients have included large companies, start-ups and family businesses, government and public agencies, and schools and health care systems. Despite their differences, many of their dilemmas are the same. We have helped our clients close plants with dignity, develop careers, build teamwork and participation, reengineer divisions, reframe research and development agendas, redeploy their human resources, develop educational ventures, and increase people's ability to manage and master change. As behavioral scientists, we draw our models from the study of the dynamics of individual change, organizational design, and systems theory. The individual, team, and organization all experience change. Change in one forms the foundation for change in the others. In writing this book, we are trying to develop the technology of managing people through the needed transitions.

WHO SHOULD
READ THIS BOOK?

This book is intended for managers and employees who face the challenge of building an empowered organization. There are not many employees for whom this does not hold true—from the people in the executive suite to those in entry-level positions. This book is for the people who see the need for the organization to change and who are concerned with the dilemmas and challenges they face. It is written for people who want to move from despair to action, who have decided that their best future lies in helping the organization make its future work. We do not deny that there are lots of reasons for people to feel pain in today's workplace. But our message is that there is much people can do to emerge from despair and frustration and make a difference. We want to help people manage change and respond to change with high performance rather than burnout.

Many employees of traditional organizations, often called "dinosaurs" because of their difficulty in adapting to change, are wondering if their organizations need to become extinct before the way can be paved for new types of organizations. Our experience tells us that there is hope for the traditional organization: The renewed commitment of key employees is sometimes enough to initiate a process of renewal and transformation. Thus this book is also for the concerned employee of traditional workplaces.

OVERVIEW OF THE CONTENTS

This is a handbook on how to change yourself in order to become an effective partner in changing your organization. We show you how to shift from seeing yourself as a manager or as an employee, with a limited role, to being a leader of change. What we are saying is not new. Many others have already chronicled the organizational and individual shifts we highlight.[2] But we provide a set of tools to enable you to make specific individual and organizational changes and we provide the maps that guide you through individual and organizational learning. Each chapter focuses on one key element in rebuilding commitment through developing empowerment.

In Part One, a powerful wake-up call is sounded, highlighting the importance of being a leader of change rather than a victim. The first chapter outlines the major changes taking place in the workplace, and how an individual needs to learn the four key skills of commitment, challenge, control, and connection. Chapter Two explores what people want from their work, and how personal and organizational values define the new role the individual will play in the future of the organization. In Chapter Three we define empowerment, explain the role of the change leader, and show why the individual needs to take the lead in revitalizing the organization. Chapter Four presents the process of empowerment: the linking of inner commitment with responsible action. This chapter talks about how people can learn to take responsibility—for themselves and for the organization.

In Part Two, we look at leading the process of change, providing some maps for organizational change, and showing how individuals can guide the process. Chapter Five outlines the nature of the new empowered workplace and explains how such workplaces are emerging in many organizations. The chapter shows how the traditional pyramid model for organizations is giving way to the new circle model of the empowered organization. It looks at how a company can make the shift from one model to the other. Chapter Six looks at the importance of values, mission, and vision. Because the journey from the old to the new is often upsetting and full of inner conflict and trauma, in Chapter Seven we examine the emotional dynamics of the shift from the old to the new. The chapter details how change leaders can help themselves, and the people around them, navigate through the four phases of response to transition—denial, resistance, exploration, and commitment.

Part Three focuses on building commitment together, examining how people can bring their new skills into their team and their organization and work with others to support the new workplace. Chapters Eight and Nine look at two key processes for maintaining the new workplace: partnership and learning. Although everyone in an organization must benefit from this atmosphere, the chapters look at how an individual leader can begin to practice partnership and learning within the context of his or her own work group. Chapter Eight shows how work relationships can become working partnerships by fostering collaboration, mutuality, and respect. The ways that individuals, teams, and whole organizations can learn and grow are the subject of Chapter Nine. This chapter focuses especially on how teams can learn how to create a climate that promotes learning and change, rather than stability and avoidance.

The Epilogue is a call to action, asking you to define your personal commitment to becoming a change leader.

TAKING STEPS TO THE FUTURE

By selecting this book, we believe that you have decided not to withdraw in response to current work frustrations and challenges. We hope that you will read this book because you want to make a difference and are looking for guidance in making that wish a reality.

Rekindling Commitment invites you to be a leader in the process of renewing and revitalizing your workplace and the other institutions of society. Each chapter should provide you with some ways to make a difference. If you feel helpless or victimized in your workplace, we want you to see that you have a choice: not to ignore your feelings but to engage your company directly and helpfully. You *can* rebuild your commitment and connection to your organization. We suggest that you become a change leader, see what your organization can become, and find some ways to help move it to that future. We suggest that you, our reader, are right now the most likely person to help your organization grow.

ACKNOWLEDGMENTS

First and foremost we want to thank our fellow HeartWorkers who share with us the work of transforming organizations: Catherine Anderson, Mary Diggins, Peter Howard, Renee Levi, Mary Ellen O'Hara, Kathleen Osta, Marcia Ruben, and Karen Spangenberger.

We also thank the other colleagues from whom we have learned much, including Marge Balazs, Lael Berkstresser, David Bork, Alan Briskin, Hal Colbom, Leslie Dashew, Andy Elkind, Richard Feller, Dan Flora, Sam Lane, Robert Levering, Kate Ludeman, Malcolm Macfarlane, Will McWhinney, Keith Merron, William Miller, Jordan Paul, Therese Rowley, David Sibbett, Rita Solnet, and Betty Vivado.

We are excited about what we are reading and learning about the growing field of organizational transformation. We want to thank the researchers who have influenced us, including Chris Argyris, Judith Bardwick, Gregory Bateson, Terrence Deal, W. Edwards Deming, Riane Eisler, Charles Hampden-Turner, Paul Hawken, Rosabeth Kanter, John Kotter, Jim Kouzes, Ed Lawler, Gareth Morgan, Ed Schein, Peter Senge, Bill Torbert, and Marvin Weisbord.

Dennis Jaffe's students and the graduates and colleagues at Saybrook Institute have contributed good ideas, careful reading of manuscripts, and a stimulating environment. He would like to particularly thank Kathryn Alexander, Bela Banathy, Kat Barclay, Anna Ewins, Bob Hammer, Hellen Hemphill, Tom Potterfield, Al Pozos, Richard Snyder, and Eva Vincze.

We would also like to thank Healthy Companies, the project funded by the MacArthur Foundation, and its director, Bob Rosen, for their support during the writing of this book, including the funding of the Staying Power conference held at Ford/ UAW National Education Center in 1993. This conference, under the joint sponsorship of Ford and the United Auto Workers, looked at the long-term effects of participation programs. The members of the Research Council of Healthy Companies, including Irving Bluestone of Wayne State University, Joel Cutcher-Gershenfeld of Michigan State University, Michelle Hunt of Herman Miller, Elsa Porter of Maccoby and Associates, Ernie Savoie of Ford, and Alan Westin of Columbia University, provided a forum for discussion of leading-edge ideas in organization. The World Business Academy has also been helpful and supportive. Special thanks to John Adams, Rinaldo Brutoco, Willis Harman, Michael Ray, and John Renisch.

We also thank the members of the companies in the American Management Association, The Executive Committee, the Healthcare Forum, the *Inc.* Magazine Growing the Company conferences, the Organization Development Network, and the Young Presidents' Organization for providing forums and sharing experiences and insights into high commitment. And we extend our thanks to *Healthcare Forum Journal*, *Nation's Business*, and *Vision/Action* for publishing portions of this book.

Jossey-Bass has been more than a publisher—they have been a collaborator and friend, nurturing the project from idea to reality. Bill Hicks and Cedric Crocker have been our midwives, and Cheryl Greenway, Terri Welch, Laura Simonds, and many others have been there for us. Special thanks also to Jan Hunter for her peerless editing, and to the anonymous reviewers for their helpful suggestions.

THE AUTHORS

Dennis Jaffe, Cynthia Scott, and Glenn Tobe are the founders and principals of HeartWork Inc., a San Francisco consulting and training company that designs programs and helps organizations learn to rebuild employee commitment and manage change. Their other books on organization include *Take This Job and Love It* (1988), *Self-Renewal* (1989), *Empowerment* (1992), *Organizational Vision, Values and Mission* (1993), and *Managing Change* (1994). Their programs—Activating Empowerment, Managing the Human Side of Change, The Learning Organization, Teaming for Quality, and Take This Job and Love It—have helped thousands of people inside companies learn the new competencies and build teams to create the organizations of the future. HeartWork has worked with over three hundred large and small companies to design programs for change, including IBM, ITT, Aetna, General Mills, Hewlett-Packard, AT&T, The Gap, Kaiser Permanente, Estee Lauder, Intel, National Semiconductor, Principal Financial Group, GMIS, and Dow Corning. The HeartWork video "Managing People Through Change" was selected by *Human Resource Executive* as one of the best products of 1990. The authors have been frequent presenters at conferences and executive retreats.

Dennis T. Jaffe is professor at Saybrook Institute in San Francisco, where he guides the doctoral program in organizational inquiry. He received his B.A. degree (1967) in philosophy, his M.A. degree (1969) in organizational behavior, and his Ph.D. degree (1974) in sociology from Yale University. For two years Jaffe was deputy chair of the Research Council of Healthy Companies, a national research and education effort of resources to create the new workplace.

Cynthia D. Scott received her B.A. degree (1975) in anthropology from the University of California, Berkeley, her Master of Public Health degree (1977) from the University of Michigan, and her Ph.D. degree (1983) from Fielding Institute.

Glenn R. Tobe received his B.S. degree (1978) in business administration from Columbia Pacific University and his M.A. degree (1983) in clinical psychology from John F. Kennedy University. He has been involved in developing high-performance workplaces for nearly a dozen years. He also focuses on the quality methodology of the Malcolm Baldrige process for organizational excellence.

Rekindling Commitment

Part One

EMPOWERING YOURSELF

1
Learn the New Competencies: Commitment, Control, Challenge, and Connection

If America is to win in the new global competition, we need to begin telling one another a new story in which companies compete by drawing on the talent and creativity of all their employees, not just a few maverick inventors and dynamic CEOs. Competitive advantage today comes from continuous, incremental innovation and refinement of a variety of ideas that spread throughout the organization.

—Robert Reich, *Entrepreneurship Reconsidered*

The call for organizational change resounds from many directions. Employees, managers, and executives are taking up the challenge to create environments where both commitment and results flourish. The need is for deep, transformative change for everyone in the organization. The question that begs to be answered is "What does change mean?" or, more specifically, "How must I change?"

Change is a collaborative effort, fueled by a clear vision and a lot of hard work. It requires thousands of linked steps from people at all levels of the organization, whose efforts enable the business to rekindle its commitment and restore productivity. The story of National Semiconductor illustrates the organizational and individual themes that are called into question during the process of change.

3

Facing the challenge of eleven quarters in the red, obsolete technology, and a corporate culture based on expediency and re-action, Gil Amelio waded into deep waters when he took over as CEO of National Semiconductor. When he entered, Amelio found many positive qualities in the culture: a tradition of hard work, many talented individuals who very much wanted to find a way to "win," islands of good technology, and global name recog-nition. On the negative side, he found an overly centralized structure, without mechanisms for coordinating efforts across the company, lack of clear measures to define success, no strate-gic plan for the future, and a reward system that was not tied to performance. His task was to revitalize the organization and to renew employees' commitment to making radical changes.

As National refocused its effort, it became clear that certain products would not be part of the plan for the future. One of the plant managers, Jim Baxter, realized that his job would be to phase out a product line, to keep people committed to the very end, and to close the plant with dignity. How could he take the lead on something that he did not fully support? What would happen to him and to all the people he worked with?

For Rick, who worked in one of the product development teams, the transition was equally personal. His manager was sud-denly talking about empowerment, change, and Rick's new role in the organization. What did this mean as far as Rick's job was concerned? How could he adapt to all these changes? Amid his fear and confusion, he felt his job commitment slipping away; he didn't feel the way he previously had about his job or the company—and he missed that feeling.

Along with all the others at the company, Gil, Jim, and Rick faced enormous challenges. In discussing those challenges, Gil likened the organizational cultures of companies today to three cities. The first city is a helter-skelter maze of streets, none of which bear street signs. The second is laid out on a grid with a river as a boundary. Its avenues run numerically and its streets are alphabetical, and all bear street signs. The third city has every organizational advantage of the second, but it also has a police officer at every corner who must give permission to pass.

Gil hoped to create a structure like that of the second city at National. His attention was focused on creating an environment in which people were empowered to move toward their destination within the bounds of a well-defined framework, were held accountable and responsible, and had a sense of ownership and commitment about their actions. This, he recognized, was no easy task. He knew that, in order to bring about the sweeping changes needed to revitalize the company, people would have to overcome their natural resistance. He also knew that most people value their work and want their company to thrive. They want not just to continue to have a job but to do meaningful work and take pride in their organization. Gil's commitment to National grew as he assumed progressively greater responsibility; he saw that what he had to do was at once simple and complex: He had to help everyone in the organization gain that sense of ownership and responsibility.

Everyone had to live National's values and vision; they had to become more competitive, cost-conscious, empowered, self-directed, high-performing, ethical, urgent, balanced, team-focused, and quality-conscious. This was no small order in the face of today's high productivity pressures, great customer demands, and fierce global competition. For a company to succeed, employees and managers alike must continue to learn and continue to increase ownership, responsibility, and pride.

Gil took steps to bring the entire company together as partners in the effort. He initiated processes throughout the company for creating a new vision of the future, new competencies to achieve that vision, and a deep commitment to the vision. This was a daunting challenge for Gil and his management team. Without this dialogue at every level, the vision could be little more than a statement or a slogan. It is the alignment of individual mission and vision with the organizational mission and vision that rekindles the spirit of both the people and the organization.

As we seek this alignment, all of us today, regardless of our corporate status or our company type, ask the same questions:

- Where do I find security?
- Whom or what can I trust in the organization?

- How can I find a greater sense of meaning or involvement in my work?
- How do I make all the changes I need and want to make?
- Where and how will I get rewarded and acknowledged?
- What is my motivation to work?
- What's my guarantee that all this change is right?
- What will happen to me if I don't change?

Further, when major transformational efforts are under way, some broader questions arise:

- How does an organization create an environment where people perform at their best?
- What does it take to rebuild trust and commitment in an organization where they have been diminished?
- What is the manager's role in developing the new culture?
- How do people come to accept change and be organizationally responsible and accountable?

By facing up to these questions, National Semiconductor has literally transformed itself into a different and more successful company. Managers and employees together must remain engaged in a never-ending process of change. This book seeks to provide a model of how companies can develop commitment and how employees can help themselves recommit to their organizations; it is a guide for navigating the cities in which we find ourselves today.

NEW BUSINESS REALITIES

The last few years have not been easy for people in organizations. Most of the conventional wisdom has been challenged. A third of 1970's Fortune 500 companies are gone today, acquired or out of business, and many of the blue-chip, high-performing organizations of the 1980s are under siege. In the face of this turmoil, trust in the policies and practices these companies typified has gone. IBM, General Motors, Sears, and the Bell companies were the paragons of success in manufacturing, service, planning and profits; their ways of managing and producing, of deploying hundreds of thousands of people, and of spending billions of dollars designing, manufacturing, and selling products were the models for all corporations. But as the world changed, demanding greater quality, faster response to customer needs, more complete service, and continual innovation—while profit margins diminished and competition increased—these organizations ceased to be competitive or even profitable. They were often slow to adapt, to meet emerging customer needs, and to respond to change; they were also too costly to run.

New business realities are transforming the workplace and the individual's role in it. Globalization; demographic shifts in types of workers and customers and what they want from work, products, and services; cycle-time reduction; and reengineering encourage this transformation or force it outright. Understanding why the shifts in the workplace are happening can be a personal comfort and offer strategic business information as we plan for the future. But a person may see one or more of these issues without understanding the whole pattern. Recognizing the interaction between all the issues can help to create a context for understanding that goes beyond the individual into the larger social context. Further, there is no time to stop work while organizations are undertaking change. In effect, they must rebuild the ship while it is at sea. This is a far more complex, challenging, and disorienting task than building a ship in dry dock.

MAPS AS GUIDES TO CHANGE

The goal of this book is to provide maps to guide people in redefining the nature of their own work and their relationship to the organization and to explain how they can redefine, reengineer, and renew themselves. Our maps, however, do not ensure a clear path: There are unexpected obstacles during any journey, no matter how well planned. Indeed, we believe that overly precise maps would reduce the possibilities for adventure, learning, and spontaneous discovery. Therefore, the maps that we provide are broad guides through the adventure of rebuilding and renewing the workplace. With them, a person or an organization can find the courage to begin the journey and set off in the right direction.

However, those who want to be relieved of the responsibility of making their own way will not find what they seek here. Amid the pressure, disorder, and chaos of today's world, we see a need for individuals to take the initiative and the responsibility for their own renewal and that of their organizations. Further, they must not wait until they are forced to change. They can anticipate the future and begin to prepare themselves—and their organizations—now. The maps in this book offer some suggestions about what they might change and how they can do it.

The maps we present are the stories of individuals, work teams and groups, and companies who are pioneers in creating new work processes and workplaces. We have taken these stories from our experiences as organizational consultants since the late seventies. Over this time we have helped a wide variety of organizations and employees discover their preferred future and create environments that match their vision. Our perspective encompasses personal and organizational change, recognizing that one does not precede the other; they must both happen at once. We take the best elements of both, because personal and organizational change are interdependent. In this way, our perspective is unique, for consultants and models tend to promote one or the other, often because they are strong in one area, either reengineering and new workplaces or personal awakening and transformation.

WHAT ARE THE CHANGES IN THE WORKPLACE?

The nature of change itself is changing. In the past, change was a punctuation in a paragraph of continuity. One could get through a change to a quiet plateau where one could rest and readjust. But today change is constant and continual. There are no rest periods; the pace of change gets faster and faster. We must do more than be able to live with specific changes; we must be able to live with change itself. Living with change means that individuals and organizations have to live in a world of continual uncertainty.

Change is rampant in all types of corporations, in educational institutions, in nonprofits, and in healthcare organizations. What is triggering this? Some answers come in the form of the newly emerging global marketplace; the emphasis on information, service, and speed; and the trend toward downsizing. We'll examine each of these factors briefly now; we discuss their impact in more detail throughout the book.

Global Marketplace

Today's organizations span national boundaries from the first moment of their existence. In effect, national boundaries mean little as companies move from market to market. The global organization is formed with streamlined corporate staffs that often coordinate manufacturing, marketing, suppliers and partners, and sales forces. The new global organization is often a partnership of many organizations working together on shared interests. Such partnerships extend to public universities teaming up with corporations to market their research, and to government and private corporations sharing resources.

Alliances, partnerships, and outsourcing arrangements make companies increasingly interdependent. Managers with global experience are in demand. Their ability to draw upon culturally diverse approaches gives them a range of options, choices, and perspectives that helps them manage complex organizational demands. These managers are less ethnocentric and less fixed on U.S. trends, having learned to see other ways to do things. But the new organization needs more than visionary and competent top managers; everyone in the organization needs to understand the company's relationships with its partners and its global involvement.

Primal Lite, a small novelty design firm, is a good example of a global business. The specialty lights it markets are designed by the company's owner, Sue Scott (who was named San Francisco's entrepreneur of the year in 1991). The lights are manufactured in Taiwan, assembled and packaged in Hong Kong, and shipped to sales representatives from Australia to Germany. At any moment, Scott may be communicating with potential factories in Singapore or opening up new markets as far away as Ireland. Practical matters can be complicated by the geographic range; consider, for instance, the possibilities for confusion and error given differing lighting specifications and packaging requirements. But Scott and her associates have overcome the difficulties. The network of strategic alliances—of factories, designers, marketing firms, and distribution—that Scott and her associates have developed creates and supports a web of sales opportunities through which Primal Lite has achieved international success.

The global focus of the new organization means that cultural sensitivity must extend within the organization as well. For example, Brice Manufacturing, a small company that repairs and reconditions airline seats for airlines all over the world, was at one time a mini-United Nations in its executive team. Its CEO was Scandinavian, its VP Jewish, its quality manager Latino, its engineers Vietnamese and Palestinian, its controller Sri Lankan, and its manufacturing manager a U.S. southerner with a military background. One might expect great cultural clashes, but in fact, all of them shared a common culture of manufacturing excellence and worked effectively toward that end.

New Emphases

The nature of the tasks that most people do at work is changing, from physical and production-oriented, to generating and using information. Secretary of Labor Robert Reich writes that work today can be described in terms of three types of jobs. There are production workers, service workers, and a new category of workers, whom Reich calls "symbolic analysts"—people who manipulate, generate, and deal in information.[1]

Information

The new jobs that are being created today are in service, for which the pay is low, and in information, which is the work of symbolic analysts. These analysts, whose work is considered of high value and therefore is highly paid, manipulate information or manage people and resources. Among the symbolic analysts, there are problem-spotters, problem-solvers, and strategic brokers. Problem-spotters look for business opportunities and for the critical tasks that need to be done, such as correcting specific types of customer problems by making a change in the product. Their value is their ability to ask the right questions. Problem-solvers range from software designers to factory workers (factory workers who make sure systems are operating correctly, rather than physically produce the goods). And finally, strategic brokers deal in information, create alliances, get information to customers, and work on the boundaries between work groups and organizations.

While working with a large chemical company several years ago, we saw some problem-solvers in action. The plant was huge, covering several acres, yet there seemed to be nobody there. Then, when we entered a small control room overlooking the plant, we saw five people. As they sat in the corner of the room, drinking their coffee and reading newspapers, they scanned large multicolored control panels. These people, formerly blue-collar workers, were monitoring the chemical processes occurring in the factory below; to do this, they used a giant computer representation of the factory. When asked what they were doing, they responded, "We are paid to watch the processes, and we assure you that if anything is not going right, we can spot it in an instant." People like these are being paid to think, not to do what they are told. The nature of their work has completely changed in recent years. Those who have learned to become comfortable with the "new work" in computer-assisted manufacturing have kept their jobs; those who refused to learn the new ways are no longer with the company.

The personal computer is the most powerful definer of new work. In contrast to the mainframe, which centralized information, personal computer systems are networked, and local units can call up centralized data at will. This kind of system has tremendous power. Individual units can understand their environment and see how work flows inside and outside the organization. Workers can see which of their operations add the most value to the product, manage fast and precise changes in what they manufacture, and monitor the quality almost instantly. Access to information breaks down the barriers and gives people more control over their work.

But in order to use these new systems and make the best use of these new data, people need freedom to take action. New accounting and information systems must begin with the assumption that people at any point in the organization may need instantaneous information and be able to take action. The dissemination of information to everyone in an organization thus has profound consequences; it shifts the nature of control and top-down leadership.[2]

Service

The company's focus of attention has shifted from product to service. Success comes from identifying and working with a customer to solve problems as the customer defines them. Companies are beginning to shift from seeing themselves as product-offerers, to problem-solvers; doing this involves combinations of services and products. They are seeing that the most important part of their contact with the customer is the service relationship, not the product.

As jobs disappear from manufacturing, they reappear in the form of service jobs. These people sell airline tickets and check baggage, file claims, take care of children, teach, help customers solve problems, repair machines, and so on. Service workers must be technically competent, able to create relationships with customers, and most important, leave the customers feeling that they have gotten what they wanted.

Doing this often means having the latitude to make decisions about what the company can and cannot offer and to streamline procedures and make services work in individual cases, and understanding how to solve problems that arise. For example, a trucking company we worked with authorized and even encouraged its delivery people to become salespeople. Since they delivered goods to the customers and talked to them in the process, they were in the best position to notice their needs and sell other forms of business. They became quite successful at sales, and their success was evident, both financially and in terms of morale.

The new workplace is a network of service relationships. Each individual, team, and group works for others. The service paradigm encourages workers to become outer-directed (looking to the customer as a guide) rather than to remain inner- or upper-directed (looking to a boss for evaluation).

Increasing service by responding directly to customer needs demands far more skill in personal relationships than can be learned from a book of procedures and memorized speeches. The person on the front lines of service must make decisions and create solutions. The service worker is also the person who is gathering the most important information about what the customer wants and what the company needs to do to help the customer. This should be kept in mind when products are redesigned, new services are created, or problems are fixed.

Speed

Cycle time, time to market, just in time delivery, and other time-sensitive processes mean that response to change needs to be immediate. Products that used to be redesigned every five years now have two-year product cycles; a company can go from start-up to market leader in a matter of months, not years. Such speed puts pressure on organizations accustomed to less pressing schedules. Tom Peters suggests that the pace of product innovation is so fast that all of business is becoming like the fashion industry, presenting whole new collections every season.[3] Even as a new product is being unrolled, another team is involved in creating the next product or service. Getting a product out several months faster not only captures market share but also increases profitability and competitive advantage.[4]

Such speed cannot be achieved if designers complete their work, then give it to the engineers, who turn it over to manufacturing, who finally ask marketing to help sell it. The speedy organization brings all specialties together so that they can design, survey customers, and consider manufacturing and engineering simultaneously. Because the manufacturers are part of design and innovation, the whole process moves in parallel steps, reducing the time from concept to product or service. People have to go outside of their traditional professional specialties and learn to work as partners with people from other areas of the organization. The skills of collaboration, the ability to listen and learn, and a willingness to put aside one's own professional interests and see the broader picture are necessary.

Downsizing

To keep afloat in today's marketplace companies have been downsizing; in fact, during the 1980s, 3.4 million jobs were eliminated in the United States.[5] Every organization has gone on a diet, cutting departments and levels of management, and continually paring costs. At the same time, mergers, acquisitions, reorganizations, and other vast changes have wrung even more from organizations.

Companies such as IBM, which once promised lifetime employment, were so battered in the stock market that they finally had to announce massive cuts in jobs, offices, and costs. Even companies that remain profitable, such as the utility Pacific Gas and Electric in San Francisco, announce layoffs and cost-cutting in anticipation of potential hardships and future competition. It seems that cutting costs has become a game that counts almost as much as profits. The company often finds itself having to go back on promises, cut back benefits, and make drastic changes in its operations. Many have been less than candid with employees. It often seems that soon after companies announce what is described as "the last round of cuts," factors lead them to set in motion yet another round.

Today's employees, at all levels and in most organizations, no longer feel protected. They feel uncertainty; the organization seems as transitory as shifting sands. It can't be counted upon for support or security. Anything may be called into question on any given day.

Employees respond to this uncertainty with mistrust, anger, diminished commitment, and cynicism. Further, as companies cut back, the people left behind have more to do. A professor at the University of California reports that she is teaching about five times as many students now as she was in the early seventies when she started her career. People in claims processing, customer service, and maintenance find that they have to do more and more work, for minimal or even no increases in pay.

Also in the eighties, "mergermania" hit. It was felt that companies could become more productive by buying up other companies, accomplishing economies of scale or synergy, and cutting staff. Over half of the Fortune 500 disappeared or re-emerged in a different corporate form during this decade. Yet, studies of mergers find that they only rarely meet the expectations of greater profits, synergy, or cost savings.[6] The Wyatt Company studied 1,000 companies that had restructured. Nearly 60 percent of those surveyed felt that morale was shattered as a result of the changes and said they were having trouble keeping their good people as a result. Another study of 365 companies found that more than half of them assessed their downsizing experience as negative, in terms of both future morale and organizational effectiveness.[7]

Such results, however, are not universal. How a company deals with the process of downsizing and cutting costs is key to its ultimate success or failure. There is a clear separation between companies that handle downsizing well and those that don't. The difference is based on whether the company sees the cuts as ends in themselves or as one step in a very profound process. Some companies understand that downsizing threatens the bond between organization and employee and that it is therefore important to concentrate on rebuilding with the people who are left. These companies follow downsizing with programs to help those remaining increase their empowerment, learn the skills to participate in making the company successful, and work to discover new ways to achieve corporate success.[8] Given their experiences, we believe that if the downsizing is followed by this kind of restructuring, the process may ultimately have a positive effect.

Increased Work Stress

One disturbing response to all this corporate downsizing and diminished loyalty to employees is that many companies have become far less pleasant places to work in. As every workplace feels pressure from the environment to keep up, to innovate, to do more with less, the remaining employees feel increasingly pressured. We have seen the stress level increasing in workplace after workplace. Employees are in a bind. If the organization is losing people and asks more of the people who remain, the implicit message is that those who don't give the company what it wants will be the next to go.

In 1992, Northwestern National Life Insurance conducted a stress survey of 600 workers and found that about a third of them thought about quitting because of job stress and expected to "burn out" in the near future.[9] Another study on burnout found that a great majority of employees at two large employers—one public corporation, one governmental—reported signs of burnout.[10]

This increasing pressure to produce comes amid conflicting messages, confused priorities, and impossible requests. Supervisors are pressured and unsure of what to do. As a result, they may be increasingly difficult to please. And their attitude has an enormous effect.

Burnout is associated with work groups.[11] If one member of a work group is burned-out, then the climate and style of the whole group will likely be so. The key factor seems to be the immediate supervisor's leadership style. Those who communicate, share information, collaborate, and allow some control over how work is done seem to produce less burnout in their coworkers. In short, research suggests that burnout is less related to how much pressure people feel than to how meaningful they find their work. If they are working hard at something they are excited about, then they are less likely to burn out. If, however, the task is not related to a clear goal, and if people do not have some control over how they do the work and some information about the larger picture, they feel more stress.

Clearly, job stress and morale are intimately linked. The question "Do you like your job?" more accurately predicts future health status than any other. When things are going badly at work, health problems, accidents, and other physical difficulties arise. We saw ample evidence of this when we were asked to determine the factors that lay behind a California city's large increase in workers' compensation claims for the city's employees. In analyzing the claims files that were more lengthy and repetitive than others, we grouped the cases together by supervisor. What emerged was a striking pattern: Some supervisors' groups had multiple claims; others had none. When employees felt they were being treated unfairly by a supervisor and felt helpless to change the situation or resolve problems effectively, health problems—and costly claims—resulted.

It seems then that people's feeling of connectedness to their work is a way to protect health. So there can be some bright spots amid the changes. Our task is to understand the changes and to work to make them more positive for individuals and for organizations.

ENCOURAGING
POSITIVE CHANGE

Some working conditions lead to better health even in people with the most stressful jobs. When Suzanne Kobasa and Salvadore Maddi compared the healthiest and least healthy middle managers at Illinois Bell in the high-stress period after its divestiture from AT&T, they found that no corporate level, type of job, or personality characteristics could predict that individual's health.[12] Instead, they found that three qualities, were present in the healthy managers: commitment, control, and challenge. They can be described as follows:

Commitment. Healthy people have a sense that what they are doing is meaningful. They have a clear vision about where they are going that is largely in line with their basic values, allowing them to be involved and motivated in their work.

Control. Healthy people feel free to take action to do what needs to be done to complete their job and achieve their vision. They feel that they have control over their jobs.

Challenge. Healthy people feel open to learning continually from others about how to do things better and improve their capabilities. They see change as an opportunity to develop their skills and to learn.

Other research findings on the importance of social support suggested a fourth factor, connection.[13]

Connection. Healthy people feel that they can call on the help and support of other people, and that their co-workers are colleagues, not competitors.

These four Cs—commitment, control, challenge, and connection—are all important for people who are effective at high-performance work. Although each is important in itself, when combined together they form a strong bridge to high performance in the new workplace.

Some additional findings help make the case for building an environment where trust and commitment can grow. Another study similarly found that employees who experience better health, even in high-demand environments, are those who have more control over how they do their work, participate in decisions, and have support from others.[14] If we are to be able to cope with the pressure of constant change, we must build more control and choice into work processes and policies. We must also establish opportunities for people to feel connected to one another. Work environments that foster this approach will presumably have lower health costs as well as higher levels of motivation and performance.

Unfortunately, work reengineering and redesign often do

not address these issues. Quite the opposite. The processes are often carried out in such a way that people feel a loss of control and connection. We have seen many companies engage in extensive reengineering efforts only to find that the gains expected are never attained. Often, the reengineering process did not include the involvement of the people whose work was being redesigned; as a consequence, they felt a loss of control. Is it any wonder that their performance level dropped under the new design? Similarly, should we be surprised that the promise of empowerment is not realized when it is given as a directive from above? Consider what one employee has said of empowerment: "Let me see. Employee empowerment means that my supervisor is gone and I have to do some of her work, and other people are gone and I have to do their work, and then I am responsible for helping to do more work. It sounds like a trap to me." The reality is that employees often feel that more demands and pressure masquerade under the banner of empowerment—and that they have no control over these changes. But if they are truly involved in instituting empowerment—an issue we discuss at length in this book—the changes could actually increase their commitment, control, challenge, and connection.

It should be understood that the four Cs are qualities, not personality traits, and therefore can be developed by anyone in response to the new demands of the workplace. Doing so involves changes in mindset and perceptions, which lead people toward new behaviors. By developing these qualities, people not only affect their own level of commitment and capacity to manage in the workplace but also affect the people around them, and perhaps the workplace itself.

This book will help you develop these qualities in yourself and in your organization. With them, you will have a broad and flexible framework for redesigning your work or your organization.

If the four Cs create an environment for individual health, we could posit that they would also form a template for creating a healthy organization. Let's transform each of the four Cs from an individual standpoint to that of a whole organization. The following questions might arise:

- What is the impact when a whole team or organization understands its mission and vision?

- What occurs when the organization's policies and procedures emphasize decision making at the lowest level and increase control and direct action?

- What happens when people in a team or a group have the skills to stretch themselves to meet the challenges they face?

- What is it like when people feel that the workplace is a supportive community that encourages learning and prudent risk-taking?

As the pressure and demands of the workplace increase, the opportunities to take control and make connections become more important. As people in workplaces face downsizing, reorganizations, and other factors beyond their control, they need to be buffered by environments that keep them from becoming overwhelmed, numb, and withdrawn. If work cannot become easier, then the workplaces and the individuals there need to become more skilled at managing pressure.

No workplace is immune from these changes. The question for every individual is "How do I respond to change?" Traditionally, many sat tight and waited for instructions. But this won't do today. Many organizations are not quick enough to offer detailed plans for all employees to make their way. Sometimes people at the top are as overwhelmed as those below them.

The onus is therefore on each of us to figure out how to respond to change. This is a self-preservation technique: We all need to change in order to land on our feet and succeed when the pressure increases. Finding our own way is also important because it is the people inside the organization who will help the company, school, hospital, or community organization find *its* way. An organization in which people share responsibility for helping the whole to manage change is more likely to achieve success than one in which people are waiting for instructions or arguing among themselves. The maps provided in this book will help people inside organizations, whether middle managers, individual professional contributors, or members of a work team, to help the organization renew itself in the new work environment.

In this chapter we have explored some of the reasons why individuals in today's workplace need to change their work roles and become empowered, and take broader responsibility for the future of their organizations and for their individual careers. In the next chapter, we look at why employees want more from work than just good pay and benefits. In the subsequent chapters, we map out ways of renewing the organization and rekindling people's commitment to its vision.

2
Align Yourself and Your Organization: Writing the New Work Contract

There is something in human nature that wants to soar, to be free to express itself in life and work. Many times organized life stifles or directs this spirit, forcing it to go underground and seek an outlet elsewhere. We can learn to channel this force through corporate turbines, to use the energy of our people to generate energy for the common good. We have a chance to create a self-perpetuating cycle: a company that encourages self-expression, which strengthens its ability to encourage people to fulfill themselves in a vital organization. What a life-sustaining and health-giving place a corporation might be!

—Kermit Campbell, CEO of Herman Miller

We have seen some of the factors that are driving the dramatic changes in the workplace today. We know that commitment and trust are in short supply. Morale is dropping. Yet despite all the factors that seem to destroy commitment to the organization, we keep finding people who have not given up hope and feel they can make a difference, and organizations whose value is increased by the contributions these people make. In this chapter, we explore what individuals and companies have done and can do to counterbalance what many have called a crisis of commitment.

REBUILDING COMMITMENT

How can we build a work environment where people do more than just show up—where they want to work? This is an important question because organizations today need the extra involvement and effort that only employees who are fully committed to the organization can give.

If organizations want more from their people, they have to give more of what it is that employees value. The conventional wisdom that employees want only money and power must be discarded, not only because organizations can't offer these in difficult times but also because these are not the most critical or effective motivators.

Dennis Young has suggested that we can learn from the principles that nonprofit organizations use to motivate people when they have few, if any, financial incentives to offer.[1] He suggests that the notions of being part of a greater whole, doing something important, and having a sense of control over the way the work is done are the critical components of feeling a connection to the organization, which is a prime motivator. We believe he is onto something important: People want their company and its leaders to show them respect, to treat them with dignity, to offer them jobs with meaning, to let them know what is going on, to invite them into decision making, and to offer them opportunities to control their work. Unlike money, these resources are not scarce. Any workplace can provide them without cost, although providing them means a shift in the way work is done and how workers relate to each other.

Even if people do not like their particular organizations or their current situation, deep inside they want to do something that makes a difference. In fact, individuals feel frustrated and demoralized when they see something that needs to be done, while the organization moves in the opposite direction. They may not expect to run the organization, but they feel that there should be a fair hearing, a mechanism for them to present their view and lobby for it.

President Clinton has begun to call on the altruism that leads people to want to improve their institutions. In his inaugural speech he echoed this idealism by asking people to look at change while considering "not what it will do for *me*, but what it will do for *us*." He asked people to move out of their individualistic frame of reference to get a view of the needs of the whole organization—in this case, the United States—and to see themselves as having a stake in the future of that whole. This is similar to the attitude that individuals adopt in what we call *the empowered workplace.*

We have examined the ways in which organizations define their vision of the future and their key values as activities that build commitment to the organization in themselves as well as take effective action toward the vision. Organizations that are clear about who they are and where they are going we call *essence-driven organizations.* Rather than motivate their employees by fear and compulsion, they motivate by generating commitment to a vision and values. Employees have energy to begin to rebuild their organization when they feel connected to the value of the organization's work. With this connection, they feel validated and satisfied by the long-term effects of their own work. The commitment to an organization's essence is far deeper than the traditional commitment for financial rewards alone or than mere compliance generated from fear.

Today people want to bring more of themselves to their work. They are no longer content to leave their maturity, feelings, creativity, spirituality, and unique abilities at the door. The company that invites in more of each employee gets the prize—commitment. This workplace, where the individual's values, vision, and mission are connected to that of the company, is what we call the empowered workplace. It stands in sharp contrast to the traditional organization that was structured and designed to limit involvement, not to promote it. The new workplace allows fuller expression of the human spirit. It is a place where people *want* to work. As we will see, empowerment comes when individual employees, not matter what their role in the organization, feel a sense of commitment and connection to the organization as a whole and take action to help build and renew the organization. In the next two chapters we will explore the nature of personal empowerment and the kind of workplace that emerges when what employees value is taken seriously.

Recent management literature has looked at corporations as cultures, like tribes or nationalities, that have their own rituals, symbolic events, and inner meaning to tie the work of many individuals into a distinctive style that adds clarity and meaning to all action.[2] If we like and agree with our corporation's culture, then we are willing to commit ourselves to making its goals our own. If today's organization is to have people who can solve the crises facing it, it needs to recover the roots of this allegiance, the personal commitment that encourages people to give. People give more when they commit to their own personal essences, which are the values, mission, and visions that are their highest aspirations. People less connected to the organization are not likely to be willing to give the organization what it needs. We must therefore replenish and reformulate the bond between individual and organization, so threatened by the recent changes taking place in the workplace.

BUILDING THE NEW WORKPLACE: PEOPLE AT THE CENTER

There seems to be a common direction in the emerging design of organizations that are surviving and thriving amid change. As high-performance, empowered workplaces evolve, individuals matter more to them. The employees of the organization contribute their creative energy, as adults, with the attention on the customer, not on the boss. The new workplace has a fuller, more inspiring and meaningful culture. In a wide variety of forms, new workplaces are communities where people can grow and are challenged.

People select the companies they work for not only because there is a job there to fit their skills. Today, people also look at the values of the organization, what it stands for. A study of opinions of healthy organizations found that, overwhelmingly, people wanted two things from the workplace:

1. A sense of belonging, a sense that they make a difference.

2. Acknowledgment from managers to make them feel respected and valued.[3]

For the same reasons that people have always chosen to work for nonprofits and community organizations, rather than private companies, despite their lower salaries, now people are seeking workplaces that offer more than the highest paycheck. The workplaces that are prepared to fulfill their desires are those that will benefit the most.

In part this is the result of the shift in work from production to information services; because of this, paradoxically, people have become more important, even as so many of them are being laid off and leaving organizations. As Peter Drucker explains: "In the knowledge society into which we are moving, individuals are central. Knowledge is not impersonal, like money. Knowledge does not reside in a book, a databank, a software program. They contain only information. Knowledge is always embodied in a person; carried by a person; created, augmented or improved by a person; applied by a person; taught and passed on by a person; used or misused by a person. The shift to the knowledge society therefore puts the person at the center."[4]

As an employee of a utility company said, rather poignantly, on being offered an award for thirty years of service, "For all these years you only used my hands, when you could have had my head and heart for free." Organizations are coming to see the potential that they have overlooked or ignored for many years. They have awakened to the fact that these resources—hearts and heads— are freely available, if the organizations learn to listen.

Organizations increasingly are learning to see that employees are giving them a gift. In addition to doing their work, they are also helping the organization to renew itself to change and grow. In high-performance companies that successfully manage change, the leadership creates a climate that allows employees to perform in this way.

When people feel respected, they begin to trust the organization and each other. They begin to open up, to look within themselves, to share information, and to become more available to take ownership and to struggle to solve problems. People offer more of themselves in a caring atmosphere. In the process, the people succeed as well as the organization.

Organizations that are successful tap the hidden capacities of individuals in the organization to increase the organization's competitive advantage. Organizations where the differing needs of all of the major constituencies—the shareholders and owners, the workers and the customers—are respected far outperform firms that do not have these cultural traits. In their study of 207 firms over an eleven-year period, Harvard Business School researchers Kotter and Heskett found that firms with these emphases, as compared with companies that did not have these qualities, increased revenues by an average of 682 percent compared with 166 percent, expanded their work forces by 282 percent compared with 36 percent, grew their stock prices by 901 percent compared with 74 percent, and improved their net incomes by 756 percent compared with 1 percent.[5]

What Do People Want from Work?

If we think of working for an organization as a voluntary act, workers must perceive it to be in their interest to invest their time and energy. We recognize that the organization can no longer promise to take care of the person or provide an open-ended agreement. So what can the organization offer?

Three conditions make up the firmest foundation for the new workplace. The company has to provide

1.   Fairness
2.   A place to grow
3.   A reasonable return on their investment

Organizations in trouble have had difficulty delivering on one or more of these basic conditions. But organizations can, with some effort, satisfy these conditions within clear and explicit boundaries that are specified between employer and employee.

Fairness.   Fairness means being able to depend on the organization for reasonable support and respect for the individual. Threats to a person's psychological or physical self make it difficult to work. A study of the nature of justice in the workplace defines fairness as having nine elements: trust, consistency, truthfulness, integrity, clear expectations, equity, influence, justice, and respect.[6] These are the same conditions that make for a fair, just, and free society.

These values are honored by many companies, but there are often large gaps between the word and the reality. Empowered workplaces are more likely to make the values explicit, and to give them teeth. For example, Federal Express has a written, guaranteed fair-treatment policy, which is given to each employee on their first day of work. As part of the policy, everyone is entitled to a review of any management decision by a board of their peers. The CEO, Fred Smith, personally reviews the decisions of these boards regularly.[7]

Some elements of fairness may seem harder to offer than others. Top managers sometimes find it difficult to be open and candid with employees; this hurts their credibility. Or middle managers and key people in an organization do not understand how to support the work and well-being of their employees in general and thereby develop a workplace where management practices range from unsupportive to abusive. But the argument that a company cannot afford to give its people fairness, justice, and information about what is going on at higher levels is as suspect as the argument that a police state is necessary because people are not ready for democracy. How can they become ready, or show they are ready, if the basic conditions are not offered them?

A Place to Grow.   Because people invest an enormous portion of their lives at work, they increasingly want to work in an environment where they grow, learn, face challenges, and use their abilities. Even with new production and service workers, instilling the desire to make decisions, help the company improve its processes, develop real relationships with customers, and be seen as a contributing member of the firm is key to their continuing commitment. Training and development are basic requirements for the employees. Allowing employees to grow and develop their talents is the core of empowerment.

Reasonable Return.   The third essential for employees is a reasonable return on their personal investment. A company has many people to whom it is beholden, and a wise and judicious company distributes its value to all of them. The owners of the company are due a fair return, but so are all the employees who make the company a success. The community in which the company operates also is due more than just tax dollars. Socially responsible companies have begun to offer as much as 5 percent of their profits back to the community. Suppliers and customers should also benefit from fair returns for their companies—the best possible prices, which are also a way of sharing value.

In talking about the basic values of his company that were driving its transformation into the new organization, Kermit Campbell, CEO of Herman Miller, said: "We believe in equity for our customers, investors, vendors, dealers, and ourselves. We believe that excellent financial results must be earned and that good stewardship of resources is everyone's responsibility. If we as senior managers are to expect everyone to become more like leaders, if we are to expect everyone to work for the common good, we must believe—and show it—that every employee has a stake in our companies. Both a financial stake and an ownership role."[8]

Dividing up the value is one of the most important activities of today's company; it must be offered fairly to all of those who have helped the company reach its current success and offered in such a way that future success is supported. If people or teams do not see the rewards for their service or that the compensation is related to the value they gave the company, their commitment will decline. They will also be less willing to sustain their commitment when the company is struggling. When the federal government bailed out Chrysler Corporation, workers were enthusiastic about helping the company turn itself around. Their feelings changed when they heard that top managers were getting huge bonuses in a difficult year. They felt that they were neither treated fairly nor getting a fair return when they had to sacrifice and management did not. Similarly, during a time of crisis, a factory of a petrochemical company began to be much more profitable through the heroic efforts of its blue-collar employees, who made incredible quality and productivity gains. Yet they remained hourly workers. The company ultimately had to look at a salary and bonus program, to give them a fair return on the value they had offered the company, in order to sustain their commitment for the next series of challenges.

Money is a prime incentive for working, yet researcher Frederik Hertzberg and his colleagues found that more money did not lead to an increase in work motivation.[9] In effect, money is the foundation for work motivation but not the source of the commitment that binds people to the new workplace. In fact, in one workplace where people were paid far more than the people in comparable workplaces, the high compensation not only didn't motivate them to do more it also inhibited them because it made them spend time trying to make sure they kept their jobs in a very compliant and conformist environment.

Working for Meaning and Identity

If money is not the motivator, we need to find out what is. When we ask people, "Why do you work?" we receive a wide variety of answers:

1. To gain security for the future
2. To gain identity as part of a meaningful enterprise
3. To learn and enhance skills
4. To find a place to take on important tasks and be part of major achievements
5. To gain economic livelihood
6. To find relationships that validate us as worthwhile, significant people
7. To do something to help the community and add value to others

One thing we can learn from this list is that work is a major building block of identity and membership in the community. In American society, "What do you do?" is usually the first question asked at social events, and our profession is the first thing we are likely to name. How we feel about our work is one of the most important factors supporting our health and self-esteem. Our work community is the place of many of our most significant relationships and achievements. A 1989 Gallup Poll of 796 U.S. workers found that people whose jobs gave them a sense of identity worked longer, harder, and more satisfactorily than those who worked just for the money. This was true no matter what the job or salary.[10]

We might broaden the definition of work to include all of the activities in which we are involved with groups of people to produce something. By this definition, involvement in community organizations, on boards, and in voluntary associations is included. Because most of these activities do not offer financial compensation, the deeper motivation for such work is service, giving to the community, and enhancing our sense of our own personal value.

Traditional workplaces were established on the premise that people didn't really want to work, and therefore had to be controlled and watched. Further, it was assumed that people weren't very smart and didn't care about the organization. In short, workers were treated like not fully competent children. In contrast, the new workplace is a place for adults. Nobody is there to be taken care of, and both employer and employee shoulder some uncertainty and risk.

The contrast between views of human nature at the traditional and the new workplace are instructive:

Traditional Workplace	*Emerging Workplace*
Workers are treated like dependent children.	Workers are adult partners.
Workers need to be controlled.	Workers are committed.
Workers are assumed to be selfish.	Workers are responsible.
People are seen as machines to be programmed.	People are self-determining organisms.
People are replaceable.	People are an investment.
People are forced to work.	People want to work.
Few people have ideas.	Everyone has ideas.
People are conformist.	People are creative.
Workers are motivated by external rewards.	Workers are motivated by internal factors such as learning, challenge, participation.

The new organization sees, values, motivates, rewards, and engages people in a new way; it puts far more value on people's potential contribution to the effectiveness of the organization. In the new workplace, the factors that motivate good work are far more varied than in the traditional workplace. The traditional workplace sees work as an activity to provide economic support for living. Life is considered to be separate from work, even though people spend a third or more of their lives at the workplace.

The new view of people demands more from each employee, but it isn't possible to achieve success in the new workplace unless people are willing to offer more of themselves. As it happens, individual employees are probably more ready to work than traditional managers are to let them do so.

The Inner-Directed Revolution

The shifts we are seeing are evidence of a major transition in American values about work. In the fifties and early sixties, the dominant values in the workplace were quite different than they are today. The organization man was a person who, above all else, "fit in," did what was expected, and looked like everyone else. He didn't stick out in any way or challenge anything, and he did as he was told. This compliant loyalty was richly rewarded by a company that promised to take care of him. Another work value was that of power and achievement—individual success came through achieving dominance over others; with this came financial rewards, promotion, and leadership perks—the special dining hall, parking space, large office, and country club membership.

In the mid 1960s, a powerful new set of "inner-directed" values emerged to replace the earlier "outer-directed" ones. People began to ask, "What is all this for?" They began to want work that was satisfying and fulfilling. They wanted to work for companies that they felt proud of and do work that was meaningful. Instead of gaining their identity primarily by being recognized by others, especially those in power, the new inner-directed workers gained identity through what they did themselves. They wanted to be respected and have the freedom to have an impact on the workplace.

This personal-values trend has influenced the workplace in many ways. The inner-directed worker has turned out to be very different from the outer-directed, achievement-oriented employee of the past. The inner-directed worker is motivated by meaning, mission, and experience while the outer-directed worker is motivated by status, money, and promotions. As motivation theorist Michael Maccoby has observed, "The growing generation in the workplace has self-development as their primary goal at work."[11] The inner-directed group now makes up more than 20 percent of the American workforce and is growing. According to researcher Daniel Yankelovich, these values have significantly influenced an additional 60 percent of American workers.[12] What is also significant about this inner-directed group is that it represents a large percentage of high-performing, innovative employees. These are the employees who find their identities outside the organization and therefore adapt more easily to change.

A team manager in a fast-growing company, whose employees are largely from the twenty-something generation, notes, "People are changing. They want to know, 'What do I get out of my day?' They want a valuable day, to feel they've accomplished things. This didn't used to be so, but I find it's certainly true now as I recruit my staff." The proper style of working with inner-directed people involves inviting people to reach their full potential and keeping them learning.

The growth in the number of people who adhere to outer-directed work values has begun to level off, while, since the societal shift of the sixties, the growth in number of inner-directed people has been exponential. Interestingly, both sets of work values seem to have simultaneous, sometimes even conflicting, impact within the workplace today. It is not that the traditional values have become unimportant but that the new values are beginning to take precedence in many people's feelings about work.

Yet most organizations were designed for the outer-directed worker. Because most organizations contain a mix of inner- and outer-directed workers, there is a confusion about how to create an environment that will be motivating for both. Many managers do not understand this basic shift and continue to offer hats, cups, and tee-shirts: *presents* to people when what the people want is a sense of *presence*.

Defining the Preferred Workplace

Until recently, American work values had remained quite stable over time.[13] The six values ranked highest in 1968 were also ranked highest in 1981:

1.   Honesty
2.   Ambition
3.   Responsibility
4.   Forgiveness
5.   Broadmindedness
6.   Courage

The least preferred values had similar stability:

1.   Imagination
2.   Logic
3.   Obedience
4.   Intellectuality
5.   Politeness
6.   Independence

But since 1981 American society has seen changes in these values. There has been a shift away from "the organization man" to a more individual orientation.

From 1989 through 1993 we asked employees in more than a hundred work groups at all levels of organizations, from many types of organizations, and from all areas of the country to define the core values that would set the tone at the place where they would most want to work. To our surprise, there was almost no variation in what they selected from a list of fifty items. In fact, recently we conducted a workshop composed of men from a Navy supply depot and women from a high-tech company. Each group worked separately, yet they came up with identical lists. The values they preferred are very different from those reflected by the earlier lists. The new values were the following:

1. Integrity, fairness
2. Competence, ability
3. Teamwork
4. Communication
5. Personal growth
6. Creativity, challenge
7. Freedom, autonomy

People today want more participation and creative involvement in defining not just what they do, but what the organization is all about—its essence. The value given to teamwork suggests that they wish to connect their own individual expression to the needs and success of the group. Indeed, teamwork, personal growth, communication, and creativity have repositioned themselves on the list. The value on American individualism is being transformed into growth and creativity, dimensions that seem to serve both the self and the organization. People want to learn and grow within an organization. They want self-expression, creativity, and freedom. They want to make a difference. All of this requires a new work contract, which we discuss in the following section.

THE NEW WORK CONTRACT

Continual change has rubbed away much of the glue that binds the individual to the organization. This glue came from a series of often implicit promises by the organization to the employee, such as continued employment, promotions, and career progression. As organizations struggled, these implicit contracts were often redefined very suddenly, leaving many employees feeling confused, resentful, and less trusting. Some people have created a sense of solace by going off to work for themselves. Many others remain in organizations, yet feel the quandary of wanting to give more of themselves but being afraid that the organization won't value what they have to offer. Bridging the gap between expectations and behavior is a key to restoring trust, morale, and productivity.

As we've seen, the traditional workplace tended to be based on the "parental" model: It offered to "take care" of the employee, as long as the employee performed up to expectations. This has been termed the culture of entitlement, as in "I am entitled to employment."[14] Under the culture of entitlement, a job was not something you had to continue to prove yourself at, it was always there for you, along with the implicit understanding that there were periods when you could "coast" on past performance. There were costs associated with the security this afforded: compliance, silence, and, at times, loss of identity.

In every company today, the rules of the game have irrevocably changed. The psychological contract—the unspoken agreement of what we give to the organization and what it gives back to us—is vastly different. Gone is the sense of lifelong job security. The workplace of today can't protect its workers: Its "parental" power has been lost.

Instead, employees and organizations are all "adults." To keep this relationship functioning requires information-sharing, so that employees can make an informed commitment to the organization, knowing the potential upside and downside. The relationship may terminate when it is no longer workable, and as "an adult," the employee must understand that the company cannot be responsible for his or her welfare.

The rules have changed faster than many organizations' structures, policies, and cultures have, and too fast for people to develop the new skills to work differently. Top performance has to be achieved every day. In addition, the new workplace often needs to ask employees to change what they do, learn new skills, undertake new responsibilities and new assignments, and increase continually their levels of performance. For inner-directed employees who want challenge, responsibility, and growth, this may be welcome. But it may also be scary because it is less secure than traditional employment.

For example, for many years, a value at IBM was "respect for the individual." Traditionally, this meant that people were not laid off and weren't confronted directly if they were poor performers; they were merely moved to a position in which it was hoped they could perform. More recently, this definition of respect is no longer operative; a new definition is required to respond to greater competition and the need for productivity. This change created a heated dialogue, the result of which is that people are respected for the value they add to the organization, not for their mere presence.

Although this shift makes perfect business sense, it seemed shocking and unfair to many IBM employees, for when they had entered the company, they had been promised something different. Coming to grips with this change required overcoming the learned expectation that they deserved to be protected. Letting go of this expectation without feeling disabled by fear and anger was a challenge. Indeed, on a larger scale, the journey from entitlement to empowerment will be one of the major challenges of the 1990s. Moving from blaming someone in the organization to taking responsibility for empowered action requires a profound psychological shift. It requires relinquishing blame, embracing self-responsibility, taking risks, and having the courage to take action. Employees must take responsibility for themselves, their careers, and their futures.

New Mindsets

In a vision of the future of labor/management relations, Barry and Irving Bluestone, son and father, economist and labor leader, suggest that whereas labor and management have previously built agreements guaranteeing certain jobs and work environments, and limiting involvement of workers, the new workplace will have worker and manager collaborating on all aspects of organizational policy.[15] They see the era of labor and management as antagonists ending, and they suggest that productivity and success lie in the more complete and far-reaching collaboration allowed through empowerment. They advocate the evolution of the traditional labor/management contract into a joint governance agreement that they call a "compact." This compact provides a legal and moral basis for employees to be full partners in the design and management of every dimension of the organization. As empowerment grows, organizations will find appropriate ways to reward this heightened initiative and the employee's expanded role.

The new work contract is, once again, one of an adult contracting to another adult, for their mutual benefit. The adult employee is in effect a self-governing unit who enters into an agreement with another self-governing unit. Either side can make changes, if circumstances dictate, within the framework of the document.

Because the new work contract means accepting responsibility for one's own future, not waiting for the company to provide it, more people are on the march from company to company, looking after their own welfare. When early retirement or severance packages are offered, which employees are the first to leave? We have found that the people who leave are on both sides of the performance bell curve. If the company is lucky it can persuade or force its poorest performers to move on. However, also among the first to leave are the top performers, who know that they are quite employable elsewhere. Sometimes this group includes high performers for whom the company is not changing fast enough; as a consequence, the company loses important champions of change.

Employees must build their own sense of security within themselves. This security will increasingly be based on the ability to learn, change, innovate, and adapt. Companies that can no longer guarantee employment can at least strive to enhance their employees' "employability." They can offer opportunities for employees to learn new skills and to learn how to be effective learners. People have to become responsible for their own future, by maintaining their own employability.

An example of a factory that has successfully adopted this new "compact" to the benefit of workers and management is the New United Motor Manufacturing, Inc. (NUMMI) auto plant in Hayward, California. In a collaboration between Toyota and General Motors, a GM plant that had been among the least productive and most problematical turned into a model of quality production and collaborative management. The plant began with a new contract between the CEOs of GM, Toyota, and the president of United Auto Workers. Instead of a long, complex, and limiting agreement between union and management, the plant began with what was called a joint governance agreement. Union and management agreed to cooperate on decision making at all levels. These meetings are not run on majority rule. There must be consensus for a decision to take effect. Under this process, by the time a decision is made, there are no questions about people being willing to carry it out.

To raise efficiency at the new plant, an operations style called "lean production" was used. Every employee had the power to stop the line and to make necessary decisions. The company worked with suppliers to make parts available on a "just-in-time" (as needed) basis. This meant close coordination between every employee in the production process and levels of direct collaboration that were unheard of in a traditional auto assembly line. This collaborative process cut costs of inventory and speeded up production. The lines could change models and retool in a matter of weeks rather than months, because new model manufacturing processes were designed with plant workers involved in the design and engineering. Speed, quality, and efficiency increased dramatically thanks to fuller use of the skill and intelligence of every employee of the plant.

The responsibilities of the new work contract were made clear at NUMMI: Union members would share with management the responsibility for the quality of their work, while management would be committed to job security. Layoffs would come only as a last resort. In 1987 there was a slump in the auto industry, but instead of the layoffs dictated by management, the labor-management councils, who were steering the venture, together created a program of vacation, job rotation, planning for increased effectiveness, and most of all, training to develop everyone's skills. The workers all helped the company weather the downturn because they were involved in planning and they knew all would be done fairly and equitably.

Thus, the new organization that is evolving in many companies seems somewhat like a democracy. Employees increasingly make decisions in peer groups and in cross-functional teams. Steering committees or councils integrate various ideas and create policy and organizational vision and designs. These councils are like the legislative and executive arms of the government and when they are clearly and adequately formed they seem to exercise their power very effectively. The new organizational citizen takes on some responsibility for the whole organization and its future, in addition to his or her own. This form of corporate governance has been found to increase employee motivation, reduce stress, and enhance health. It also appears to be the best arrangement for organizational effectiveness in highly complex and changing environments.[16] However, it requires some work and retooling by everyone involved.

New Skill Sets and Career Paths

An article in *Fortune* magazine offers the following point of view: "Hereinafter, the employee will assume full responsibility for his own career—for keeping his qualifications up to date, for getting himself moved to the next position at the right time, for salting away funds for retirement, and, most daunting of all, for achieving job satisfaction. The company, while making no promises, will endeavor to provide a conducive environment, economic exigencies permitting."[17]

Wise employees take every opportunity to learn, to develop skills, and to seek challenging assignments. Rather than trust the organization, or good fortune, they take care of themselves. This viewpoint is summed up by Chris Jones, an aircraft mechanic who is studying for his engineering degree while working: "Of course my job is never really secure, but I hope this training will help me stay here for a longer period of time. If not, it will help me get another job."[18] His fear of the future is diminished by having taken control of some aspects of his future.

Career development has a new meaning in the empowered workplace. It is not a gift from the company; it is a necessity for both the employee and the organization. Continual learning is critical to success.

Because of the changes in organizational structure, a "career" no longer looks like a ladder—for many it seems more like an escalator or even a conveyor belt. How do people explain this to themselves and to the people around them? How do people find their identities when their jobs are not stable and their career paths not predictable?

A study of career paths and values of AT&T executives during the 1960s and early 1970s found that as AT&T moved from its traditional style of organization, managers moved toward a project focus in their careers.[19] Instead of job titles, they focused on the various challenges they had managed and the projects they had been associated with. This was a clear indicator of a shift from status-by-position, to status-by-achievements. People would say, "He was part of the redesign project team for marketing and he helped design the marketing campaign for the wireless products" rather than "He's an executive VP."

Increasingly, people are seeing themselves as brokers of a portfolio of skills that are "sold" or brokered[20] to different parts of the same organization or even to different organizations. In response to their uncertain futures, employees seek to upgrade themselves and maintain their marketability. Workers are paid for the number of skills they have rather than their seniority. At the Nissan auto plant in Smyrna, Tennessee workers are compensated for the number of skills their job requires, skills such as technical capability, problem-solving, and integrating information. Employees with more varied skills are considered more valuable, whether within or beyond the walls of the organization. Companies that want to maintain their own effectiveness do so by offering continual training to employees.

Both the company and the individual benefit from this. The increased flexibility, diversity of skill sets, and ability to shift and learn creates an environment where both the organization and the individual employee have maximum capacity to follow market demand.

FOUR RESPONSES TO THE CHANGING WORKPLACE

The new work values, work contract, and career progression mean that individuals have to respond to work demands and pressures in a new way. They need to focus on doing not just what the organization wants but also on what is meaningful, important, and helpful to themselves. They can only focus on what the organization needs and wants if the latter are connected to their own personal needs. To illustrate the new work styles, which focus in varying degrees on the values, needs, and demands of both the organization and the individual, we can generate a grid showing four types of workers (see Figure 2.1).

Follower: Running in Place on the Treadmill.   Followers place organizational needs over individual needs. They are good soldiers; they try to maintain themselves on the treadmill, doing more work and trying to get better results working in the old way. Followers try their best to do what has been done in the past, what was expected. This often leads them into the trap of working harder and longer on what may be a failed solution, rather than turning their attention to new ways or innovations. Continuing on this path gets to be draining and tiring; it often leads to an individual's sense of overload or burnout. In doing what is expected of them, these people become trapped by trying to keep up but falling further behind. They may eventually do what is needed, but they have less and less control over their own jobs.

Drifter: Disconnected and Adrift.   Drifters tend to withdraw, stop trying, and give up, reasoning that they are in a no-win situation. This response is one of despair, silencing the internal desire to make a difference or to do good work. Drifters are unmotivated and apathetic; they turn their brains off. Drifters are often burned-out followers: Once they discovered they could never succeed, they gave up.

Maverick: Out for Oneself.   Mavericks are those who respond to difficulties in the organization by lapsing into selfishness. Since nobody else cares, they believe, why should they? As a result, they follow their own personal agendas. They take advantage of other people, taking credit for others' work, getting results on the backs of their colleagues, or simply making it look as if they are getting results. This response creates distance between themselves and other people. However, there is a lot of life in mavericks: They focus on their own needs and how to get the job .done. Instead of listening to the organization, they listen to themselves and discover ways to succeed. The maverick is creative and energetic.

The workplace needs to get mavericks to go beyond their narrow self-interest, to begin to bring their energy into helping the organization to grow and succeed. But all three responses, although satisfactory in the short run, lead to choices that foster neither individual nor organizational health. The path that we see leading beyond mere adaptation is one that embraces the need to change—by both the individual and the organization.

Figure 2.1.   Styles of Response to the Workplace.

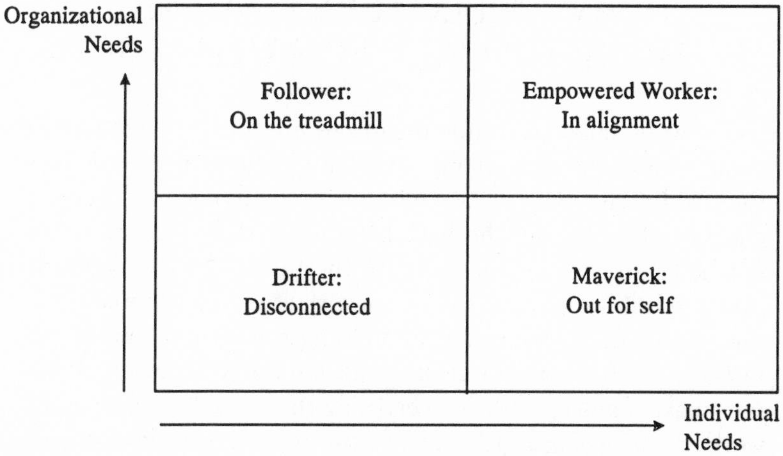

Organizational Needs ↑	**Follower:** **On the treadmill**	**Empowered Worker:** **In alignment**
	Drifter: **Disconnected**	**Maverick:** **Out for self**
	→	**Individual Needs**

Only the fourth response, that of the empowered worker, generates real personal commitment to the organization.

Empowered Worker: Aligning Self and Organization.   The empowered response balances individual and organizational needs. Individuals increase their net worth while the organization reaches its goals. The empowered response requires individuals and the organization to push beyond "business as usual" by changing what individuals do and how they do it.

It is this fourth response that will yield a committed individual and a healthier organization. Empowerment connects two basic needs: organizational and individual. Followers try to respond to the organization's agenda by reaction, without considering their own needs or agenda. Mavericks follow their own agendas, ignoring or paying lip-service to the organization. Drifters do neither.

Our intent in this book is to chronicle this fourth path—to empowerment—to anchor it in business examples and provide a template for people and organizations to build the organizational environments that will support the United States in the global marketplace.

HOW EMPLOYEES GET THE WAKE-UP CALL FOR CHANGE

As the world changes around organizations, the people inside the organizations need to change. As Phil Quigley, the president of Pacific Telesis, said at a 1992 meeting about management change, "The people who have been successful in the past may not be those who are successful in the future."[21] The organization needs its employees to have new skills in order to make it in the new work environment. Rebuilding the organization is not just a shift of the organization chart and a few behaviors. It entails making a deep shift in everything that once held true about work and adapting a new set of assumptions, expectations, reflexes, and behaviors that would have been problematical in the traditional organization.

Even the most satisfied organizations today will not be able to coast on past successes tomorrow. Everything needs to change: the people, their relationships, and the nature of the whole organization. How does one begin a shift to where employees refocus their energies and attention—to try out new ideas, take risks, and upset tried-and-true strategies—without crashing? Much as it is hard for individuals to change, it is even harder for a fully formed organization to change. What can you as an individual do? There are always avenues to change; here, we outline three.

- *Change yourself.* Changing may involve learning new skills, acting in new ways, or changing your perspective on the situation. Changing yourself may make you more valuable or more effective to your organization, or to other organizations.

- *Change other people by changing the way you relate to them.* Encourage other people to try things, set an example, influence their decisions, or even teach or coach them in new behavior.

- *Change the organization's procedures, its expectations, or its structure.*

Under the old entitlement contract, the idea of changing the organization was practically unthinkable. But now no one else is to blame for not doing things differently. Thanks to empowerment, the best way to change the organization is by changing yourself, and changing others by the example you set and power of your relationship with them.

There is sometimes misperception all around about these choices. People feel that *they* want to change, but the organization, or their superiors, won't let them. They feel that unless the organization changes, they cannot or will not change themselves. Feeling like victims, they overlook or do not understand the levers they can pull to initiate or support the necessary change. Or the organization (in the form of its top management) may feel it wants its employees to change, but unintentionally frustrates and limits their ability to do so. People at the top can get angry and blame the people at the bottom, and people at the bottom can feel that top management is uncaring, selfish, or incompetent. The result is a stalemate, with both sides dug in, waiting for the other to make the first move.

In reality, everyone who works in an organization needs to look at how they are reacting to the need for change. No one can stand on the sidelines, watching the spectacle. And we cannot postpone the time of reckoning. We must not continue to keep trying the same things, using the same techniques, assuming that they will eventually succeed: this is folly. As Jungian analyst and philosopher James Hillman has said: "Insanity is doing the same thing over and over again and expecting different results."[22]

Of course many organizations have deeply wounded their people and given them many reasons to withdraw just at the time when they are needed most. But we are suggesting that withdrawing is a disservice to yourself as well as to the organization. If you are going to remain in your organization, the best way to get yourself reconnected to it is to become a change leader and help the organization meet the challenges of the new work environment.

In Chapter Three, we better explain the path to commitment through empowerment by defining a new role for employees in the new workplace: the change leader.

3

Release Your Personal Power: Becoming a Leader of Change

The world now needs a multiplication of leaders in every domain—leaders to redesign societies characterized by spreading knowledge, leaders who empathize with yearnings for fairness, leaders who can reconcile the global imperatives of technology with the protection of human diversity and individual human rights. The day-to-day risks taken by "transformative" leaders—men and women who make a difference—are the key factors in the dynamism of a single organization or a whole society.

—Harlan Cleveland, *Beginning the World Again*

$\mathbf{W}$hat makes the United States a leader in management education, despite the fact that our organizations appear to be at least as troubled and struggling as those of other nations? One answer has to do with the nature of our culture. Deep in our culture is a perception that if things are not working, individuals can take it upon themselves to make changes. Ours is one of the few national cultures founded upon a self-initiated, planned organizational change. The United States also appears to balance the value it puts on independence and autonomy in the individual and the respect it gives the needs of the organization. Unlike Japan, where harmony with the organization is valued over the needs or ideas of the individual, in this country there is respect for the organization and for the individual as well. Allowing individual growth is our most distinguishing strength.

47

Literary critic Leslie Fiedler highlights how American mythology is steeped in individualism: The cowboy, the war hero,
the private eye are all loners, people who espouse a just cause
and take things into their own hands against unjust forces in the
community.[1] According to our mythology, individual rights take
precedence over societal needs. Individuals feel, in theory at
least, that they have the right to struggle against injustice and
unfairness. Expectations of such rights seem to extend into the
organization; employees feel it their right to speak out.

As we look for workplace models that can be effective in the
emerging global arena, we need to look at the individual for the
roots of change. The people who work inside organizations must
be hardy enough to learn new behaviors and ways of working.
People who look to the organization, for directives from the top,
to show them the way, are not likely to be as effective. The new
model of the organization is premised on activating the initiative
and the power of the individual to make the organization work.
At a time when individual commitment to the organization is
precarious, the new models of organization all entail the person
finding not only a reason to reconnect to it but also a deeper and
more global commitment to making it work. The individual must
become *empowered*, that is, able to harness his or her own drive
and fervor to help make the organization grow and succeed.

If American culture popularized nothing more than selfish,
unbridled individualism, we would never have created organizational giants with the power to generate global empires. The corporation is the largest and most powerful goal-oriented entity
ever created. When it is successful, it coordinates and harnesses
the energy of thousands of individuals into one overall purpose.
Empowerment means bringing the American hero back into the
organization, not as a lone cowboy ridding the corporation of cor-
ruption, but as a member of the community working with others.

EMPOWERMENT: RESPONSIBILITY
WITHIN COMMUNITY

The ability to create large communities to which people voluntarily commit their energies has always been part of the Ameri-

can culture. Indeed, the American organization has always been able to compel more than mere obedience; at its best, the organization's employees identified with it and were deeply committed to its goals. The corporation created meaning as well as products and services. Each corporation had certain values and those who worked there identified with them. But the image of the organization has changed. We cannot overcome the crisis facing organizations today unless we redefine the entire nature of the connection between individual and organization.

One of the fantasies that doesn't die, even in the new age of organizations, is that of a leader with vision, competence, and respect who will emerge to solve the organization's problems. Recent books on leadership also give the impression that the captains of industry are the sources of the wisdom and power to redesign organizations, if only *they* would begin to change.

We are not denying that such people can have massive impact. But given the overwhelming pressures on corporate leaders just to keep their organizations afloat, the official leader may not be the likeliest source to meet the challenges of the future. The story that people tell themselves about how an organization succeeds must shift from one about the heroic CEO or inventor to one about teams and groups working together to create amazing results. The organization must find ways to support people coming back into the fold, even as they have done many things to frustrate and push them away. Paradoxically, what is needed is a drastic shift that can come about quickly.

Companies have found that a small semiautonomous group of people from every department of the company—from technical to marketing—can develop new products and get them to market in far less time, with far more success, than can a large bureaucracy with many departments taking the project from each other in sequence. Cutting teams and people loose from some organizational control, allowing them to innovate and take the initiative, have become the keys for organizations that want to change fast.

In but one example, consider the classic team story of the creation of the Eagle computer for Data General.[2] In less than a year, a team of people created a completely new computer design. The organization had freed them from restrictions, with only the expectation that they would find a way to succeed. The leadership was shared; every member of the team acted heroically. Every individual felt fully engaged and able to take action; every action was deeply connected with the discoveries and the work of the others. The group's success came from individual commitment to the team and from the freedom to act with no constraints.

But for many organizations, such a phenomenon does not come easily. For one reason, as organizations have grown, the control at the top has tried to direct more and more groups, each of which performs in different environments. Over time, management has become synonymous with more and more power to control. These control processes limit the vitality, creativity, and ability of organizations to adapt and change when circumstances demand it. Something has to change.

Often the process of loosening up doesn't start at the top. In August 1984, the largest corporate restructuring in history was initiated when AT&T agreed to split into seven smaller corporations. It also would lay off 21,000 employees, something that had never been done before. Shock was far too mild a term to describe the response of longtime employees who had come to work at "Ma Bell" precisely for its security, predictability, and tradition. Now, in one consent decree, everything changed.

We were brought in to help individual branches of one part of the new AT&T renew themselves. We entered what could be described as a field of devastation. Branches had been amalgamated, people had been let go, and the direction and future of the new company was a cipher. What were people to do while they waited for direction? "Well," one team member in one of the branches said, "we can sit around and wait for orders, but I think we know that the people in the regional office don't have the slightest idea what to do. Or, we can just look at what has to be done, and do it as best we can." This was a revolutionary concept in a company that had been built upon doing things by the book and getting approval for any deviation. Now, with chaotic change, the rules were called into question. At this team meeting we first heard the phrase, "I'd rather beg for forgiveness than ask permission." The team became energized and excited as, for the first time, they began to think of ways to do things rather than follow the mouldering established methods, some of which they thought self-defeating or foolish. Initially, they had a real business challenge—to sell equipment that was more expensive than the more technologically advanced Japanese systems.

The team members got excited and even began to forget some of their confusion and pain as they defined for themselves the best method for selling phone systems. They then sent a copy of their handbook to the regional office and waited to see what would happen. To their surprise, that handbook was made the guide for the whole organization.

The branch unit had shifted ground and begun to think of itself as the originators of policy and ideas rather than as the receiver of them. In their pain, and despite their frayed connection with the whole company, the group substituted a new perspective in which they were creative, innovative, and able to act on their own. The team members' connection was rebuilt, not with the whole company at first, but with one another, each of whom days before had been strangers.

The shift in perspective that this team made is the essence of what we mean by empowerment. Empowerment comes about when individuals feel deep commitment to the organization or the team; when they feel that they are working beyond constraints to solve a problem that is important to the company as a whole.

Reconsidering Power

The case at AT&T was unusual in that consent decrees are rarely the instigating force behind such changes. But, however begun, such changes require a shift in how power is viewed.

The Manager's Point of View.   Power is the ability to get things done. Traditionally, power came from one's position and was assigned to individuals in the organization in carefully measured increments. The higher you were, the more you could give directions to other people, make your own decisions, and be less controlled by supervision. Power meant the ability to tell others what to do, and have them obey. It meant you didn't have to learn.

Thus managers are used to experiencing their power only in terms of control: control over resources, information, and people. They keep control by keeping other people powerless; to them, power is a zero-sum game. This is a notion of the organization that has held for thousands of years, and despite the fact that such exercise of power may be counterproductive today, it is far from extinct.

But the new realities of the workplace may push this notion into extinction. If, because of rapidly changing environments and technology, the boss is not sure what to do, who has the power? The boss? Or the person who knows what needs to be done? In such cases, which are everyday events in today's work life, power is shared. It is important that both parties know that this is the case.

People in all positions—from the manager, who used to have all the answers, to the new employee—are struggling with a feeling of loss of control and powerlessness. Empowerment has a special promise for such people: It sees power as something that is not given but can be created by individuals.

Operating an organization by letting go of control and trusting the people below you to come through is a difficult proposition at first. Yet the new form of power—empowerment—means that people in organizations must do so. As a result, the organization will begin to gain the help of people by their voluntary commitment, not through fear and compulsion. And, as we are seeing, this has very beneficial effects. The level of commitment of the person who has a hand in a decision is probably higher than of the one who is told what to do. He or she is more willing to do the work and therefore more likely to succeed at a complex and demanding task.

Rosabeth Kanter noticed that much of the controlling, demanding, and even abusive, manipulative, or hostile behavior of middle managers was not an expression of their superior power and status, but rather an expression of their frustration and anxiety at not having the power to get the job done.[3] In their anxiety, they leaned on their subordinates, who in turn withdrew, disobeyed, and limited their commitment, putting even more pressure on managers. Thus the cycle of control began. How is this cycle broken?

Both the cycles of control and of empowerment (shown in Figure 3.1) begin with pressure on the manager to perform. The change from a controlled to an empowered workplace often begins with a shift in the manager's response.

In the control cycle, the manager tells people what to do and exerts control over others. This leads the employees to do what they are told but also to become passive, uninvolved, even angry. They give less than their potential and do not offer the manager any help. The manager has total accountability and responsibility, creating still more pressure. The manager therefore continues the cycle by becoming more controlling. The control cycle leads to low results and low morale.

The empowerment cycle similarly begins with pressure on the manager. However, instead of trying to control others, the manager gives them trust and brings them into the problem as partners; the manager shares resources, information, respect, and control. After a time, everyone gets involved and helps achieve results. Performance levels rise and morale is boosted.

If the differences are so dramatic, why is the traditional control cycle maintained in so many organizations? A major factor is that the shift to the empowerment cycle involves start-up costs in terms of investment in people. Many companies feel that they do not have the time or the money to make this investment and instead accept low performance. Another factor is that managers either do not know that another cycle is possible or do not have the skills to make it happen. They do not know how to motivate by inspiration. It takes time and effort to learn such methods. Also the manager has to make the first move, which is a scary thing to do, because people have never had the experience of acting in a way that empowers others.

The Employee's Point of View.   The real power in the new organization belongs not so much to the people in high positions as to the people who make things happen, who are able to mobilize themselves to get things done, and who inspire others to work with them. Potentially, everyone in the organization can do this. Power can be created by the people who use it.

Figure 3.1. Two Cycles: Empowerment and Control.

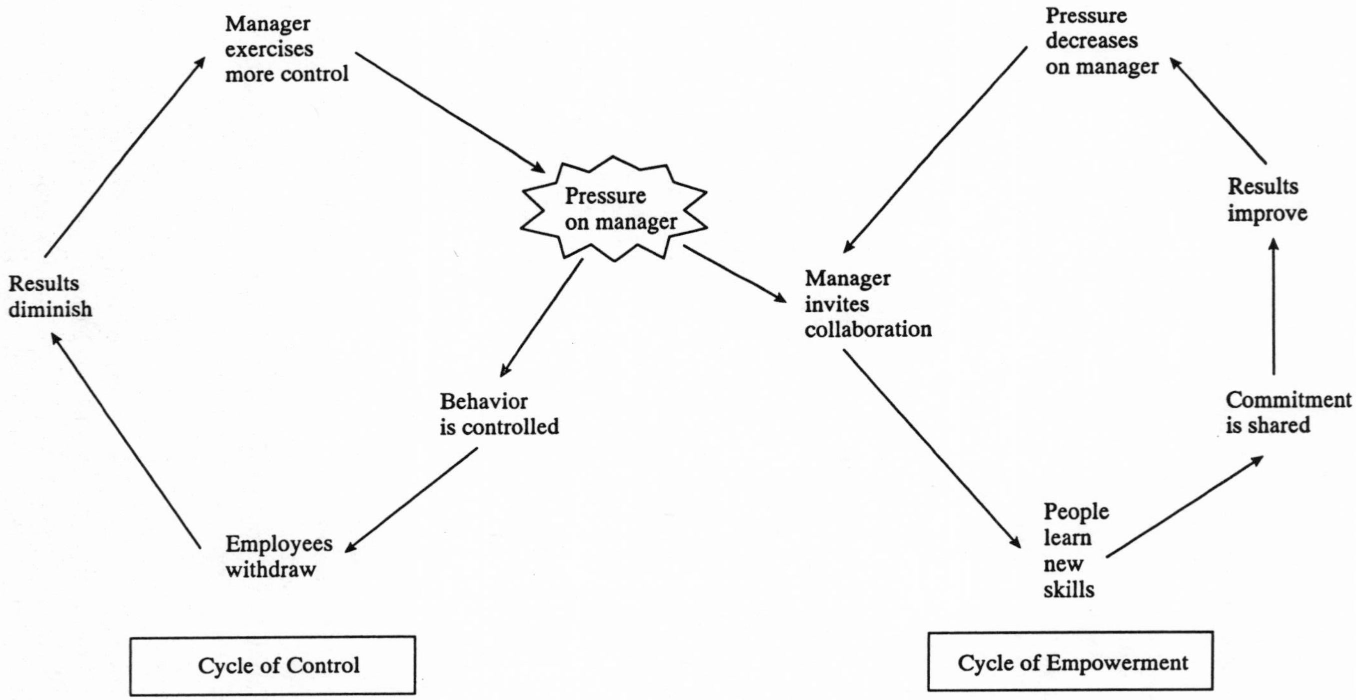

There are three ways of gaining power:

1. You can take it yourself. This is personal power—self-empowerment. You express it directly through your skills.

2. You can give it to others, by the way you relate to them and manage them. You thus empower others.

3. The organization can give it to you, by giving you the position and offering you the procedures to confer power and responsibility. It creates an environment that supports and values power in everyone.

The first two methods can be taken by individuals. A person can decide to be empowered without getting permission from the organization. The empowered person has many sources of power, which we call "power tools"—tools he or she can use to get things done. Power tools include the following:

-   Gathering information
-   Persuading others
-   Saying no
-   Asking for help
-   Creating a vision
-   Showing people a new possibility
-   Developing a new skill

Thus, a power tool is anything that enables people to get something done. The new power tools have unique qualities: They are readily available, do not have to be taken from others, and do not take power away from others. In fact, as some people in the organization begin to create power using the available power tools, many other people throughout the organization get more power.

The third method leaves it up to the organization to create an environment that empowers people. However, this support, because it demands a paradigm shift or major transformation of the organization, is not likely to happen until *after* many people in the organization have already changed. As the company evolves and people learn to communicate directly with other groups and carry out their own projects, people other than those traditionally in power become the real sources of power. Thus, the empowered workplace reflects a fundamental redefinition of power and its expression.

THE CHALLENGE
OF EMPOWERED LEADERSHIP

There is always a lag between the workplace that people envision and need, and the one that they have. How do we move from here to there? We believe that people at work, no matter the level or role they have, need to respond differently to the new pressures and changes in the workplace. Consider, for instance, the following questions:

- Can you begin to look at the organization not in terms of what it is and has been, but in terms of what it can be?

- Are you willing to see yourself not as a victim but as an active force helping to propel the organization toward a preferred future?

- Can you see part of your work role as acting as advocate for change rather than as supporter of the traditional way?

- Can you become an educator in the organization, taking the knowledge that you have gained in work groups and in contact with your customers and using it to help the organization grow?

    The new leaders of the organization will be the people who bring a new style and design to the organization. In most organizations in the early phases of change, the new leaders are not necessarily the people at the top; they emerge from anywhere in the organization.
    The major changes that need to take place in the next gen-

eration will come from these new leaders, people who at any level have effectively shifted their view of themselves and of the organization so that they are empowered to do their best. This requires new skills and the courage to put those skills to work. Other people will only change when they see that they need to grow. Changing yourself and how you work is the most radical step in organizational redesign.

Managers, Employees, and Empowerment

Thus the traditional employee and manager roles need to be rethought to allow for the new realities of empowerment. In fact, both terms are being redefined. For example, in many companies, the term "employee" has come into question because it implies the traditional familial pattern, a parental organization and a child. The new word used by companies such as Federal Express, W. E. Gore, Wal-Mart, Honda, Herman Miller, Ben & Jerry's, and The Body Shop is "associate." This implies collaboration across levels and work groups.

As we see it, the traditional role of the manager is endangered. That is not because there isn't something important about these people who were linking pins between groups and maintainers of performance. It's just that with full empowerment, the nature of the manager's job will change completely. No longer will the manager be responsible for another person's performance. The tasks of communicating the needs of the people at the top and directing how the work gets done will become less important as more employees or (or associates) begin to manage their relationships and their work themselves.

Where does all of this leave the traditional manager? Many feel they have the most to lose in the move toward empowerment. If their employees are empowered, managers lose the familiar world where they felt in control by defining for others how things would be done. As their employees gain power and authority, managers lose some of their power and status. The fear of this loss can lead managers to fall back, even retreat into traditional controlling behavior, in a time of stress or crisis.

The fear of change has many causes for middle managers.

They are reluctant to give up the perks of their role; it is a very comfortable role and they feel they have earned it. Underlying this may be a fear that they will not be able to learn new ways. "I have been acting this way for a long time," one manager told us, "and I don't see myself changing very much." Or they may believe that they have changed and even point to specific differences. Yet their team members haven't noticed the change. Finally, the greatest fear for many managers is that as they let go of control they may be overshadowed by the people under them. As one manager of a large company said, "The fear of empowerment is that I may have to let my people know that I don't know the best way to do a job. And I may find out that one of them knows better than I do, which is very difficult to admit." And this fear is well grounded, because the reality is that those managers who didn't add much value to the company and whose power was negative will be unmasked once the people they used to manage become empowered.

There will always be a need for people who link cross-functional groups, who help other people perform, and who mediate between individuals and the organization. We see these people as being the synapse, the coordinators. But they are not managers in the traditional sense; instead, their role can be coach, partner, helper, consultant, facilitator. Anyone in a group can take on such a role.

Managers must face up to empowerment as it comes to the fore. For example, middle managers in a large telecommunications company recently heard their choices in very stark terms. They could go in one of three directions:

1. They could become teachers, or coordinators, who would inspire large numbers of people to become empowered and supervise by liberating people's potential. They would have less formal authority and function as servants to their staffs.

2. They could join teams as members or as technical sources. In this case, they would have to overcome the feeling that they had been demoted and learn to perform a service to the team rather than direct it.

3.   They could leave the company.

Even in the organizations that try to hold onto traditional
ways, the fact that the individual manager now has many more
people to supervise provides some interesting dilemmas. One
military group was talking about how its work had changed. In
the old days, the colonel (top management) would say, "I want
you to do things my way, and if you deviate you'll suffer." Now
the colonel has many more officers reporting to him and isn't so
sure how things should be done. When an individual group
makes a proposal or wants to do something a certain way, the
colonel is more than likely to say, "As long as you get results, do it
whatever way you think is right." In the new workplace, control is
no longer desirable.

The "glue" for the new workplace is employee empowerment. Yet how many people in an organization see what needs to
be done and don't say or do anything about it? Because management does not see them as innovators, they stop seeing themselves as potential forces for change. "Checkers checking checkers," was the traditional organizational orientation; the game was
to avoid responsibility as much as possible by sending it up to
one's boss. Now, however, the roles of employees and managers
in the empowered organization include broadened and increased
accountability and responsibility. This step of taking responsibility is something that few employees have learned and that few
workplaces have demanded.

The new distinctions between manager and employee continue to be worked out as we find our way. Also important are
the concepts of "leader" and "manager" and how they are
changing.

Redefining Roles of Leaders and Managers
Zalesnik first made the distinction between the leader and the
manager, a distinction that is key to the new organization.[4] Stable, predictable organizations needed managers, people who
made sure that everyone acted consistently, according to the pre-
scriptions of the organization. They were responsible for a small

number of other people. Their task was to keep things consistent and to limit change, which could be seen as a variation from the norm or the traditional way of doing business.

The differences between the leader and the manager are often symbolized as in Figure 3.2. As the inward-pointing arrows indicate, the manager works to maintain boundaries and to do things precisely as prescribed. The manager's role is to contain and focus individual and team effort. In contrast, the leader takes on the task of helping the organization grow and change by broadening its possibilities, learning new ways, and creating and innovating; the leader's role is to move people beyond the boundaries of their jobs to produce results for the organization.

If an organization is continually changing, the old-style managers can be the least helpful. An organization that is changing needs leaders who help others move beyond traditional ways to discover and adapt to new realities. Further, in the evolving organization, leadership becomes an expectation of all employees, not of the manager alone. Every contributing member of the organization is called upon at times to exercise leadership, that is, to help move the organization beyond into new territory.

The ability to maintain a vision of the future, to know where you want to go while living with the tension of the current situation, is central to success. Added to this are two additional qualities:

Figure 3.2.   Changing Roles: Manager and Leader.

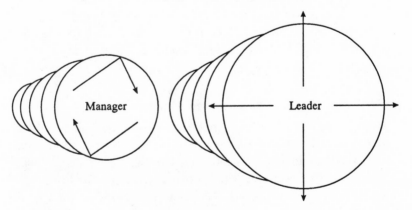

1. Dealing with the diverse and different views and voices of people in the corporate community, and

2. Developing a "big picture," a broad perspective of what is happening and how to make the organization successful

In the changing organization, the only way to keep despair and frustration at bay is to develop these new competencies to respond to growing pressures.

Depending upon the group and the moment, there is also a need for different leadership skills. To create the future a visionary leader is needed, one who can create a context and develop a picture of the desired future so that everybody sees the need to change. At other times, a leader is needed who can broker and link the group to other groups in the organization, gathering information and resources, and taking the group's cause to others. This is what Andre delBeque has called the *interface leader*. At still other times, a *statesman* leader is needed, one who can negotiate different interests and come up with a single focus and task. And a change leader may be a *healer*, a person who helps others overcome hurt and trauma and regain their commitment. Because there are too many roles for one person to take on, a strong and effective team draws on diverse competencies of different people at different times to fulfill the various roles.

The Change Leaders

The traditional organization looked to the formal leader, the CEO and his consultants and staff, for change leadership. These people came up with a strategy and introduced it to the organization. The usual pathway to change began outside: Experts would tell the CEO, and then the whole organization, what they should do, and then they would do it. This model of change is based on the person as a machine that simply needs to be placed on the proper path by an outside designer. But this model leaves us dependent on leadership in the form of CEOs and we may fall into despair about the possibility of change: If the leaders don't seem to get it, how can the organization change? And if CEOs last only a few years, how can change really work?

A recent article introduced the concept of substitutes for leadership.[5] Instead of looking at leadership as coming from the top, what if group members divided up the functions of leadership among themselves? Leadership became decentralized, no longer embodied in a single person of authority and wisdom. If leaders aren't leading in the traditional sense and the group members see an opportunity, they can exercise leadership by influencing the group in a new direction. That is what we mean by change leadership. If one person has a new idea that would enhance the capacity of her group, she should sell it to the group. The top leader may be persuaded to step aside and let the experiment run if the other team members can be persuaded to back it.

In this way, the company can become better able to face the two tasks of every organization in today's world:

1.   To develop the specific products, services, and capacities needed to succeed in a difficult, competitive marketplace

2.   To develop the organization's capacity to keep on growing and reach the next success

Many organizations are effective at task 1. The winners in the long-term sweepstakes are those who succeed at task 2 as well. To accomplish these results requires leadership that is abundantly available everywhere in the organization.

Every organization is engaged in some form of renewal process as it lurches fitfully toward its own version of the new workplace. Renewal as we use the term means "making new," discovering a new form that fits the deepest intention of the organization. The key to renewal is broadening the role of all employees, thereby enhancing their commitment and gaining their involvement in making change work.

THE CHANGE
OF EMPOWERMENT

One of the obstacles to empowerment is the misperception by some that other parts of the organization are not open to change.

We conducted an empowerment program for the staff of a new Macy's store. The top management group was very excited about the prospect of empowered employees at all levels, but they voiced concern that although this was exciting to them, they didn't feel their associates (associates in the new sense) would "buy" it. In the next room, the new associates were going through the same scenario. They wanted empowerment and a new role, but they had a similar concern: They were certain that top managers would not buy into the concept. We were able to pass this information back and forth to both groups so that they could see that each was projecting its fears and concerns onto the other. Without someone in that intermediary function, how could change come about?

One way to build commitment to the organization is to see it not as a static entity but as one moving toward the image of what we would like it to be. If you can see your company evolving toward more empowerment and toward more attention to the core values that you hold, then you may find yourself able to forgive it for its past disruption and put energy into helping it move toward that image.

In short, if you want change, become it. This means acting out of a sense of how things might be done in the new paradigm, creating an empowered organization through the example of your own work. People who feel this ask other people at work, "Why can't we do this?" or "Why don't we do it this way?" rather than gripe about how they can't get things done or how the organization doesn't support them.

If someone's organization lags behind his or her images of its possibilities, and if that person has ideas about how it can be a better place, that person has three choices, described more than a generation ago by Albert Hirschorn:6

1.   Exit and go elsewhere.

2.   Remain in the organization, voice concerns, values, and desires, and become involved in change.

3.   Remain in the organization and be quietly loyal to it, keeping silent.

The final choice—loyalty—supports the old ways and limits a person's potential to lead the organization into the future. Therefore, we see only two choices today: exit or give voice.

Imagine that a work group in which you are involved does things in a certain way, but you see the possibility of a vast improvement. If you keep silent, you diminish the group, and your own feeling of commitment to the organization. Keeping silent says that you do not feel connected enough to the organization to share your ideas. Keeping silent—exhibiting what has long been known as "loyalty"—only deepens the rift between your own feeling of what is right and possible and what the organization actually does.

"Giving voice" means speaking out and trying to influence others to consider what you have to say. The key to voice is to become a change leader—to mobilize transformation starting with oneself and one's own way of working. Change leaders see their jobs in terms of facilitating organizational change in the direction of a social mission and a set of values; working within an organization thus carries with it a responsibility to hold the company to its stated values and aspirations, and to work to achieve success within that broader definition of success.

Empowerment means taking full responsibility for getting the results you want in the organization. It means that you do not blame others for what you can't do, but take responsibility for what you can do or what you feel is important. This is sometimes terrifying and confusing for a person used to a traditional role in a traditional organization.

Empowerment means moving out of a reactive style of work and adopting a strategic focus to examine what you want to accomplish in your work. By doing this, you no longer see yourself as a helpless victim, waiting for the organization to tell you what to do. Just as your team and your company have a set of goals and a vision, you need one for yourself as well. Looking ahead toward your goals and vision, you define the steps to take toward them. From your own proposals, you negotiate and work with others to fit your personal vision and goals into the vision and goals of the organization. This alignment, a win-win orientation, is the essence of empowerment.

Succeeding at Change

No matter the changes in an organization, a person can see change as originating from outside or inside. An *outside* change might be an order from above or a reaction to a catastrophe. An *inside* change might be a personal inspiration or commitment. Some people are entirely reactive, and see all change as coming from outside. They are overwhelmed, because they feel things happening to them but lack the skills to respond. All they do is keep up with the changes that are imposed on them. They hardly get a chance to breathe.

Others, those we call the change leaders, find ways to anticipate or ride the leading edge of change and align their own values and vision with the change process. They push back at change, molding change in the direction of their own sense of where they are going. They are not victims of change but struggle to become its master. They discover they can keep from being demoralized and helpless by acting on their own values. If they believe in a new way, then they begin to act in ways that support the new direction. Change leadership becomes an add-on to their regular jobs in the sense of broadened responsibility.

The manager becomes an empowering leader by learning to let go of control and share information, responsibility, power and rewards with the team. The manager begins this process, knowing that when the team experiences such a change, they will become higher performers and increase their level of success.

The individual team member becomes a change agent by releasing his or her creativity and vision of what the organization can be and sharing it with others. In so doing, the individual reaches out to other parts of the organization, builds coalitions, listens to customers, and builds new teams and groups to get jobs done. The individual becomes a networker, a fountain of new energy for others in the organization. This process is infinitely more effective than waiting for the CEO to make the "big change" happen.

In the face of each frustration and problem, and each seeming limitation, the empowered leader finds a way to take action. The most frequent obstacle is the gap between what is desired and the resources offered to get it accomplished. People every-where in organizations see that their companies or its leaders want change but don't commit the needed resources to get it to happen. Often there is no congruence between policies and in-tentions, or between words and actions. But empowered groups and people find ways around these limits. They seek ways to get started with few resources, ignore the rules, find ways to get the job done within the established budget. This produces a shift in the spirit of a group and the spirit of individuals. They feel ener-gized, as though a burden has been lifted. And, indeed, the bur-den of feeling controlled, powerless, and helpless to do the best possible work has been lifted.

If we could trace organizational innovation back to the first note of change, rather than start from when it becomes policy or a new program, we would see clearly that change begins with individuals becoming empowered. People become active rather than passive, take the roles of mastery and leadership rather than of victim, and begin to move the organization toward the new form.

For example, a product development group was frustrated by the lack of participation in their activities by the marketing department, which was the far higher-profile and seemingly more highly valued group in the organization. The development group felt that its initiatives were rebuffed by marketing. But the group persisted in inviting the marketing group to its meetings until cooperation began. Then the group did the same with the manufacturing group. Thus the group's leadership, rather than that from above or from other groups, led to the development of cross-functional cooperation.

Roles and Competencies

Thus there is no single role for change leaders. There are a num-ber of ways that a person can exercise positive power to trans-form an organization.

Crisis-Spotter. The person who is able to spot a crisis on the horizon can help the organization overcome denial and see that it must move outside its comfort zone. Focusing attention on possible bad news was never honored in the traditional organization; it was downright dangerous. But crisis-spotters are effective at bringing information to everyone's attention and helping people see the need for change. They are constructive in helping find ways to respond to the crisis. Crisis-spotters tend to build support for doing something rather than simply blame people who have not seen the crisis.

Idea-Generator.   The idea-generator comes up with new possibilities and options. This is the person with entrepreneurial vision. Like the entrepreneur, the effectiveness of the idea comes from his or her effectiveness in bringing it to the attention and interest of other people.

Broker/Sponsor.   The broker/sponsor sees the need for change and has the ability to build a coalition to gain the momentum and resources to take action. This is the person who can get things done in an organization, who bonds with the crisis-spotters and the idea-generators to get action.

Tinkerer.   The tinkerer helps develop and build on new ideas to make them practical, to deal with objections or obstacles, and to make them work. The tinkerer is often the unsung hero who works in the reflected glow of the individual hero. In the new workplace, tinkerers are critical team members who make a new initiative a success.

Process Leader.   A new role, about which more will be said in the following chapters, is that of the process leader. Process leaders focus attention on and question the way things are done; they have the skills to help groups operate as empowered teams. They know how to build environments that help people to behave in empowered ways and to learn together.

Whatever the specific role, the key skills of a change leader are learning how to learn and being able to master change. More specifically, the new competencies of the empowered leader include the following:

- Seeks information when needed, from anywhere inside or outside the organization

- Moves across boundaries to connect to whichever people are important in achieving a task

- Develops the new skills that are needed to do the work, on personal time if necessary

- Shares concerns and expresses contradictions between current operations and those needed to achieve success in the organization

- Listens and learns from others, never feeling that his or her own insights or ideas are necessarily the last word

- Supports and affirms the power of others and respects their work

- Takes risks by sharing new ideas and hunches rather than trying to get them perfect before seeking feedback

- Willingly challenges, confronts, and informs people at higher levels about what is needed to get the job done

Imagine that a small group feels that the organization needs to change and begins to apply appropriate new competencies on its own. By acting differently, members take responsibility for doing what has to be done. The effect of their initiative is to begin a process of transformation within the whole organization that gains some support and involvement from others. The cycle of transformation thus begins based on the responsible action of a few individuals. In the next chapter, we will look at such self-empowerment in action. We describe how people can initiate empowerment in their own thoughts and deeds, and begin to create a workplace that fits their deepest personal values.

4
Take Responsibility: Linking Commitment to Action

I would rather be ashes than dust!
I would rather that my spark should burn out
in a brilliant blaze than it should be stifled by dry rot.
I would rather be a superb meteor, every atom of me
in magnificent glow, than a sleepy and permanent planet.
The proper function of man is to live, not to exist.
I shall not waste my days in trying to prolong them.
I shall use my time.

—Jack London

In our era, the road to holiness necessarily passes through
the world of action.

—Dag Hammarskjöld

No matter how significant the position people hold in an organization, if they do not prepare themselves for a deep and fundamental shift in the way they themselves do business, they will not be prepared to lead others into change. If individuals do not change, the changes they try to bring about in others and in the organization will not amount to much. People need to modify their own sense of who they are at work, what they are capable of, and how they assume responsibility in order to fit into the emerging workplace. This chapter discusses the basic shifts that are necessary in preparing to be effective at change.

THE GENE OF
ORGANIZATIONAL RENEWAL

In the traditional organization, the amount of personal freedom was very small indeed. But once people begin to see themselves as the source of the action, taking responsibility both for themselves and for the organization, the personal freedom expands. The way they see the organization, their job, and what is possible changes because they see that they can make a difference. The way one acts changes as one finds new pathways and avenues for achieving goals.

Self-empowerment (or personal empowerment) begins when people ask themselves how they can contribute to making things better. If they don't currently have significant power in their organization, they go out and get it. They may take a chance and do what has to be done or they may respectfully suggest another way to get a job done; they don't simply accept a task that they believe will produce less than the desired effects.

Our view is that, given the nature of the challenges facing all companies, the people who initiate empowered action are those who will eventually take a company onto a new path. If the company does not enter a new path, the chances are that everyone will be needing new jobs—even those who played it safe. But those who are empowered may have a jump on those who don't prepare. We must therefore provide a caution: *empowering yourself is not without risks.* Self-empowerment means challenging, taking risks, and sometimes even creating problems for oneself and for others. Self-empowerment offers many rewards, but it also means walking on a tightrope. Any person who begins to suggest change and new ways will stir up controversy. People cannot expect that their new ideas or actions will automatically be embraced by the organization. Empowered people must learn to build support for their ideas, persist in their work, and most of all, present new ideas without dismissing the efforts of the other people in the company.

Personal empowerment means discovering in oneself the sources of power needed to get the job done. It means finding and asserting one's own authority. It usually begins when people look for the sources of power that can get them what they want, rather than focusing on the limits or barriers. Personal empowerment contains two necessary dynamics:

- *Inner transformation:* the discovery of new ways of seeing yourself, the organization, and possibilities
- *Responsible action:* doing what is right and thereby having an effect on yourself, other people, and the whole organization

We discuss both of these in depth in the rest of this chapter. We conclude with specific strategies for self-empowerment to help underscore the chapter's meaning and make it immediately useful.

INNER TRANSFORMATION

One of the things that a traditional organization does very well is resist, or deny, the need to change. The organization has developed what we term "limiting beliefs," which are widely held assumptions that encourage people not to try to change things. The traditional organization is maintained because employees internalize a set of boundaries they never cross. They implicitly agree not to challenge these limits, so the whole organization acts as if the limits are inviolable. To go beyond these limits would demand that people question the assumptions (assumptions like, "The organization will take care of me," "Don't rock the boat," "Get along by going along," "Don't ask why") that kept the old ways working.

Empowered people question these limits, realizing that there are many ways to make a difference in an organization. They look for the creative possibilities. But new possibilities aren't sitting there, asking to be seen; they need to be discovered. To do this requires an internal shift that enables people to see the organization and themselves differently. In this section, we explore three dimensions of this shift:

1. Looking at the organization differently and discovering new ways to have impact

2. Moving out of one's own, and one's organization's, comfort zone

3. Developing the inner faculties to see creative possibilities

Empowerment sometimes means challenging the organization's limiting beliefs. With an attitude that we call *breakthrough thinking*, people can challenge themselves, their team, and their organization to find ways to do better. Instead of seeing the organization as a given, they see it as something that they can question, perhaps by asking: Could we do it better? Are our assumptions correct? In raising questions, their voice and personal behavior can change. Their speaking up may encourage others to begin to change as well. Ultimately, when enough people have made the leap, the culture of the organization may change as well.

Changing the Inner Hologram

Every employee has an internalized image of the organization, a hologram of sorts through which they carry the organization within themselves. This hologram depicts the organizational culture and rules, which are accepted as givens.

To see how the inner hologram can be changed through questioning, let us take a simple example. Ruth has worked for five years in a work group that is known for its poor performance. There are many negative company norms that encourage such low performance: "Don't work too hard," "Nobody cares if you do any better," and "We'll just get more work if we do any better." The group's results create a self-fulfilling prophesy and come true—its members are slow to respond to customers, don't meet their goals, and generally are known within the company as "slow." Ruth decides that she doesn't have to wait for the whole group to change; she is just going to make a change in her own performance. She begins to look at her work as if it mattered and view the work of other people with the same interest. Some people think she is crazy: They know that her group can't do any better. But as Ruth persists, her work begins to change, and her perception of herself also changes. Her production rate goes up; her scrap rate goes down. Ruth is becoming an experiment in initiating a different result from that expected within the prevailing hologram. Her supervisor and people in her group begin to notice. Her single example of change begins to influence the behavior of an entire group.

In many cases, however, the initial response to any new behavior may not be positive and enthusiastic. Initiating a challenge to any of the organization's cultural norms is, in fact, likely to provoke resistance. For instance, entering a team meeting with a suggestion such as, "Why are we meeting alone? Why don't we call in the members of the marketing group to meet with us?" is likely to provoke criticism, even derision. "If they wanted to meet with us, they would have told us," one person will likely say. "We asked them and they never sent us a date," another will chime in. These past events or nonevents have become encrusted into limiting beliefs, so that people assume that yesterday's experience must become tomorrow's reality. Until someone acts, they will not change.

The journey to personal empowerment begins when you begin to believe that your organization can become something new and better in the future, that it is not sentenced forever to operate within limits of today. First, you need to begin to notice, and root out, all of the ways you yourself maintain the organization of the past. Within your job, in what you say, you have the opportunity at every moment to maintain the old organization; look for the ways that you do this:

- What do you notice and consider when you have a difficulty?

- How do you go about finding things out?

- How do you respond to your intuitions about how things ought to change?

You can use more than just imagination as a guide. People seeking empowerment frequently discover relevant models by reading, talking, and observing. When they look around they are able to discover a world of alternative possibilities. Taking action on those possibilities may require an individual to step out into unfamiliar territory, out of what we call the comfort zone.

Moving out of the Comfort Zone

Our internalized images also tell us about ourselves and what we believe are our own possibilities. Our limiting beliefs are the stories we tell ourselves to keep from growing. Perhaps we tell ourselves that we have advanced as far as we can go, that we cannot learn a new skill or are too old to learn—then we act as if that limit is real. We keep ourselves from changing and growing.

Many people carry around limiting beliefs that may have started back in grade school. "I'm not smart," "I'm not good at math," or "I can't speak in public," are among the most common. These become self-fulfilling prophesies, keeping people within familiar and safe limits of behavior: the "comfort zone." For example, when Sam has difficulty deciding which computer program will best suit his needs, he applies this myth, "I can't determine this because I'm not smart enough." When he gives up and doesn't try to analyze the benefits of various programs but chooses one based on price alone, he has stayed inside his comfort zone.

A comfort zone encompasses all of the familiar activities that we can handle easily, competently, comfortably. Within the comfort zone, we do not question or pressure ourselves to change, and we perform without fear. The organization also has a comfort zone, which includes its norms, the types of activity in which it engages, and its ways of doing things. People and organizations find it easy to live inside their comfort zone. Unfortunately, living in the comfort zone means not growing and not changing. Growth and change require moving outside the zone, or at least enlarging it.

Many people accept their limitations, and those of their team and organization, because they do not believe themselves capable of changing them. Change is triggered when a new situation arises for a person, a team, or a whole organization. The challenge can come from the environment or from within a person. For example, when people find themselves facing a physical challenge, they may find some of their inner limits vanishing. Change also happens through the vehicles of personal relationships (such as new marriages), children, personal loss or adversity, and psychotherapy. Each of these vehicles helps people see themselves and the world differently, and break free of their inner limits so that they can see themselves acting differently.

Without some impetus, denial and resistance may prevail and keep the individual or organization inside the comfort zone. People may deny that change is happening or they may ignore it. Or they may continue doing things the old way, feeling that their "right" way will eventually triumph. In a rapidly changing environment, breaking through denial and resistance quickly and beginning to deal with the new situation increase the chances of being successful.

Recent business history is full of stories of organizations that tried to stay within their comfort zones: American auto companies ignoring the engineering and cost achievements of the Japanese; computer companies believing that people would always need mainframes; a retailer's belief that a store's location, status as an "institution," and customer loyalty would protect it from new kinds of competition; an abusive manager thinking that discontent was gone because he or she stopped hearing it.

Moving outside the comfort zone means moving into an area where you will feel strange, scared, and very uncomfortable. This is the "risk zone," the area where you are learning, where your new behavior will be tentative, anxious, uncertain, and probably not very effective at first. Your performance level will be low as you begin a new behavior. After telling yourself that you will no longer feel bound by the limits, you begin to learn, grow, try new behaviors, and extend your own capacities.

We saw some powerful examples of people beginning to grow out of their comfort zones by challenging their limiting beliefs when we were consultants to a high-tech plant with a thousand employees that was being threatened with termination by the parent company. The plant employees had been told that if they increased their performance and quality to the highest level, the company would retain them. Then, with a new CEO and the economy still in the doldrums, the decision was made to close the plant anyway. People felt angry, betrayed, and fearful.

The workers, mainly Latino women who had children, were largely formally uneducated but had developed high levels of technical skill in their years of work. Their perceived limits revolved in a small circle: As they saw it, their skills were not good for any other job; they were not educated, so they couldn't get new jobs; they had to be home with their children, so they couldn't get a formal education; they weren't smart enough for college, and anyway, their husbands wouldn't let them go to school, and they wouldn't get jobs even if they were educated. Obviously they were left feeling very helpless and vulnerable.

In our work, we began to challenge them. First, we found some examples of women from the company who had disproved the beliefs. They had taken the risks and gone to school while still taking care of their families. They had found new jobs, surprised at the number of new companies that were relocating to their area. Second, we helped the workers put aside their limiting beliefs and look at their possibilities. How could they arrange to further their education? What kind of education did they need to augment the skills they had developed on the job? In exploring the environment, we found that the educational level expected in new technical jobs was indeed much higher than that needed when they had gotten their jobs, but the financial rewards were substantially higher. In addition, there were many ways that their current company, and other sources, would support their education. After a while, the sense of helplessness and fear was replaced as several active support groups of people began empowering themselves to take care of their future careers.

In an environment of continual change, the chances of staying in one's comfort zone for a long career with one company are as likely as the survival of traditional organizations, which is to say quite small. The old comfort zone of protection, along with the culture of entitlement, is disappearing. Yet leaving the comfort zone is so frightening that many people don't do so voluntarily. Then when the environment forces them out, they do not know what to do. People need to learn and exercise the skills of personal empowerment, rather than feel paralyzed by their denial or the fear or anger of their resistance.

We made a choice to take ourselves out of our own comfort zone when we established our consulting firm, HeartWork, Inc. Each of the three authors of this book has a different natural ability. The synergy of our skills offered us two ways to form our organization. The traditional way would have been for each of us to specialize in his or her strong area, thereby deepening our individual strengths and leading us to become dependent on one another. This would have kept us within our comfort zones. It would also have led to a traditional organizational structure at the top, where we each developed a different "department." Instead, we chose another possibility, requiring each of us to develop all the skills. Although each one of us is still stronger than the other two in some area, everyone can now step into every job. We feel more empowered, more skilled overall, and more creative and connected with our mutual abilities. We are not saying that it has been easy, only that it is possible and rewarding.

How can you cultivate the habit of moving out of your comfort zone, when everyone feels better remaining within it? First, be ready to explore and act when circumstances thrust you outside your comfort zone. Second, find ways to send yourself outside the comfort zone, by learning, developing new skills, and challenging limits, so that you will be ready for change. Although change can seem very surprising and unexpected, its general trajectory can often be seen in advance—if you're paying attention and not using excuses or denial to ignore it.

Remembering the Future

Self-empowerment means a change from "I'll believe it when I see it" to "I'll see it when I believe it."[1] It is a process of listening to oneself, to a voice that is often drowned out by the louder voice of the organization's limiting beliefs. The limit to the degree of empowerment is then simply the limits of one's imagination. People have usually grown up in traditional organizations that do not change very fast or support empowerment. By "organization," we include our families, our schools, and our entire work experience. Because we have never seen anything else, it takes imagination and courage to believe that it might be different. If we can't imagine an organization being different, then we certainly can't create deep change in the culture.

In traditional, nonempowering organizations, people focus on pleasing the authority figure by sensing what he or she wants. They are not oriented toward looking inside or exercising independent thought.

During personal growth several avenues of potential within people open up. First, they open to things they may not have previously considered. This can happen by looking inside and asking about one's values, talents, and inner images of what might be. When people are asked to set aside "reasonableness" and practicality, and think about the place where they would most like to work, incredible pictures emerge. Very often, people have almost never listened to their inner voices. For example, we held a workshop with health professionals—physicians and nurses—people who are particularly prone to burnout. We asked each of the participants to recall the time in their lives when they first decided that they wanted to go into health care. They recounted very early decisions in their lives, remembering great idealism about helping and healing. This contrasted sharply with the work they found themselves doing, where they felt that they did little that fit their idealism about healing. Empowerment meant returning to their ideals and moving their current practices in that direction. What did they need to do differently in their current practices to match better their inner sense of what ought to be? These discussions generated a wealth of creative innovations, many of which turned out to be practical after all.

Another dimension of empowerment is the discovery of outside models. Employees who have worked in the same company "forever" have severely limited their horizons. The way things are done seems like the only way. The way people behave in their company seems like "human nature." Like fish that would never discover water, they would never discover the limiting nature of their environment. But once they begin to visit other companies, new possibilities open up. They see, for instance, that in other companies doing similar work there are self-managing teams and few supervisors. In other companies there are people who feel that they want to make the whole company better. In other companies the same work is done with fewer people, and fewer mistakes are made. The empowering excitement that comes from seeing models in action is enormous. They see how different the worlds of work can be. After this experience, the same employees can imagine with some clarity just how their work could be different.

Catalyzing Action

Personal empowerment often grows out of a difficult challenge in one's life that old ways cannot solve. It can be a business problem, a personal performance issue at work, or a difficulty in one's personal life. In our work we have discovered a four-stage model for self-empowerment.[2]

Stage 1. Awakening: Crisis and Pain. Without a need or a reason to look inside and change, it is hard to do so. It is therefore not surprising that there is always a "wake-up call," an event that old, familiar ways cannot solve, that leads people into crisis. It may come from one's boss saying, "You have to change or go." But not every crisis leads to growth. One can—as many people do—go into denial and not face the dilemma directly.

Stage 2. New Possibility and Vision. The existence of a crisis doesn't tell people how they need to change or what they need to change. Luckily, connected to the crisis, there is usually also a vision that there is indeed another way. This gives direction. For example, an empowered person in one organization may see that nearby organizations are trying new things, bring this to the attention of her boss and her colleagues, and then suggest change. Because everyone is enthusiastic about what the other company is doing, her suggestions fall on fertile ground.

Stage 3. Dialogue and Challenge.   The third stage is also a period of learning. One takes risks, learns new behaviors, and receives feedback from others about whether one is on target or not. The learning process is almost never solitary. For change, a person needs to consult others and work with others. People need to hear how they are doing. For example, a manager may tell his direct reports that he wants to become more collaborative but that it is hard for him. He invites people to tell him when he's slipping up, even providing avenues to get anonymous feedback and suggestions.

Stage 4. Commitment to New Ways.   Finally, having successfully learned a new way, one's comfort zone expands. Learning is nearly irreversible: Once you know something new, see a new possibility, or expand your capacity, you cannot easily "put the liquid back into the bottle." There is no real ability to *unlearn*, although a person can be forced not to use a skill.

With layoffs and uncertainty about the future, companies are espousing new rules and looking for new solutions. The people who shift from crisis into awakening to empowerment are usually the ones who land on their feet. Because their lives and their future are at stake, they don't need their company's permission to take the path. But curiously, the people who do not become mavericks (see Chapter 2 for a discussion of individual responses to change), but whose empowerment brings benefits to their organization as well as themselves, are often more able to adapt and are more satisfied with the results.

EMPOWERED ACTION

Translating inner possibilities into reality puts people at risk. By moving to action, they take a risk within the organization. Because the forces that frustrate and limit change have the power to punish and reward, often the people who do not challenge are the ones who are rewarded. So there are real risks in becoming empowered. But given the experience of people who have taken risks for what they believed in, the possibility of success is great, usually greater than anticipated.

Empowered action involves finding ways to redefine work activities, take action, and become an innovator. In this section, we look at how you can free yourself from organizational constraints and blinders that may keep you from acting; we show how you can take empowered action to move the organization in a new direction. We discuss this process, including

- Taking responsibility for what you do; in effect, becoming the CEO of your job
- Challenging the organization's values with your own, acting out of a sense of what the organization might become
- Extending your web of influence to become a teacher to those around you, especially those above you
- Building an example of what you want, an alternative culture

Becoming the CEO of Your Job

Today's workplace requires more than just surviving and becoming more savvy in living within the organization, the old philosophy summed up by such books as *Looking Out for #1* and *Power*.[3] The organization of today and of the future needs empowered people who have a new sense of responsibility for events far beyond the scope of their jobs.

As a step toward this, imagine that you are not an employee but a company of one. You are an entrepreneur and your success lies in adding value to the service you give your customers (the people with whom you work in a large company). You will not succeed by just showing up or carrying out tasks. As an entrepreneur, you need to be alert to opportunities to add value and you need to continually assess how you are doing. You get paid (employed) only if you satisfy the market (your company).

Empowered action means stepping outside of your job as it exists and seeing how it might be in order to add more value to your organization. It means deciding to take responsibility for helping your company succeed rather than hiding and hoping that things will work out. Like a company that is struggling to stay competitive in a world that is ever more exacting, you as an entrepreneur have to see your own personal company as competing and continually improve your own ability to stay competitive.

An employee of the federal government who operated as an empowered person within a very controlling and rule-bound department reported that a newly appointed boss had told her she had the authority to take a certain action. She said, "I told him that I never knew I didn't. Not only that, but I had long ago delegated the authority for that kind of decision to my people in the field." She had assumed she was the CEO of her job from the beginning. Her experience highlights another potential of empowerment: She took her authority and shared it with others. She assumed that together they would get the job done well.

To act as the CEO of your job, you need to grapple with the following questions:

1. Who are your clients and how do you add value for them? If your client is a unit of an organization or serves several teams, you need to look at the nature of your value and what you are doing to ensure your continuing value. What is unique about what you are doing? How are you helping your clients achieve their goals? Who is your boss? Is your client the organization itself or the customers of the organization? In the traditional organization you had only one "customer"—your boss. In the evolving organization, this is no longer true. For example, as a human resource generalist, your customers would be the employees and the whole organization because you would be responsible for helping people reach their highest levels of performance.

2. How can you add value for your clients and support their work? Take the initiative and draw up a strategic plan with your clients to support and add value to them. Brainstorm ideas and possibilities with your clients. Talk about the issues; do not just assume that things are fine if you do your job as usual.

3. What is the big picture? Step back from what you have always done and look at the goals of the larger system, the group that you serve, and the company as a whole. What are they trying to achieve? How are they excellent? What can you do to maintain that excellence? What is your special competency? How can you develop your unique contribution to a higher level?

4. What are the drivers, your key activities that achieve the greatest impact? How can you do more of that and less of other things? Simplify. Determine where your greatest impact lies. Prioritize, then keep your priorities in focus.

5. As an entrepreneur, you are part of strategic alliances with other entrepreneurs to serve a large company. Who are your strategic allies? How do you work with them? Are your agreements clear? Are there areas of tension or differences in priority or approach?

6. Do you maintain a personal learning and development program? Do you add to your skills continually rather than resting on last year's laurels? Are you continually growing and extending your personal mastery?

As you ask these questions, you will begin to focus on yourself as an active force in creating your work and in re-creating the organization.

Laura Neisius, the computer manager of Clarke Home Nursing, told us about how a shift in her way of seeing her job led to a deeper sense of personal empowerment. At first, new to her job and feeling a little over her head, she saw herself as a data person who was called upon to fix complaints. She felt frustrated, put-upon, and completely reactive. Then she began to shift her perception of herself and what she was doing. She began to see herself as a teacher and a leader. Instead of fixing complaints, she began to anticipate the needs of the people who worked in the agency. She began to focus on providing service, asking each person—whether they had reported a problem or not—what their needs were. She became a teacher, making others more effective. She felt she could use the good ideas that she got from her talks with others to improve internal systems. She shifted from a reactive to an empowered role.

When you become your own CEO you are no longer muzzled and helpless. Instead, you put yourself into a strategic alliance with your work team and your boss to create value. Your task is to solve problems, not to follow orders. This means that the power and authority relationship begins to shift. Even if the organization and your supervisor see you as a traditional employee, you see yourself as an entrepreneur. You structure your job more from your new inner image than from the traditional expectation.

CHALLENGING THE ORGANIZATION'S VALUES AND VISION

The transformation from a workplace that operates through control and in which you feel compliant and deenergized, to one where you feel vital, energetic, excited, and committed occurs when you feel that the organization is doing what you believe is important or that your job reflects what you believe is important. When your personal values and vision of what you want yourself to become in your best possible future are in alignment with the organization, it is like tapping into an inexhaustible energy source. You find that you feel good about your work and your workplace and you no longer are susceptible to burnout. In fact, this kind of attitude may even keep you alive longer.[4]

Connecting your work with your values is key for this shift to occur. To do this, you must fit your own job into your personal values and vision and hold the organization to its espoused values and vision (the values and vision that drew you to it or that you care about). In other words, live by your values and challenge the organization to live by its own.

Hellen Hemphill studied women who rose to the highest levels of large organizations and found two distinct styles.[5] The first Hemphill called the *corporate* style; it is very similar to the style of the person we called the *follower* in Chapter Two. Half of the women Hemphill studied had this style. These women were achievers who got to the top by doing exactly what the organization wanted—and, as they said, doing it better than the men they were competing against. They never questioned their drive; they just did what was generally accepted as needed to get to the top. When they got to the top, they all had the same response: "It wasn't worth it, because I lost so much of myself along the way." This is the pathway to traditional achievement and it is disconcerting to hear that those who took it believed it was not worth the energy, and that they wouldn't do it again.

In contrast, the other half of the women had what Hemphill called the *vanguard* style, another term for what we call empowerment. Vanguard leaders were involved in the process of their rise, rather than strictly focused on the outcome. At each stage of their careers, they listened to their inner voice and values, and challenged the organization to do what they felt was right. They were ambitious but confident that they had other options if the organization rejected what they had to offer. If the organization accepted their gifts, they advanced; if not, they left. They were driven not by fear but by doing what they saw as important for themselves and for the organization. They took risks, they helped the organization grow by their presence. These vanguard leaders felt fresh when they reached the top and weren't bitter if they didn't achieve the highest levels of success, because they felt good about what they had done at each level. Because they stayed with their values, they did not get burned out in their journey.

Organizations trying to transform need vanguard leaders. We can certainly assume that many vanguard leaders do not scale the corporate ladder—or as much of the ladder as still exists—but are short-circuited because the company does not want what they have to offer. The key is that the people whose challenges are not accepted by the organization do not define that as failure; they don't feel defeated. They know they have done the right thing. Also, because they have built their skills and expertise, they have no shortage of other opportunities.

In one example, Gloria Garrett, the director of Home Health Care Aides for Clarke Home Nursing, told us how she had seen that the community needed a way to find health care help and that her agency could give back to the community by providing this service. Her idea was that Clarke should start a caregiver hotline, with its own money, within its office. She persuaded her boss, Ken Clarke, that it would be a win-win community service. It turned out to be a powerful innovation, an instant success; there were four hundred calls by the second month. The visibility of the company's help quite clearly helped it develop new sources of referral, although that had not been the intention. In addition, Clarke employees now love providing the service and the referral resources love it too.

Again, acting on one's values has an element of risk. Whatever its espoused values, most companies are somewhat reticent to confront their shortcomings. They bring this attitude to their culture, creating a norm where people do not take risks or challenge standard behaviors except in very limited, tentative ways. Yet, this lack of listening and learning is what makes organizations slow to respond to change. Organizations that have grown and changed have employees within who challenged the status quo and took risks to do so.

John Graham, a former foreign service officer, and Ann Medlock, a journalist, initiated the Giraffe Project in 1981, to honor people who "stick their necks out for the common good."[6] They sift through nominations, looking for those who have risked their necks as well as done some good in the process. They often honor community activists who risk their livelihood and money for something they believe in. They challenge employees to develop the qualities of "risk, caring, and sharing" because finding ways to make a difference and risking one's neck do not stop when one enters the workplace.

Harvey Hornstein studied two hundred instances in which executives acted with courage within their organizations.[7] The executives took action that challenged the organization, questioned policies and directions, even blew the internal whistle on questionable ethics. Hornstein expected to find that such instances, because very dangerous, were infrequent, but to his surprise he found the opposite. More than 80 percent of the risks were deemed successful by the initiator, in that the organization addressed the issue and the person's job was not threatened. Hornstein found that the people taking action were very careful to maintain a respectful and open communication with the people they questioned, listening and learning, negotiating and remaining patient rather than becoming angry and defiant. The most surprising finding was that, almost universally, the people taking action reported that their stand was the most important action of their career and that their sense of personal self-esteem and integrity grew as a result of what they had done. They also felt more powerful.

Extending Your Influence: Manage Change Upward

If your boss is feeling pressure to get the job done in a complex environment and reacts by getting more controlling, how can you decrease his or her anxiety so that you can be seen as a resource rather than as a problem? There are several ways to convince your boss to give you more freedom and allow you more autonomy. Interestingly, these are the kinds of activities that those who are already CEOs of their jobs—for example, consultants and small-business owners—use to firm up their fragile relationships with partners and customers.

1. Keep your boss informed. Don't just say you'll do the job; make it clear what you will do and how. If you inform your boss, he or she is more likely to feel comfortable to allow you freedom to act.

2. If you want to amend or shift your responsibilities or actions, make clear how your plan fits into the overall objectives and how it will be helpful. Instead of just accepting an assignment, you might talk about how you could be more successful with it by making some changes.

3. Let your boss know if he or she is doing things that limit your ability to be effective. This is the cause for many people to lose power in an organization. They are asked to get something done, but the rules or ways by which they are

expected to do it make it difficult to be successful. By being firm and presenting your case clearly, you can sometimes find yourself innovating rather than being frustrated by procedures. You might have to say something like, "When you go to the people that I supervise and tell them what to do, or ask them what they are doing, you make it more difficult for me to work with them as a group to get the job done." A warning: Offering feedback of this type to a supervisor generates a lot of anxiety, and is certainly a step out of the comfort zone.

4. Get help from other people. If you can't convince your boss at first, you might work with others who are part of your team to make your case. When several people make a request together, and make it clear that they take responsibility for success, they are often more successful than one person acting alone.

5. Just do it. This may be the riskiest path of all. But corporate innovators are like CEOs in that they take action first, from a deep inner conviction that they will be successful, and then they come to the higher levels of the company when they have succeeded. The stories of corporate innovators are full of people like Chuck House, of Hewlett-Packard, who had an idea for a new type of video terminal.[8] Told to stop his experimenting, he borrowed equipment and worked on his own time, eventually developing a breakthrough in video technology that was a great success as a new product for the company.

Building Alternative Cultures

Self-empowerment must be tested in action, rather than in fruitless arguments about whether certain actions should be done or what will happen if they are done. Discussions of hypothetical changes are more often about people's fears than about real consequences, because change is so complex and unexpected that it is hard to predict what a new method will actually look and feel like. That is why conversations are so often negative when a new idea is proposed. People can come up with lots of objections and questions, but it is hard to visualize the real effects of the change. And in fact, the problems that come up when a change is made are usually not the ones anticipated during planning.

It is also difficult to be sensible about hypotheses when we are considering change that may challenge all of our everyday assumptions about the organization. For example, people whose careers are spent in traditional organizations will scoff at the notion of self-directing teams or will say that people just won't take charge of their own work. Or they will fear that with so much freedom and so little traditional control, chaos will result. Or they will say "We tried that; it didn't work." There is no counter-argument to such fear-based projections. A productive response may be, "I disagree with your view, but instead of arguing, why don't we try it on a small scale and see what happens?" This is challenging the current paradigm with the hard data that will be produced.

Empowered people find ways to create models-in-action. They don't wait and wonder "what if" but act out of an image of the possible organization. Empowered people know that with innovation, especially transformational shifts, people have to be shown new ways to get comfortable with them. So empowered people find ways to reach out to like-minded people and to try something rather than just argue about how effective change could be. If it is a large scheme, like a new cross-functional team model, they might conduct an informal meeting of one relevant group and let the group discover how working together can speed up their work.

About 20 percent of people in the organization are always trying new things, are excited about learning and change, and are open to new information. We call these the *pioneers*. They experiment without knowing the outcome in advance. They see change as an opportunity to move toward the vision. These are the empowered person's natural allies, the people to whom one needs to reach out across the organization. They have objections to ideas, but their objections are premised on the need for change and their desire is to make it work. Their objections are different from those of the people who wish to kill an idea or stop a project from taking place. For example, in one company, people were told about the quality approach: They needed to have extensive data to back up any new idea they proposed. Although this sounds reasonable at first blush, if a new idea has not been tried, there are no back-up data. In effect, this culture was using the quality rubric to kill change.

Once the pioneers are on board, empowered people need to find a way to initiate a trial of an experiment. At this point, the new project needs to be isolated from the rest of the organization that is doing things in the old way. This is the incubator period, the special environment necessary for people to learn new ways. There is a start-up period for learning new skills and getting the project together; people need to get it up and running. At this phase, the effective manager or project sponsor is not touting the new idea around the organization, but running interference and keeping the new project safe within its own boundaries to see if it will bear fruit. At this stage, the new project needs to be separated out, to be able to fail, to try new ways, and to get people who are not pioneers on board. This is the period where the new project needs as little outside interference as possible. After it has become a reality, and shows real results, then it is time to move outward and begin to get other parts of the organization on board. The new project thus becomes what is termed an "alternative culture," a newly transformed group within a larger culture.

The story of organizational change is the story of small groups coming up with new ideas—projects, ways of working, new marketing thrusts—that larger and more fully staffed groups do not sense because of the blinders put on by their previous successes. Sometimes the small group is a start-up company with a new idea and a deep commitment to make it work on a shoe-string budget. Sometimes it is a small group of people working far from the center of the company, with fewer company controls and demands on them. Peters and Waterman aptly described the Lockheed new-project group as "skunk works;" it kept Lockheed on top in technology and new products for many years.[9] Whether a start-up or a small group within a larger organization, such groups are critical to transformational change. Innovation seems to be both less costly and more effective with a smaller group, another paradox that is sometimes ignored by large companies as they try to change.

Sometimes the alternative culture must be initiated by a group without direct permission from its bosses. In one organization, a group was concerned about the negative effects of "ranking" individuals on a team in order of their contributions. One team discovered that if everyone was to perform fully then ranking was no longer relevant, so they simply stopped doing it. Every group has some directives that it chooses to ignore. They felt strongly that following the corporate ranking system was counterproductive for them. They found that this change, done quietly and without major fanfare, boosted their performance and morale.

In another example, a marketing team began its own alternative culture. Without announcing a special program or getting extra resources for it, they simply began getting together to design a more customer-centered service system. The team manager started the project, and the team invited other pioneers from other teams to join in. This was done quietly and informally. They began to change rules and try new ways without directly challenging the whole organization. Then they began to show results, and many of their innovations spread to the whole company.

One important reason for the pilot experiment is to allow the people involved to develop the new competencies they need to be part of the project and to allow them to work together to iron out unintended difficulties. The participants often find themselves using skills they haven't yet fully learned and therefore needing time to develop them. They need to learn such skills as adopting a systems perspective, working as a team, learning as a group, helping each other, and so on.

Once the pilot project is successful in its own right, the next step of the change leader is to bring it out of its shell and integrate it into the wider organization. This is the more difficult of the two phases because the resistance and differences that the project runs into will be very stressful and challenging. The project will be held to unreasonable standards, will be implemented ineffectively and too quickly elsewhere, and will be tested by changing personnel and pressuring its champions or by forcing the change on people in other parts of the organization who are not ready for it. As we will see in the next chapter, the emotional dynamics of introducing change into an organization are more important than the actual effects of the new change.

Cutting groups loose to innovate while maintaining enough connection to the central organization so that they are clear about their mission is the ongoing task of the new cluster organization. Maintaining the connection between the innovating group and the rest of the organization needs care and effort, for the traditional paths of communication do not usually support innovation.

Initiating change at the group or team level supports self-empowerment:

- The people who are being changed by events are asked to become change leaders, designing their response to change; the difficulty of getting them involved is overcome.

- The sense of powerlessness and of being manipulated by the organization decreases; people are part of innovation.

- The group deals with the problems it is closest to and that it has the best information about.

- The group reaches out of its own will to other groups that are part of a difficult situation, rather than having the organization create special structures for that to happen.

The ability to experiment with alternative cultures, images of the future, and the anxiety that emerges when the comfort zone is breached is central to the development of both self-empowerment and organizational transformation. Personal change—even a small one—is at the root of organizational change. It is the willingness to take one step on the journey toward self-empowerment that matters.

Strategies for Self-Empowerment

The journey to self-empowerment begins with you. Take the initiative and make the first move. From your own inner values and visions, begin the process of changing the organization. Then your skills as a salesperson will come into play, as will involvement from others. Can you hang on and remain an advocate of a new path, building support and energy toward change?

Here are some strategies to help you move toward your own empowerment:

1. Learn to live with uncertainty. Look at what is happening; try to keep your eyes open. Do not retreat into the conventional solution or the old ways. Take a wider view; try to see the broader pattern, the coming changes.

2. Look for new possibilities, new ways to get things done. Learn from others, listen to everyone, become open to learning.

3. Realize that despite the limits placed on you, there are many ways that you can do what you think needs to be done. You are not a victim. Take a strategic, creative view of the organization and of yourself.

4. Hold the organization to your values and vision and to its own.

5. Become a teacher to the people around you. Push your influence upward. In times of great change, the people at the bottom become the teachers to the top. This is a difficult role, but seeing yourself as a teacher is one of the keys to your own empowerment.

6. Understand or find out the need, or the reasons, for change, and create awareness of the crisis in others. Every organization will want to play down the degree of change that needs to take place. Let yourself become one of the pioneers who sees the need for real change and faces up to the crisis that may lie just over the horizon.

In the next chapter, we look more fully at the nature of the empowered organization and discuss how to create an organizational environment that sustains empowerment and compels employee commitment.

Part Two

CHANGING YOUR ORGANIZATION

5

The Empowered Workplace: Learning the Dynamics of Change

We have only just begun the process of discovering and inventing the new organizational forms that will inhabit the twenty-first century. To be responsible inventors and discoverers, though, we need the courage to let go of the old world, to relinquish most of what we have cherished, to abandon our interpretations about what does and doesn't work. As Einstein is often quoted as saying: No problem can be solved from the same consciousness that created it. We must learn to see the world anew.

—Margaret Wheatley, *Leadership and the New Science*

This chapter offers a picture of how the new workplace is evolving, what it looks like in action, and some of the dynamics of change as an organization moves from the old to the new way. It will be useful to you as a change leader, for if you know where all the change is leading, you will be able to put your organization's change into a broader context, and even chart the direction for your own initiatives.

We look at the structure of the new workplace—the empowered organization—and the process of its evolution from a more traditional structure. We begin by looking at the nature of the deep and total transformational shift, from one style to the other, and then at what some of the organizations that have begun this journey look like and how their empowered employees make them successful.

WHO SUCCEEDS: THE EMPOWERED ORGANIZATION

In looking for models of the new workplace, consider *Fortune* magazine's list of most admired companies.[1] Companies are selected not just for their profitability but also for their success in dealing with change, for the quality of their results, for innovation, and for the way in which they manage their people. The more admired companies, while strikingly different in many of the ways they operate, share certain qualities. Previously, the key markers of competitive advantage were strategy, marketing, and technological edge—how the organization affected its environment. Now, increasingly, with the speed of response and the need to maintain continual creativity and adaptation, competitive advantage is based on a company's internal coherence—how it mobilizes its people.

Fortune's most admired companies, which include Wal-Mart, Levi Strauss, 3M, Corning, GE, Johnson & Johnson, Harley-Davidson, and Herman Miller, can be distinguished by the quality of their relationships with their employees. These companies have maintained the respect of their employees even as they cut costs and people. Some of the qualities of companies including those in the admired group that stand out include the following:

- They are clear about their corporate values. These values include not just their values in the marketplace but also their treatment of employees and their methods of working together. Levi Strauss recently decided that its values demanded that it stop producing several million pairs of jeans in China because of China's human rights record.

- They value participation and teamwork, and they build participation into every aspect of policy and decision making. They share information throughout the organization and solicit input from every part of the organization. People feel a sense of partnership, of being on a team that shares problem-solving and has many skills. Although individuals are allowed to shine, people feel an allegiance to their team, not just to their single boss or manager. The team focus of factories like New United Motor Manufacturing Inc. (NUMMI) and Saturn, two plants that are leading the renewal of General Motors, results in levels of commitment and quality that far surpass any of its other factories.

- They have moved from a centralized hierarchy to small business units with lots of control over every aspect of their business. They let individual business units chart their own futures and they push responsibility down to the units, who are accountable for their results not their methods. They are lean in centralized corporate staff. Companies like Johnson & Johnson are made up of decentralized, almost entrepreneurial, business units that are loosely connected.

- They are focused on the customer, not on pleasing the boss; employees' decisions and actions are determined by this goal. They are open to new ideas from the people on the front lines and minimize the levels that must sign off on a new initiative. Jan Carlzon, CEO of Scandinavian Airlines, was able to bring his company out of a slump by giving every employee the power to do what it took to help the customer get what he or she wanted.

- They respect the basic rights of the individual employee, treating people fairly even in the event of layoffs, letting people know about policies that affect them and even considering alternatives. They do little things to show people they are valued, and these are substantive and continual things, not just window dressing. For example, Levi Strauss has a "statement of aspirations," the values it will uphold in relation to its policies, practices, and employee relations.

Along the continuum from most to the least admired organization, we see a range of styles that runs from the emerging organizational model—which has been called *the circle, the network,* or *the cluster* model—to the more traditional hierarchical model.[2] The least admired companies operate according to the principles of the traditional hierarchy: They keep control, tell employees little, rigidly prescribe jobs and behavior, treat people

like replaceable machines, and change as little and as late as possible. In contrast, Robert Levering proposes a model of the
healthy workplace based on observations of successful companies that also have positive employee morale.[3] This workplace
is characterized by trust, participation, progressive human resource policies, and shared rewards; companies run along this
model also significantly outperform the Standard & Poor index
of financial performance.

Change Versus Transformation

In discussing the shifts that organizations are undergoing, it is
helpful to clarify what we mean by change. A change of the work
culture in which a whole new form of organization is created is
transformation: It is not just what people say and do that
changes, but how the organization works as a whole. It is more
than a shift in policy or structure, more than a reorganization,
new program, new mission or vision, new leader, or new compensation, information, or performance evaluation system. Each of
these provides new contexts or new experiences for people inside
an organization, but limited programs don't create transformational change.

Creating an empowered organization occurs through transformational or breakthrough change. The organization termi-
nates a certain style and set of values and begins to adopt new
ones. It begins to respond differently to its people and its environment. Breakthrough change doesn't happen along a linear
path, in a simple series of sequential steps. It lurches ahead, falls
back, makes a false start, gathers steam or falters.

The difference between linear change and breakthrough
change has been described as follows:

> There are two different types of change: one that occurs
> within a given system which itself remains unchanged, and
> one whose occurrence changes the system itself. To exem-
> plify this distinction in more behavioral terms: a person
> having a nightmare can do many things in his dream—run,
> hide, fight, scream, jump off a cliff, etc.—but no change
> from any one of these behaviors to another would ever ter-

minate the nightmare. We shall henceforth refer to this kind of change as first-order change. The one way out of a dream involves a change from dreaming to waking. Waking, obviously, is no longer a part of the dream, but a change to an altogether different state. This kind of change (is) second-order change.[4]

The shift from the traditional to the empowered organization cannot involve only first-order change; it must involve second-order change. Transformational changes move the organization the most—and begin with questioning assumptions and raising possibilities. In fact, the way one thinks about change is how one changes. If people see themselves as working together in fundamentally new relationships, then they may not need a reorganization to validate their perception, they may simply become partners working equally. When people begin to see the world transformed, other kinds of change may begin naturally. So a major transformational change can take place within one person or team, whereas a major organizational initiative can result in no real change at all.

Shifting Paradigms

To guide us in making such an enormous shift in how we work, we can look to previous experiences of total shifts in world view. In 1970 Thomas Kuhn[5] studied what he labeled "paradigm shifts" in science, where everything that had been accepted as true was overturned as another view of reality took its place. Kuhn observed the shift of scientific world views such as the Copernican view of the sun as the center of the solar system overtaking the earth-centered concept and the round-world perspective overturning the flat-world perspective. The flat earth was as reasonable to people who had never looked through a telescope as organizational pyramids are to us, who grew up seeing nothing else. Who could question it? It is hard to visualize a round earth when all you have seen is the land stretching out to a flat horizon.

The transformation begins when a few courageous, visionary, and surprised researchers begin to notice "anomalies," data that do not easily fit into the traditional paradigm. An example of an anomaly in the corporate sense might be the increase in customer service that comes from allowing employees to use their own judgment, or the increase in effectiveness when teams regulate themselves and are not controlled by a supervisor. Traditional organization theory and practice would predict chaos, poor results, and confusion under such conditions. But when the experience doesn't fit the paradigm, these researchers say the theory or perspective needs to change.

Yet Kuhn observed that it takes at least a generation for the new view to win out. Most traditional adherents don't change, they just die out, and a new generation takes over. The people who adhere to the old world view simply do not accept the new data, and hold onto their own perspectives by dismissing the results of the new guard. Kuhn was pessimistic about people changing paradigms within their own lifetimes. Just as the scientific academies studied by Kuhn were the most reticent about researching the new ideas, today there are management schools that teach the old organizational perspective and ignore the new models.

Yet the organizational paradigm shift today is somewhat different from Kuhn's scientific paradigm shifts. For one, people today have learned to make major shifts and are more comfortable with change. Change is not unthinkable, it is just difficult or imprudent. The pace of change in technology and knowledge has accustomed us to vast shifts—for example, our widespread adoption in one decade of personal computers. It may be that people can actually learn to shift paradigms, at least once in their lifetimes.

For another, the anomalies that challenge the traditional, dominant view of the organization are so obvious and the premium on learning the new ways so immediate, that major change is encouraged. If people are faced with losing their jobs or if they see other people getting results in their teams while members want to leave theirs, they may not be able to deny the need to change. People are finding that traditional methods cannot maintain sales or new product developmet; they are therefore forced to learn new ways. Donald Peterson, former CEO of Ford, writes about how he was persuaded that the workers could become partners, not antagonists, in every aspect of product development, design, and manufacturing.[6] The lesson of his success has not been lost on the CEOs of other large companies.

There are other problems during the process of change. The change from one paradigm to another, from one way of working with others to another, is so far-reaching that many of the people who think they have changed or who try to change are not able to complete the action. A company gets enamored of a quality program, and begins to ask everyone for new ideas, but responds to the changes according to the traditional hierarchy—getting permission from higher levels, not allowing the changes to challenge the most basic ways of doing things.

For example, the director of a group of work-team managers in a company was transferred to another post. While the team managers waited for the position to be filled, they found themselves reaching a new level of cooperation and creative exchange. It began to dawn on them that, according to the new model of organization, they would be seen as a self-managing team, a group that coordinated its own activities. They calculated that eliminating the director post would save the company about $200,000, or allow for adding one additional position to each of their individual teams. But their executive vice president was interviewing people for the director job and had difficulty believing that they could get along without one. He was caught in the traditional paradigm. Despite his proclaimed commitment to "total quality" and "self-management," he was reluctant to let them emerge right below him.

Two kinds of change are necessary for organizations to shift fully their paradigms. There is the breakthrough change, as occurred in the team just discussed when they realized they had the power to make a difference. This is an instantaneous, "Aha!" experience, where the world shifts before people's eyes when they change the way they see it. But there are also many incremental, gradual steps in redefining every aspect of the organization to fit this new sense. Many consultants and employees are so excited by the breakthrough that they feel frustrated or confused when they also face the many incremental steps they need to take to make the breakthrough part of the fabric of the organization. Yet often incremental changes precede breakthrough changes. An organization that is making many incremental steps, such as allowing greater and greater participation from all levels of the organization, may well reach a point where the sum of the small changes leads to a breakthrough change.

Organizational Cycles

Organizational growth and development thus proceeds through both incremental (first-order) and breakthrough (second-order) change. The organization goes through a developmental cycle that follows the S curve development of all living organisms. This cycle is show in Figure 5.1.

First, there is a period of inner development, slow growth as the system develops a new idea. It is the period where the company is designed, develops its product or service, and gets it to market. After its founding, an organization can experience fast growth and development, as it exploits the results of its innovative product or service. But after the period of fast growth every

Figure 5.1.   Stages of Organizational Growth.

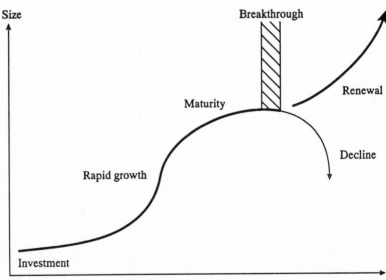

living system, from people to organizations, reaches a period of maturing, in which growth slows. At some point, the environment creates an equilibrium. After its initial period of creative excitement, the organization or group enters a period of stability or managed growth. Organizations at this developmental stage predictably become set in their ways and lose the ability to innovate and respond to the marketplace. Eventually, there is a feeling in the company that the magic has gone out of the work and that now it's "just work." The product can no longer be refined or fixed in order to compete; or the way a group works is no longer efficient enough to beat the competition, or everyone feels they are getting stale and exhausted without any really new ideas or innovations. When the group enters the flattening period of the growth curve, it has reached a point of diminishing returns. It seems that nothing the group does makes much of a difference. The only possible ending for a system that does not have a major change is decline, or even death.[7] To avoid this, the system—meaning the group, person, or whole organization—needs to have a breakthrough and initiate a new S curve.

The system must question its values, its mission, and its methods and look for a way to break from the past and change its very nature. A good example of breakthrough, second-order change, is that accomplished by the Macintosh computer. Before the Mac, computers were technical tools used by engineers; they were difficult to work with and mysterious to the general public. Then came the Mac with its new system—a "mouse," a "desktop," a "trash can"—that made it ridiculously easy to use. In fact, it made it fun. People began to name their computers and to feel they had a personal relationship to them. This was more than a product: the Mac established a new relationship between layperson and computer that has grown and continued to this day. The old S curve of technical computers was supplanted by a new S curve of personal computers, which took on functions different from those traditionally associated with this tool. Once we accepted personal computers, they helped us find new dimensions in typing, making the typewriter obsolete; they helped us use graphics and design; they helped organize our lives; and they helped communicate around the world. This was a breakthrough shift in the public's perceptions.

Any breakthrough leads to a need for new systems, new design, in order to achieve its possibility. The new Mac needed new software systems to encourage us to take the time to learn them. In another example, after the recent breakthrough of "freedom" in the Eastern bloc, people are now facing the enormous task of redesigning political and economic institutions.

Breakthroughs are almost irreversible. Once one sees the world in a new way—as the Mac user did—one cannot return to the old perspective. Once one recognizes that everyone in a team is a resource and a potential leader, one cannot return to seeing oneself as a mere cog in a wheel. Having made the breakthrough shift into empowerment, it is difficult to go back to the old way without demoralization and great discontent.

At a recent conference of companies with more than a decade of experience in employee participation, we saw several examples of the interplay between breakthrough and incremental change.[8] At first the change was incremental, as a company instituted various forms of problem-solving groups in the manufacturing plant. The groups were heavily regulated. Then there was a crisis: The groups began to question basic assumptions about how the company was governed and policies implemented that neither union nor management had intended. They began to shake the foundations of the assumptions of the hierarchical organization and deal with issues such as work rules and grievances, which had been excluded from the agreement.

When the breakthrough came, the participation process expanded to become a new way of doing business. The teams agreed to look at any and every issue that they deemed relevant, such as financial information, the basic management structure, and whether a company should outsource parts of a process. Instead of a traditional hierarchy with a few "circles" or "clusters" in the form of teams, the structure of the whole plant began to look like a series of circles, as teams looked at such issues as the vision of the future, large-scale problems facing the whole business, and ways to become more profitable. Successful participation programs became joint governance processes, and new paradigm organizations. Other participation programs, those that were not able to make the breakthrough, found the initial commitment to change dying out after a year or so, as it reached its natural limits.

THE NATURE OF
THE PARADIGM SHIFT:
CIRCLES AND PYRAMIDS

This new organizational path to empowerment represents total discontinuity from the old organizational style. It entails a major shift in the way people view and draw upon the commitment of others and the way they see the organization and how it works. Yet the new ways are not really so new; people have been talking about some of them for over a generation.[9] What is new is that today they are essential for success.

It is very much like the shift from the mainframe to the personal computer. The mainframe was, in many ways, like the CEO: under central control and unable to be accessed without special authority. In contrast, the personal computer makes information available to everyone, everyone has access; power goes to those who can use the information and solve problems.

But the traditional organizational pyramid has a familiar look to it, since organizations have been designed as pyramids for over two thousand years. Such hierarchies were very efficient ways to distribute power and messages quickly to a large group of people. Basically, the pyramid works with the leaders at the top giving only the necessary information to the people lower down. If information moves from the bottom up it is considered insubordination.

The assumptions behind this structure were that people didn't want to work and had to be watched, that every task could be broken down into individual steps, and that these steps were relatively unchanging. Breaking down tasks and activities into parts, with coordination at the top, was the essence of bureaucratic effectiveness. People felt secure because they had a secure structure—boss, peers, and subordinates under them. If they were union, they did their job and no one else's. People were safe.

The downside was that hierarchies created overspecialization, narrow department loyalties, turf wars, excessive administrative control, and much compartmentalizing.

Pyramids have been a powerfully successful model for organizations within a stable world environment. So what's wrong with the pyramid? Why does it need to change?

While the downsizing, shrinking middle management, and mergers of the 1980s were attempts to fix the inefficiencies of the pyramid, all these changes did not change the organization into a new form. As Lawrence and Lorsch noted in the sixties,[10] when the external environment begins to change, the pyramid is less successful. Such a structure cannot support increasing emphasis on the customer. In the traditional pyramid, the customer was often invisible. Instead, the customer of the hierarchies was usually the hierarchies themselves; they were self-contained. In the pyramid, information cannot flow up, even as people on the front lines learn about customer needs and new possibilities. Coordination between departments such as marketing, engineering, and manufacturing does not exist, in part because the people in those departments do not even know each other.

As one example of its inefficiencies, Boeing discovered that its traditional sequential and vertically managed technical specialties produced enormous waste. Of its total labor costs, some 30 to 50 percent reflected wasted effort: rework or repairs. One engineer out of every three was fixing mistakes made by others. The traditional organizational structure wasn't very efficient and it wasn't giving the company what it needed: speed, quality, and adaptiveness.[11]

These are today's needs. The world has reached a unique point in human evolution in that we are now living with enormous amounts of personal, environmental, global, and business turbulence. As change becomes omnipresent, evolution is leading to new organizational forms. These new organizations are built around the customer's demands and requirements and on operating within continual flux and uncertainty. Even the definition of customers has changed. Every work group has its internal customers and internal suppliers and must operate within an internal economy. Given all of these changes, organizations are creating models for working in cross-functional teams.

Moving Toward the Circle

In this generation the pyramid is evolving into the empowered workplace that focuses on customer needs. In such organizations, activities that do not serve the customer are questioned and discontinued. In the new empowered workplace, individuals and teams take more control. There is an environment where individuals or teams take responsibility for linking their work to others' efforts and satisfying the customer and the organization. Functioning in this kind of organization requires the management of a complex set of relationships and a lot of feedback.

As organizations experiment with the new ways, they see that there is no "right" form. The organizational form is not cast in stone but a product of people's intention that can be changed at will.[12] Indeed, most organizations are blends of two models, with some qualities of each. The pyramid and the circle represent two ways of thinking about organizations, not organization charts. We have seen organizations that have created circles with pyramids and pyramid structures that linked circles together. Organizations evolve in numerous stages, combining and modifying these qualities to support their needs. In general, the rules, structures, and assumptions of the old hierarchical model and the emerging circle model of the organization can be contrasted as follows:

Hierarchical Model *(control)*	*Circle Model* *(empowerment)*
Stability	Continual change
Small change	Breakthrough change
Resistance to change	Embrace of change
Now	Future
Motivation by control	Motivation by commitment
Individual leaders	Teamwork
Separate departments	Cross-functional teams
Individual results	Team results
Products	Processes
Upward focus	Customer focus
Downflow of information	Free-flowing information

The changes inherent in this shift take the form of new initiatives, values and aspirations, and models for future success. Organizational changes are matched by equal amounts of individual change. In the new workplace, as Walton[13] describes it, control gives way to commitment. People "want to" work rather than "have to" work. They want to work because they feel a sense of connection and purpose, and that they make a difference.

For example, AT&T and the Communications Workers of America Union have been working together to define the "organization of the future" that fits the personal needs of the workers and positions AT&T for success.[14] The new paradigm is being designed into division after division as a partnership between union and management. It represents a realization by both that the future of the company is a shared responsibility and that its success is in both of their interests. The new model consists of leadership councils and different steering committees and teams for each part of the organization. In order to create this new structure, operating values, roles, and ways of working need to undergo massive changes. The partners are committed to a major training effort and anticipate the ups and downs of the process as people make the new design work.

Service-oriented companies that have attempted to turn the pyramid upside down find that their focus on the customer needs to be reinforced and retuned periodically. To this end, Balazs Analytical Labs has made the transition from a circle to a pyramid to a circle again. When Marge Balazs founded the company to provide support for the manufacturing phase of the semiconductor industry, she formed a customer-focused, team-oriented organization. As the company grew, there was a need for more "business" practices and differentiation between staff roles. In an endeavor to add more professional management, a COO was hired. In the course of the COO's tenure, many systems and standards were put into place—so many that they began to impede the flow of vital information and to stifle the employees' creativity. In less than two years, the customer-focused team culture was in danger of eroding. Employees were dissatisfied, sales were slipping, and the COO knew something was wrong. The culture that had developed did not embody the values that Balazs had been built on. A drastic change was necessary to restore the previous spirit and productivity. The COO decided that the values and the direction that Marge Balazs wanted to take the company were not in concert with her organizational philosophy and decided to leave. What was left was the need for a major organizational redesign around a more collaborative form of decision making. A transition team met daily to focus on operational issues and keep catastrophes from happening. This team acted as the keeper of the organizational spirit and focused on restoring teamwork and customer focus. The outcome of this transition process, which took over six months, is an organization focused once again around customer needs and a nonhierarchical team system; an organization that looks at the overall work process across functions, not just individual jobs and departments.

The empowered organization runs by creating networks, or circles, which are groups working together to share information, make decisions, and share responsibility; in them, people begin to rediscover their voice and their spirit. A circle can begin simply when team members begin to talk about shared problems. Instead of complaining about how bad things are, they start to think about how things can be different. They go beyond their levels, titles, and other divisions to consider how their work can be done better.

In one medical-surgical service group at UCLA Medical Center, a nurses' group established to talk about overcoming burn out began to consider that burnout came from the fact that they weren't doing what they wanted to do—touching and relating to their patients. Instead, they were glorified maids, following largely meaningless rules. They wondered what would happen if they stepped back and questioned what a medical ward should be like in order for them to be healers. This discussion led to a breakthrough; they began to see that the old rules were no longer necessary and that many of the rules took away the dignity and the control that was needed by the patient. Why didn't patients eat together? Why couldn't they get snacks from the refrigerator? Why couldn't they help themselves more? Why weren't there classes and presentations in the lounge? These questions led to redesign of the whole medical ward, to the delight of the patients and of the physicians, who had been initially skeptical.

The circle concept affects top leadership as well when the major issues and steering of the organization are passed from one person at the top to a network of steering committees and ad hoc groups that are set up to resolve issues. People at all levels participate in the decisions. The team doesn't necessarily make the final decision, but they work on the problem. If they don't make the decision, they at least hear about it directly from the decision maker, along with the reasons for the decision. Everyone is considered a contributor to governance. The circle concept does not mean unbridled democracy—there are limits and boundaries to every group's charter and scope of their decision making. But the shift is away from top-down control.

Thus, changing an organizational form is a process, a series of steps. A few of them are transformational; many are incremental. Ford's Sterling plant has been evolving from a rudimentary union/management employee-participation program to a whole new style of circle organization.[15] Having started with several problem-solving groups in the plant, the plant now has more than 250 teams. The shift has affected every way they do business. First, the plant is perceived as a partnership between union and management; the two are not antagonists. Over the past decade, they have gone from an organization chart with a traditional pyramid to a series of circles, each one connected to the center, the plant joint steering committee. As the model has evolved, there has been increasing use of teams for broader policy and planning functions, which would have been the domain of top management. For example, a "future vision" group is undertaking planning for various possibilities and challenging once again the way the company does business. The new system is motivating to both the company (which now has a highly productive plant with low costs) and the workers (who have high morale and whose grievances have dropped to zero). There has been no single leader in this evolution; instead, the vision formed the core around which many people's efforts produced the result.

Other workplaces are developing along the same lines as Sterling. Despite their diversity of form, they share several common elements:

- Management gave up power as employees proposed and implemented a partnership.
- Everyone felt a sense of empowerment to take action.
- There was consensus around values and vision rather than rules.
- Teams worked together and had control over their work.
- Information was widely shared and policy was debated.
- People felt that they were treated with respect.

As the empowered organizational form develops, the organization chart must be redrawn to show the new linkages and structures. Instead of presenting a series of authority relationships, the new designs focus on what the organization does and how the core tasks interconnect. The new organization charts are more free-form and varied; the new organization cannot be contained within traditional boxes and levels. It contains much looser boundaries than the traditional organization and its structure is more difficult to pin down. A person may be a member of one team and also a member of several steering committees or councils. The boundary of any group is always open. Indeed, the boundary between inside and outside the new organization is often very fluid. Customers and suppliers at companies like Motorola and Herman Miller are part of the planning for new products and work together to cut costs and provide parts quickly and accurately. Contractors and suppliers may even have offices in the customer's company.

Corning has adapted the circle model in part because CEO Jamie Houghton, the fifth-generation heir in this family business, decided over a decade ago that the focus and style of relationships in the whole company needed to change. He charted a course of evolution in the nature of the organization that was based upon increasing respect for diversity and better management of change. Toward that end he created methods of developing awareness of new possibilities and needs and then encouraged each group to redesign itself. The result is an organization where individual units and teams feel a deep sense of empowerment and a clear and powerful connection to the rest of the organization.[16]

One of the most advanced models of the new organization is Semco, which rebounded from financial disaster in 1980 to become one of Brazil's fastest-growing and most productive manufacturing companies.[17] The company has eliminated the differences between salaried and management employees to leave only three types of employee: a core circle of five counselors who steer the whole; a ring of five partners, who are division heads; and everyone else, who are associates. The values upon which this organization is founded are democracy (employee involvement), profit sharing, and information sharing. Every vestige of the hierarchy is gone, from the rules to management decisions to levels of authority. Every associate is empowered to participate in major decisions and to help guide his or her work area. People are responsible for designing their work and for their results; if they succeed they share in the profits, which have risen 500 percent in the past five years of this experiment. Semco sees each of its employees as contributing adults and draws upon their full capabilities and capacities, thus earning their commitment.

Forming the Circle

There is an adjustment period that is sometimes rocky even if the rewards are great. As the organization shifts and asks people to act differently, people may not necessarily change their behavior. They need a new mindset, they need to learn and practice new behaviors, or there will not be a real change.

Our recent work on a team from a prominent museum presented a microcosm of what happens when the organization begins to move from pyramid to circle. The team had three responsibilities:

- Consulting to specific exhibit groups on maintenance
- Putting together the museum's big project for the year
- Being part of a five-year new building development project

The director of exhibitions, Betty, wanted to reorganize the structure of her department so that her people would not be so overworked. If only the team reorganized the structure, she felt, things would be solved. Like many clients, she wanted us to show her the way to redraw her organization. We did several things that she didn't expect. We began by helping her create a "living" graphic diagram, a work-process map—not an organization chart, but a representation of how things actually were being done. The chart also included the customers and the suppliers. Our whole team—including people from different departments who were only partly involved (such as contractors, part-time employees, volunteers, and outside people)—created this work-process map. In doing so, we all drew a representation of how work began and ended in the unit.

As it turned out, there was a need for different organization charts, one for each of the team's three primary tasks, rather than one overall design. People could have different roles in different projects and people who were on one team might have two jobs. We found, for example, that the informal organization contained a person outside the group, from the education support group, who spent 90 percent of her time with the team, as a writer. She worked with the new construction person, but there was friction between the two. She wasn't considered a real "member" of the team and didn't act like one, even though she worked in the team. She had two jobs and didn't know how to handle the split responsibility.

Our team felt that our "customers" were the top managers and the supervisor, the staff from other departments who ordered consultation, and the visitors. Thus we might be called a team that was trying to operate as both a pyramid and a circle. One problem was that visitor feedback took longer than top management feedback. Top managers felt that they were the customers because they were spokespeople for the visitors. We began to resolve that problem by sorting out the relationships.

How could members of the team best allocate their time among our three tasks? How should we plan for each of them? How should we all coordinate? Who was in charge? The museum had a steering committee of top managers who had to sign off on plans, and if they were on vacation, it could hold up things for a month. Also, members of the top management steering committee and Betty, the director of exhibitions, tended to micromanage, not just setting policy but deciding on minor details, and, most frustratingly, to change their minds frequently.

We showed that the problems that came up were usually ones of interface between people or groups and that therefore they couldn't be solved by our team alone but needed to involve people from several teams. With these task force groups, we looked at ways to overcome them.

Betty saw that she had to manage relations with top management in a better way and had to press for clarity about its role. One way to do this was to ask the exhibit steering committee to review the year's project. With this change, the data would come directly to them, rather than leaving Betty to sell it to the top managers. Our team's members began to make more decisions themselves, and to get visitors involved early on, via focus groups, inviting them to meetings and into the planning process for new exhibits.

Motivational issues had to do not with the pressure of the work, but with how much freedom of action the team had and how much permission was needed. We talked about a policy in place at Sun Microsystems: If people didn't show up, the action in question could be taken without their approval. The burden was on the individual to be there. The museum team began to see why the organization was more likely to block new ideas than to support them.

In an update several months later, we found that the "customers" (the people who visited the museum regularly) felt more connected to it. Further, as the museum team we had worked with began to see itself in a new way, the planning, design, and implementation processes proceeded more smoothly and every team member felt more powerful.

In sum, this section of the book has given an overview of the group as it evolves from pyramid to circle. Throughout the book, we will present more information on the steps to take along the way.

THE NATURE OF
CHANGE IN ORGANIZATIONS

A context is an environment in which people act. The organizational context is the set of expectations, understandings, behaviors, and methods that people instinctively adhere to within any group. In the pyramid organization, the context is established by the management team. People who don't learn these ways, or who challenge them, are either forced to leave or become very controversial. This is why the person who becomes a change leader encounters difficulty: he or she is challenging the organizational context.

Setting a New Context

An organizational context is set in very subtle ways, but it reflects the organization's deeper rules and values. For example, in meetings, do people sit in rows or around a circle? Does the leader talk first or does he or she listen to the others? What happens if a person enters and challenges the norms? For example, if you come in and begin to share your idea, or change the seating arrangement, you may be taken aside and told that you shouldn't have done that. Or even more aggressive action may be taken. What if a person stands firm and offers a rationale for his or her action, explaining that it's a change that might be important to the group? Then that person has entered the realm of the change leader and will have to influence others to adopt the changes, rather than merely impose them.

Sometimes a shift in context is perceived as more powerful than the content of an intervention. For example, if instead of solving a problem on your own, you get your group together and say, "We have a problem, here is the information I have about it. How can we begin to work on this?" you have changed the context. Mike Doyle, a consultant, says, "The change you start with is the change you want." If you want people to act according to a circle model, you should create a circular context.

In one example, we were creating an event for the two hundred top leaders of a division of a large company. The leader of the group talked about empowerment and sharing, but his behavior was very controlling and he limited feedback and interaction. Instead of letting him show the one hundred transparencies that he had brought to outline his "vision," we took his arm and marched him off the podium to talk with everyone and answer questions. Every time he wanted to get back to the front to show his foils, we brought him further into the group. That event represented a profound shift for everyone. The leader learned a new way to relate to a large group of managers; the managers heard answers to some of the tough questions and found that their leader was open to give and take. The group now tells the story of the event as a company myth explaining how they have changed.

The Systems Perspective

Transformational change can take place only if the individual within the change can step outside of the current context and see the self, the unit, or the whole organization differently. One of the more important steps toward such a change is taking the systems view of the organization.[18] The systems view begins by looking at the organization from the broadest vista. The popular phrase "think globally, act locally" suggests that one can initiate change by getting an overview of how the organization works at a level larger than the one for which change is desired. As systems theorist Bela Banathy says, redesign of systems begins when one "takes the largest possible picture in the largest possible context."[19] Change in an organization cannot be taken at the level at which it is intended. It must always involve people at the next highest, or broadest, level of the organization. It must always have a larger boundary than the change itself.

There are two ways of breaking out of a limited system to see the whole. One is by opening the system and inviting others in to participate. The second is by looking at the system's design to see how it inherently causes a certain problem rather than blaming an individual. Both of these pathways are difficult.

Transformational change cannot occur unless someone, and preferably many people, steps outside of their ordinary perspective to look at the wider system. The question then is not "How can we fix this problem?" but "What are the reasons in the broadest sense that lead these things to happen?" Asking the second question leads to the search for new information.

People need to learn how to shift their perspective from their narrow self-interest and the welfare of their own job or work team to the needs of the whole organization. This is not altruism, because the success of the whole organization is really a higher form of self-interest. In a merger, for example, the tendency is to see the new organization from the vantage point of one's own system. Breaking this pattern requires effort. In the merger of Sperry and Burroughs CEO W. Michael Blumenthal wanted to create the best possible organization, not have fights between the two cultures. During the executive retreats, anyone suspected of pushing the old Sperry or Burroughs solution was sentenced to wear a hat with the logo of the other company for a week. The message was clear: Step out of your narrow perspective and see the whole.

The systems view also asks the individual to look at problems in relation to the role they have in maintaining the system. This means, to assume that in some way the system is designed to create the problem and then to find the flaw in the design. This is a contrast to looking for ways to fix a system by changing the areas where there is difficulty or by using the most common method, blaming someone for a problem. In one hospital, when there was a medication mistake, the nurse who made it was identified and disciplined. This happened repeatedly. Finally, the systems perspective led the unit to ask how the medication system itself was flawed. Instead of blaming individuals and avoiding responsibility as a team, unit members began to look at aspects of the unit that created pressure and led to mistakes. The team came upon many factors, such as shift changes, organizational changes, and poor communication between physicians and nursing staff. They were then able to improve the unit by seeking strategies to avoid such errors.

A dramatic method for taking a broader view of systems problems and moving toward transformational change is gathering all the key stakeholders to explore the possibilities of change.[20] In a retreat for all of the faculty of a school district, with administrators and a representative group of parents, students, and community members, the dilemma of how the school system could become more of an ideal learning system was raised. The committee on the vision of the future had convened the conference, after continued conflict among the stakeholders, problems caused by funding cutbacks, and lack of consensus about what the district was trying to achieve. The key part of the two-day event was the identification of an ideal model that was widely agreed upon. They also found that many of the dimensions of the model would not require increased funds or resources, but could simply be initiated if the people were all agreed in making the changes. By discovering agreement about the design of the whole, people felt they could make changes; they knew they were all connected.

Supporting Organizational Change

To implement change, personal comfort must be overcome and satisfaction with past success must be disturbed. It is not entered into lightly, and organizations have tremendous ability to dissemble changes. The corporate landscape is littered with quality initiatives, new compensation systems, and corporate commitments to new missions and value statements that began as a high-profile positive response, but in the end changed nothing in the company. We must therefore ask what causes a change to be implemented and what can be done to ensure that it is.

Organizational transformation is elusive because it involves changing a dimension of the organization that is hidden from direct observation; it involves changing what lies behind what is said.[21] The invisible level drives the visible; it forms the culture, the infrastructure, the values, and essence that live at the core of the organization. If a visible change, the institution of a change program, for example, contradicts some of the invisible norms, it will probably not "take." Thus we cannot change the visible without changing the invisible.

The Visible	*The Invisible*
Mission statement	Culture
Behavior	Values
Style	Purposes
Decisions	Thinking patterns
Language	Assumptions
Action	Paradigms
Writing	Attitudes
Procedures	Beliefs
Policies	Norms

Another issue in trying to change a large organization is what we call the "ceiling effect" or the law of rising expectations. When one initiates a change, one often sets up an ideal goal. If, for example, there is talk about a program moving toward empowerment, participation, or customer focus, then the gap between the program and the ideal must be dealt with. That is why, when a program begins with a request for involvement of employees in one issue, and they are successful in resolving it, it creates the demand for more involvement.

In a recent conference, companies that had a decade of experience in employee participation discussed the fact that at each stage of the process, the success they experienced led to a desire for more participation.[22] For example, many union/management programs began with narrowly defined activity like quality circle or quality-of-work-life programs. The groups were not supposed to go into work grievances or work rules during their discussions. Yet, as one shop steward observed, it was impossible to talk about quality-of-work-life problems without getting into the other areas. The successful groups decided to talk about whatever they thought was important. The programs had to take on greater and greater scope. If they didn't, and tried to keep the change limited, they ended up frustrating the rising expectations for change. Thus, over time, the successful programs evolved from their beginning as limited "programs" with specific rules, to participation as part of the culture, used to determine how any work process should be done.

Generally, the larger the organization, the less power people feel they have to achieve real change. In order to help develop the new organization within the old one, the nature of power and authority has to shift. Units need the power to experiment in response to their own unique demands. In the empowered organization, the direction of change may come from the top, but each unit or group is put in control of the means to achieve the changes. The CEO of the new workplace knows that the people in the unit understand how to change and assumes that their commitment will grow if they determine how to meet the challenge. Also, the assumption is that each group may come upon a different pathway to reach the goal, because each operates in a different environment.

Another issue to be dealt with is commitment versus compliance. People may be told to change behavior, but they frequently are not asked to understand why they should do so. They need to know the reason so they can develop commitment to the change. If they understand the reason, they may then have the potential to find ways to work toward change. By developing a deeper understanding, they can internalize what is wanted, rather than simply copy it.

The more people are involved in and committed to a plan, or a change, the more likely it will be to succeed. Executives spend vast sums of money to come up with good plans and almost nothing to get them implemented; many believe, as one executive said, "A good plan will sell itself." Not so. In fact, we have seen excellent plans for change fail because people were not involved in them. Further, much to our surprise, very ponderous and seemingly ineffective plans have done well when the people who were responsible were committed to them.

People must be empowered as part of the process. For an example of what happens when they are not, consider what happened when a large bank decided to undertake a massive re-engineering process. Instead of having each branch under exclusive control of a branch manager, the branch managers were given more limited portfolios. Each branch had members of three corporate-level functional teams, representing major business processes in the bank, who were part of groups. Team members could move from branch to branch. This was a very creative and sensible innovation leading toward a circle or network organization. However, it was implemented completely within the old pyramid framework—by edict from headquarters. There was great anxiety about who would lose jobs in the new organizational model and about the seeming demotion of the branch managers. Instead of helping people understand the reasons for the change and learn the skills needed to make it work, they simply gave the order. The result was anger, chaos, and outright rebellion.

Another obstacle to organizational learning and empowerment has to do with people's perception of what is possible, and what can be achieved. The horizons of their aspiration are limited. They are stuck in the low level of performance they have today, and have lost the drive and motivation to do better. People often feel this way because there is no vision of something else that is preferable and possible. If the organization also does not really seem to believe in improvement, or feel able to challenge its people to improve, this limitation is further abetted.

A related issue is top managers' denial of the need to change or lack of recognition of what change requires. Consider what many change consultants refer to as the "boiled-frog phenomenon." If a frog is thrown into hot water, it will jump out; however, if a frog is put in warm water that is gradually heated, the frog will not perceive the minute shifts in temperature and will ultimately be scalded to death. Companies often do not see the day-to-day changes, or they assume they will go away; they thus endanger the whole. A problem gradually worsens until a sudden total collapse reveals a crisis.

Until a crisis commands the attention of the top, things can get hotter in the pyramid organization without management perceiving the change. One reason for this is that top managers are often kept from learning what is really going on. In workshops, we ask people if they would bring bad news to their bosses, and if so, how they would do it. Rarely do participants feel that their leader will comfortably accept the truth. As a result, information is often withheld from them. As the adage goes, "Leaders never get a bad meal or the truth." When the crisis occurs, it is often too late to respond: The frog is cooked.

One of our clients made us familiar with a related difficulty, the "fat-duck syndrome." When hungry ducks find a deep and apparently endless source of food, they eat and eat until eventually they can no longer fly. The fat ducks have become impaired by success that they assume will last forever. Fat-duck companies forget how to listen to customers, innovate, and develop new ideas.

Whether because of the boiled-frog, fat-duck, or other syndrome, employees don't take problems to the top because they perceive that even if leadership agrees with their diagnosis, they won't be part of the process dealing with it. They'll be thanked sincerely and told not to worry about it any more. Because the leader doesn't feel the need to listen to people inside the organization, and doesn't feel that he or she has much to learn from them, outside experts are often called in to work independently of most people inside.

But renewal—systems change, real transformation—must start with the people at the front who are in constant contact with customers or the environment and who usually see more of the problems than those at the top. In fact, a study of one corporation found that the lower one went in the organization, the greater the number of basic operational problems were apparent to people. The tragedy is that the pyramid system does not allow the awareness of the problems to filter up to the top, and further, prevents those at the middle and bottom levels from becoming involved with the problems and so resolving them.

Sidney Yoshida, a quality consultant, asked a cross section of employees in a large Japanese factory to list the significant problems they knew about.[23] Incredibly, as shown in Figure 5.2, the lower down he went, the greater the awareness of problems he found.

There are many ways that leaders seal themselves in. Joseph

Guglielmi, who worked at IBM for thirty years, talked about his changed perceptions after leaving to join a smaller company. He was shocked to see how differently the world looked when he did not have two executive assistants "to deal with the details," while he looked at broader issues. Not having "servants" led him to get in much closer touch with his customers and with the issues. His privileges at IBM had isolated him and limited his ability to see. He had become a boiled frog, as had many of his peers.[24]

If this is the situation at the top, then who will lead change and how will it happen? In our workshops, we ask groups where they perceive themselves and their team in the evolution from pyramid to circle style, and where they perceive the top management of their company. People always see their group as being ahead of the company. If such perceptions accurately reflect reality, then the new model of change must allow the middle of the organization to become teachers to the top. However, if the top still sees the world from the tip of a pyramid while the middle is part of an evolving circle, there are real risks involved in taking new ideas to the people at the top.

Figure 5.2.   The Iceberg of Ignorance.

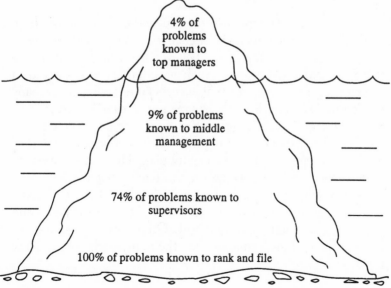

The Paradoxes of Change

One of the key obstacles to change in organizations and groups is the artificial paradox of long-term versus short-term results. As one executive put it, "We have ten-year problems, five-year plans, two-year employees, and one-year budgets." Finding the time to innovate within an environment that in effect punishes us for new ideas, and withholds development costs is difficult. The reality is that there is no incentive for change or empowerment for a plant manager or group member who has to keep productivity up on a day-to-day basis. This situation leads people to accomplish superhuman results in the short term, satisfying stockholders and top management, but leaving themselves exhausted and impairing their ability to get up and achieve even better results tomorrow. Groups that come through with incredible efforts often self-destruct when they try to do it on a more continual basis.

As shown in Figure 5.3, from time T1 to T4, the performance of the controlled group is higher than that of the empowered group. This is because it takes time for people to become empowered. The experiments and thus the time necessary to develop new initiatives inevitably decrease productivity in the short run. The benefits of empowerment become apparent later, at time T3.

As Charles Hampden-Turner suggests, work groups have further limited the possibility of change by posing alternatives in either/or terms.[25] They falsely believe they can do one of two things in order to improve, such as offer better quality or a cheaper car. He points out that success comes when a company or a group learns to do both, as Japanese automakers learned to do in the eighties. He suggests that groups trying to change see the two elements not as opposites but as two values that they need to incorporate into a successful plan. They must have high performance and few people on the team; that is, they must achieve a better product in shorter time. Then the group imagines how they might move toward each element of the pair—and then how they might approach both. Often this exercise leads to breakthrough transformation in their methods of working together.

Many either/or dichotomies limit our ability to change. A common dichotomy is feeling that we can't change toward our vision and get things done to respond to immediate pressures. Or that we can't change without more resources or time. Or that we can't serve people well and be profitable. Or that we can't serve customers and employees, or stockholders and employees, at the same time. Each of these supposed dichotomies can be challenged: There are many examples of groups or companies that have successfully done both things simultaneously. The companies that overcome these imagined dichotomies are in control of their destinies, even in an uncertain environment. When a group stops dismissing change by hiding behind the dichotomy and begins to engage the dilemma and explore ways to deal with both parts of it, transformational change can begin.

Maintaining Change

What is the difference between reversible and irreversible changes? How is a change maintained and supported? One of

Figure 5.3.   Time Needed for Performance Improvement with Different Management Styles.

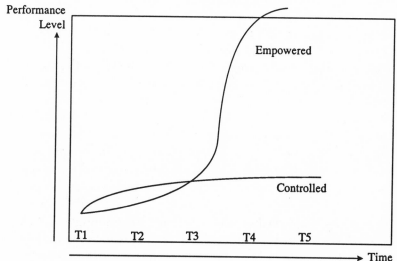

the greatest challenges in transformational change is to reach a point where the shift is largely irreversible, where it is so much a part of the culture that it is never questioned or only questioned appropriately, in terms of how it helps the organization achieve its overall purpose. So many of the changes that organizations initiate seem to be reversible when the change leader moves on or seem to degenerate over time. What makes a change strong enough to stick?

There are many answers to this question. First, change has to be deeper than a single person. If a single leader holds it together, then it is fragile. When change becomes transformation, it embeds itself within all of the people in an organization. If everyone supports and benefits from change, then it will be sustained by the whole group.

Several types of activities help the organization sustain the transformation:

Moving the Ceiling.   As the skills and capabilities of the organization grow, there must be wider empowerment, participation, and sharing of responsibility. When done effectively, empowering an organization creates an appetite for more innovation, in effect raising the ceiling of possibilities. The original limits imposed on an activity or change need to be questioned, and moved upward.

Shifting Streams.   If a change stalls, it is often because the innovation has focused too much on one project or activity and needs to spread out. If partnership has been the focus, there may be a need for more individual responsibility or for better learning skills.

Internalizing a Transformation.   The paradigm shift has to keep moving in the organization so that the transformation is internalized by all; every individual must be imprinted with what the change is about and must take responsibility for its success.

Shifting to Focus on Essences.   Change sometimes gets stuck because it is too focused on practicalities and has lost sight of its values. The process of stepping back and renewing the process by asking the deeper questions "What are we trying to do?" and "How well are we doing?" must begin again.

Developing a New Work Contract.   Another way to sustain change is through a legal or morally binding contract or agreement. The terms of the transformational change may be set down in some form of operating agreement between the company and the employees. If a change is codified (for example, like many labor/management innovations) in legally and morally binding terms and set out for everyone to see, the chances increase that the innovation may be sustained after the initial commitment and excitement dies down.

Learning New Relationships.   Many organizational structures are reversible, but relationships are not. Once people have learned to work as partners and talk directly, it is hard to have them revert to silence. Once a group learns to work together, a leader who tries to go back to directive leadership will get great resistance. This resistance is based on the team's natural wisdom, their ability to sense for themselves the best course of action, and their understanding that they have learned to be effective.

Supporting Maintenance Activities.   Maintenance activities help people remember, affirm, and support the heroes of their values. When an organization goes through a transformation, it needs to design activities to support it. For example, if a team style of leadership has evolved, then the most successful teams should be rewarded, not individual champions.

There is always a tendency to regress even after a successful change. If a new source of outside pressure arises, or a new crisis hits, it is still possible to regress to the directive, secretive behavior of the old pyramid form when one is under stress. The second generation after a change often fumbles or finds things drifting back. New programs wind down, innovations fade, a new leader enters from the outside and cancels everything. We must guard against a tendency to react to problems by moving the organization's boxes around without making real change. This is not a new phenomenon, as the following quotation from Petronius's writings[26] in 60 A.D. shows: "We trained very hard, but it seemed that every time we were beginning to form up into teams, we would be reorganized. I was to learn later in life that we tended to react to any new situation by reorganizing, and a wonderful method it can be for creating the illusion of progress, while producing confusion, inefficiency, and demoralization."

How, then, can we be sure we are making real change? Ernie Savoie, the director of the employee development office at Ford, writes that renewal is a critical dimension of a successful transformation.[27] After a period of activity, even the most transformational change seems to get dry, and people forget its original intent. They need to get back in touch. He notes that affirming the structures and behavior expected after the change is not enough. The group needs to go back to the original vision behind the change. Next, they need to explore the obstacles that have emerged: New employees who are not trained in the new values and skills? A new competitive situation? A change of leadership? They must discuss what can be done about the specific obstacles. Then, they need to ask how they might solve the problem in a way that fits their original values.

In effect, they are redefining the change and renewing their group or organization. The new organization cannot establish itself and then coast. It needs continual periods of questioning and renewal. After each of these periods some new understandings, pathways, and structures may evolve, even if the values remain the same.

The new organization is not based upon specific structures or ways of doing things as the pyramid organization is. Instead, it is based on a set of values, a vision, and a purpose. Respecting these values, it then forms a design for acting in accordance with them. In the next chapter, we will look at the process of creating a vision and a mission as a means of determining direction.

6
Organizational Purpose: Defining Values, Mission, and Vision

The best way to predict the future is to invent it.

—Alan Kay

A vision without a task is but a dream,
A task without vision is drudgery,
A vision and a task
are the hope of the world.

—From a plaque in a church, Sussex, England

In this chapter we look at the soul of the organization in the three aspects of its essence: values, mission, and vision. These form the underlying core of the organization's identity, the glue that keeps people, teams, and organizations responsive and innovative in new situations. Together, they give meaning to inspire and connect people; they keep an organization continually growing and focus people on the important tasks.

THE ESSENCE-DRIVEN ORGANIZATION

We call the company that is organized around a deep sense of values, mission, and vision the *essence-driven organization.* Such organizations provide a foundation that allows individuals to make clear choices about the environment they will be working in. Organizations that are essence-driven provide a foundation for the following:

- Bringing people together
- Eliciting greater commitment
- Coordinating the work of many people
- Making difficult decisions
- Encouraging business planning
- Challenging current thinking
- Making incongruent behavior more noticeable

Harmony and coherence of effort are the results when an organization is essence-driven; such organizations also have more flexibility to respond to internal and external changes.

The first step in creating such an atmosphere is to invite the hearts and minds of employees to join the company. One of the vital things people look for in their work is meaning. They want to see the connection between their task and its purpose. For example, volunteers often stay involved in such mundane tasks as stuffing envelopes because the reason for their work—rather than the work itself—sustains them.

Meaning and purpose can also help employees when they make business decisions. We worked with a small construction company, started by artists, called the Flying Turtles. Their vision and mission was to serve, be creative, have fun, and be ethical. The problem was that a friend and competitor did not share the same ethics but instead cut corners and used undocumented workers, and was able to undercut their prices. The Turtles felt frustrated because their values seemed to make it difficult for them to compete. Eventually, they came to the realization that many value-oriented businesses come to: They would compete by offering the best work at reasonable prices. Although they might not grow to the size of their competitor, they felt inspired and committed to their decision to maintain their values.

In essence-driven organizations, people have the power to contribute directly and believe they can achieve results that are congruent with the company's values. They feel less tied to the rules and more deeply committed to the values. Shared values, mission, and vision unite people and provide a link within diversity.

Meaning can be more of a motivator than the pay scale or incentives. In an editorial reply to management guru and columnist Tom Peters, who had written in his column about his discomfort with the growing spirituality in organizations, William George, CEO of Medtronic, a medical instrument company, told how his company was organized around its mission to restore people to the fullness of life and health.[1] The company's founder, Earl Bakken, still meets with small groups of new employees to talk with them about this mission. The company takes time every year to look at the effects it has had on the people who use its equipment. Several people whose lives have been affected by its products are invited to the company's annual holiday party to tell their stories.

More recently, Medtronic has added a values statement to its mission, formulated as a series of operating principles for employees, to make it still clearer. The company has found that leading by mission and values is more effective than by objectives. The statement reads as follows:

Our values are to

1. Restore people to full health
2. Serve customers with products and services of unsurpassed quality
3. Recognize the personal worth of employees
4. Make a fair profit and return for shareholders
5. Maintain good citizenship as a company

The statement covers Medtronic's relationship to every key constituency, by defining an overall outcome desired in that relationship. Each team and individual in their work strives to clarify how that value is defined in their own work.

In an organization with an overarching vision, the task of each individual and team is to determine how what they do is in alignment with that vision. If the two are not aligned, sooner or later, people will experience tension and frustration; in contrast, alignment produces commitment. Alignment is supported by access to information about the precise nature of the mission and vision.

In the aftermath of the Loma Prieta earthquake, companies around San Francisco underwent supreme tests of how closely their people were aligned with their missions. Because of the crisis, there was a period in which it was impossible to reach employees—they were on their own, empowered to take action. Employees from Pacific Bell rallied to the challenge. They knew their jobs and made needed decisions. They knew what to do and how to get it done. They acted with little supervision. They were able to do this because they had the skills, and they were clearly aligned with the company's vision and mission.

All elements—mission, vision, and values—are interconnected and do not necessarily need to be clarified in sequence. However, there are times when it is important to stress the sequence of values, mission, and vision. If the organization is out of focus, it needs to return to its foundation (values), then update its purpose (mission), and finally, stretch itself toward the future (vision).

In this chapter, we will discuss each of these aspects of the essence-driven organization. The creation process is what we call "visioning."

VALUES: THE BEDROCK
OF THE ORGANIZATION

Value is defined in Webster's dictionary as "a principle, standard, or quality considered inherently worthwhile or desirable." The root is the Latin *valor*, which means strength. Values are sources of strength because they give people the power to take action.

A person's values evolve in response to the question, "What's important to me?" They are the deep-seated standards that influence almost every aspect of people's lives: their moral judgments, their responses to others, their commitments to goals. People make decisions based on value systems. Values are deep, often unconscious, and often difficult to change.

Values are among our most distinguishing characteristics as human beings. Because of them, people act not only in service to personal needs but also out of a broader sense of what is important and meaningful. Sometimes we mistakenly think of values as "shoulds," telling us what we can and cannot do. In fact, values are energizing, motivating, and inspiring. When we care passionately about something—when we value it—we can spur ourselves on to great achievements.

Values help organize our lives. What is most important to us to accomplish at work, in our families, and in our personal lives and careers can be described in relation to our values.

A company cannot get the job done today without clarity about its values for dealing with its customers, the community, and its own employees. As employees face increasing responsibility, making more complex and far-reaching decisions, a corporate values credo provides guidance for their behavior. Traditionally, employees were compliant in the face of procedures and standards of behavior controlled by supervisors. Today, with greater autonomy for individuals, they need to be guided not by rules or by a supervisor, but by values. If a decision is in accordance with the company's values, then it is right.

One of the most important keys to greater commitment is a close link between personal and organizational values. A survey by the American Management Association of 1,460 managers and chief executives suggests that an understanding of this relationship provides new energy for corporate vitality.[2] Shared values between the individual and the company are a major source of both personal and organizational effectiveness. When there is little relationship between the two, it can be a breeding ground for conflict and cynicism.

If we all had the same values and the same priorities, it would be easy to work together. But in most teams, there are many different values and beliefs. In order to help us work better as a team and make decisions that lead to commitment and action, it is necessary to see the range of values that are influencing the decision-making process. While there will always be some differences, consensus about key values is important for any group.

Values are the bedrock of corporate culture. Values provide employees with a sense of common direction and guidelines for their day-to-day behavior. As Robert Haas, chairman and CEO of Levi Strauss, noted, "We've learned. . . that the soft stuff and the hard stuff are becoming increasingly intertwined. A company's values—what it stands for, what its people believe in—are crucial to its competitive success. Indeed, values drive the business."[3]

Values define the way that people actually do things in an organization. Deal and Kennedy[4] note the following: "If employees know what their company stands for, if they know what standards they are to uphold, then they are much more likely to make decisions that will support those standards. They are also more likely to feel as if they are an important part of the organization. They are motivated because life in the company has meaning for them."

When people work in an environment where their activities are aligned with what they consider important, greater energy, motivation, desire, and will to achieve even the most difficult tasks emerge. If our most important values remain somewhat hidden from us, or are unclear or unknown, the result can be conflicts and contradictions that make us feel confused, blocked, and frustrated. In contrast, as Schmidt and Posner have reported, when managers' values are congruent with the values of their companies, their personal lives are in better shape, their approaches to their jobs are more optimistic, and their stress level is lower.[5] Clarifying personal and work values can therefore be a great resource for an organization. We must first clarify our values for ourselves, and then for our team and our organization.

Clarifying Personal Values

Our earliest values revolved around our parents and the people who took care of us. As we grow we develop other values revolving around school and the larger community. These learned values are associated with our basic growth and development.

Later we develop values that are related to working and becoming self-sufficient. Later still some people develop values that are related to the human community in general.

Personal values are like the steering mechanism on a ship: They help us stay on course even in the midst of turbulence. Many people find that clarifying their personal values gives them added strength when confusing situations arise. Our ability to express personal values in work strengthens our commitment to the action.

Clarifying Organizational Values

Values don't mean much if they are kept secret. If you share your values with the people around you, you are more likely to actualize them. It is important for people who work together to share their personal values and thus determine together which values are central to their shared work.

Some values are in conflict with other values. What if a company values honesty but also values a high sales volume? How or when does the value of honesty supersede the value of making a sale? Many companies have been deeply wounded by such value conflicts, most often because employees did not feel that they had a forum to discuss these conflicts.

For example, one company with a strong values orientation was given a huge order from a tobacco company, but only on condition that it eliminate its no-smoking policy. The company debated the order within every work group, balancing the need for the order with the challenge to its corporate values. The different work groups finally achieved consensus that their values on health promotion were more important than making the sale, and the company turned it down rather than change its policy.

More than anything else, the values of a work group or team help its members work together. Values also define how the team relates to other teams in the organization. In most organizations, the core values—how to work together, how to treat other people, and what is to be the overriding focus of attention and concern—are understood but seldom discussed. Most organizational and team values are *unconscious* in that they lie below the surface and are not openly explored. Bringing them into the light of day enhances agreement and connection.

Personal values exploration helps make individual differences explicit and leads to the building of a team values statement. When a team crafts a values statement, it is taking control over an aspect of its own process and deciding that it can create its own work environment, as long as it is aligned with the organization's mission. One method we've used to facilitate crafting values credos is shown in the following:

CRAFTING A VALUES STATEMENT

I. Select Key Values

Each person in the team should define his or her own values. It is then time to define team values. Each person should select five values that he or she wants expressed in the workplace. Not all personal values will be appropriate for the workplace. Each person should select ones that he or she is willing to live by in the workplace.

2. Share Key Values

Going around the room, each person in turn reads off his or her first, most important value. One person records each value on a flip chart. When any value is repeated, the recorder puts a check after it on the flip chart. When all have named their most important value, a second round begins. The process continues until several rounds have taken place. Now the key values have been recorded. The number of check marks after each indicate how many people consider it a key value.

3. Rank Key Values

The values are arranged in a list, from the one with the most check marks to the one with the fewest.

This becomes a list of the team's key values. It is best to come up with a limited number: five to seven seem to focus a group. The team might also look at some of the important values and cluster together those that are similar.

4. Discuss Gaps

The team now can use its list of key values as a basis for a discussion. For each key value, some of the ways that people express it in their work can be discussed.

5. Determine Neglected or Unexpressed Values

Often a team espouses certain values but feel they are not really acted on. They might select the values they need to develop or those that are expressed but too often neglected in activity. People can then select ways to begin to practice that value in the group.

6. Create a Group Credo

An organizational values statement or credo can be a powerful influence to align everyone with the organization's core principles. A values credo expresses the values that are important: It is not a mission statement. The statement should be readily accessible so the team can refer to it, using it as a reference point for decison making.

7. Align Behaviors with Values

Values come alive when they are expressed in behaviors. Therefore, the behaviors that exemplify each value and those that contradict it can be discussed. Such a discussion provides a way for a team to clarify how it will evaluate each member's alignment with the values.

A powerful exercise that we have used to help clarify values involves inviting each person, in order of their tenure in the organization, to speak about the values and the culture that they found when they entered. By recording their recollections, we create a map of the evolution in key company values. We can then use this information to clarify the values that are currently important and ensure that they spark individual commitment.

For example, the faculty of a primary care training program in a prominent medical center started their yearly retreat with a reiteration of the values and culture that each member found when they joined the program. The founder of the program led off with a story explaining how she came to have the values that provided the foundation for starting the program. This history gave the faculty a starting point to clarify the values around which they would build a new program to train physician's assistants and nurse practitioners to work in underserved rural areas of California. The following values statement was developed:

- The means are not separate from the ends in the practice of health care.

- Self-care, self-awareness, and self-referenced behavior are essential practices for educators in order to "teach" these skills to our students.

- Relationships with our patients are focused on assisting them to return to a state of physical, mental, and emotional well-being.

- The real art of health care is based on the humanistic application of scientific knowledge.

- A desire to reemphasize the importance of attitudinal, interpersonal, and self-care issues is necessary in the education of health professionals.

- The task of educators is to provide the best possible technical training as well as to transmit and articulate ideas and values.

This statement caused some deep disagreement among the faculty. Some realized that these were not values that they could support and hence chose to leave the program. Further, the statement gave potential students a way to see if their personal values matched those of the program to which they were considering committing several years of their lives.

When people compare their personal values with those that are clearly defined by a work team and by a whole organization, they can pinpoint areas where there is alignment and areas where there is strain. Only when they are aligned with their organization's values, can they empower themselves to take action to help the organization reach its goals.

General Electric has taken an additional step to ensure alignment between personal values and corporate values by adding their values to the performance appraisal system. The top officers' ability to manage and perform in accordance with the values of the organization has become an important criterion for success.[6]

FROM VALUES TO MISSION

Values form the foundation for behavior; the direction of behavior is formed by the mission. People who understand the reason for their own or others' actions experience less distress, even if they don't agree with the action. A mission provides the overall reason for behavior and helps organizations face challenges that arise. The mission helps people make choices, set strategies, and stay on track, rather than simply react to outside pressures.

Personal Mission

Once again we begin with the personal. A personal mission statement articulates an individual's unique reasons for living. It answers the existential question, "What is it I'm here to do?" When a person defines his or her personal mission, it acts as an emotional touchstone that unleashes powerful feelings. It is a statement of core purpose. A mission is not a single goal but an overall guiding direction. Sometimes people do not want to clarify their mission for fear that they will be held to it. A personal mission should not be seen as a restraint but as a fuel propelling them toward their vision.

The match between individual and organizational missions often makes the difference between a high-performance organization and one that is just getting by. When people find an organization that is an appropriate vehicle for their personal missions, their energy and excitement multiply.

Organizational Mission

Discovering a group's mission is just an extension of discovering an individual's mission. The mission should distinguish the team or business from others, making clear what is unique about it.

The mission also provides a guide for developing strategy, defining critical success factors, searching out key opportunities, making resource allocation choices, and pleasing customers or stakeholders. It focuses energy and clarifies the importance of the actions to be undertaken. The mission is a synthesis of what the customers' and employees' perceptions of the business, of goals for the products and services, and of understandings about the customers and the value the organization brings to them. It also takes into account what the larger environment sees as the organization's purpose and how specific job tasks fit into the whole. Once the organization has gone through the process of defining its values, developing the mission statement becomes easy. The specific statement is an outcome of lots of previous work. The mission's definition determines the way that a business is structured. For example, one way to define the mission of a railroad company is that it maintains the railroad, another is that it is engaged in the freight transfer business. A change in mission resulted when the leaders of Federal Express decided that they were in the transportation business rather than in the package-delivery business. To set their business on this new mission required two big changes:

1. Reevaluating the assumption that all packages should travel the shortest distance between pick-up and delivery

led to a new system whereby all packages are flown to a hub city (Memphis, Tennessee) and sorted and redirected for final delivery there.

2. Developing a new and dedicated information system allowed the company to have concrete real-time information on the whereabouts of every package.[7]

A mission, then, is often not the first answer to the question, Why are you here? When a group of nuclear technicians was asked what it did, the members said, "We build bombs." To have stayed with that answer would have produced a less than inspiring mission. By asking, Why? again and again, the group eventually discovered the real reason they did their work—to learn to use science and technology to serve the needs of the nation. This mission was one that could sustain them. Today, as their laboratory moves to convert from defense to civilian research, they find that their mission was broad enough to focus their transformation.

Missions work best when they are grounded in the past and project into the future. They become more essential and inspiring when they focus less on what individuals do now and more on what they will do in the future. For example, consider the following mission statements:

> By defining and solving problems of the working and healing environments, we aim to improve the quality of our customers' lives and become their reference point for quality and service. Through personal competence, participation, research, and design, we strive for excellence in each aspect of our business.

> Our mission is to prevent harm, to help people survive, and to be nice.

The first is the mission statement of Herman Miller, manufacturer of high-quality office equipment; the second is that of the Phoenix Fire Department.

Many organizations have returned to earlier mission statements and reworked them to make them more vital and energized. For instance, one school district had as its original mission:

> We are dedicated to serving the educational needs of pupils within the community. The board of trustees, staff members, and the state share in the responsibilities for the education of pupils. The commitment is to provide a free public education in order to maintain a literate populace which is the basis for a democratic society.

After a group process of redefining its purpose, the visioning group came up with a deeper, more essence-driven mission statement:

> We are committed to providing the necessary resources and inspiration for each student to develop a command of learning, social responsibility and critical thinking. We are dedicated to motivating students to achieve their maximum potential and to value lifelong learning.

Some organizations develop successive mission statements and none of them seem to stick. Often this is because the missions are created quickly without commitment to it by employees of the organization. Also, in some cases the mission does not get at the core of what the business is really about. For example, a restaurant team was asked, What would you be doing if 70 percent of your resources were taken away? The team answered that what it really would be doing would be "entertainment" rather than food service. This determination helped them focus their activity. They began to focus more clearly on their atmosphere and style of service.

It is important that each draft of the mission be reviewed by as many people in the organization as possible, and with all key stakeholders. One way to do this is the following:

1. Have a design team consisting of representatives from different groups within the organization draft the mission.

2. Have a larger group (often everybody) critique the document.

3.   Have the design team synthesize the feedback into a revised mission or a set of alternatives.

The mission emerges from a process of getting feedback from
customers and employees, and then comparing it with the organization's own views of what it is doing. In many cases the organization thinks it is clear about the mission until it really analyzes
the work that it is doing. What an organization or group does
might not fit the original mission statement. Revising the mission can strengthen the resolve of the people in the organization.
It is likely to take several drafts to draw up a mission statement.
The time spent is well worth it, for those who craft the process
own it.

Clarifying one's mission is not a risk-free enterprise—it can
often increase people's frustration with where they are and where
they would like to be. To be willing to talk about mission is to
revisit past disappointments and disillusionments. Therefore, for
some people, looking at the mission takes courage.

A recent study of mission statements has found that one
that is not backed up by action is probably worse than none at
all, because people get confused and do not know if the words or
the actions are desired. The study suggests that the company's
leadership define a direction and take action before codifying it
into a statement. The source of a company's strength is doing
what it does well; the mission simply makes clear what is already
happening in the company.[8]

Some people feel that a two- or three-word slogan is a mission statement. Slogans focus attention but they do not give a
sense of purpose. Slogans tend not to carry the enduring power
of a mission statement. A mission statement should evoke feeling and passion. It should say who the company is and why it is
passionate about its mission. Companies must put the attention
on a broad-brush view of the spirit of what it does. The mission
should be brief and so clear that on a really bad day, when people
remind themselves of it, it will keep them from walking out and
quitting.

Once the mission is formulated, it is time to envision the

future. Some groups have experimented with trying to get an image of the future—their vision—without referring to their mission. Often that vision becomes impractical because it is not grounded in the mission. The mission statement is directly linked to an analysis of the customers and the environment; it therefore makes sense to look to the future within the context of the mission.

VISIONING THE ORGANIZATION'S FUTURE

Visioning refers to the process of focusing on a powerful mental image of the future—in our own lives, in our work team, and in our whole organization. It is a journey from the known to the unknown. We design the future from a montage of current facts, hopes, dreams, dangers, and opportunities. Visioning is challenging, letting go, soaring, and engaging the heart and spirit in asking: "What do we want to be? What is the best we can be?" It is revolutionary because it steers the organization by reference to what it wants to become rather than to what it is; so it invites us to look at the organization in new ways.

It is important to extend the vision farther than seems possible; it should, in fact, be "a stretch." A modest vision is not worth committing ten years to create. Even though a vision tends to evolve, it needs to be big enough at the outset so that it does not change substantially every few years.

Although our vision directs us toward the future, it is important to remember that it is created in the present. Powerful visions are never an escape from reality; instead an awareness of today's reality helps the vision avoid becoming disconnected and powerless. The tension that comes from comparing the desired image with today's reality is what fuels the organization to action. Visions enable us to explore possibilities; they become an overarching framework for what we want to create, guiding us in our choices and commitments.

Envisioning Excellence

A vision is a compass that can guide us when all other indicators of direction seem to be gone. A vision helps individuals and groups make sense of what is going on by stressing the core competencies on which constant improvement can be built. A vision is strongest when it focuses on an image that has enduring capability.

Visions have to be clear and inspiring. People don't get out of bed in the morning and drive to work in the dark excited about how they can "increase shareholder equity." Vision statements about return on investment and other such things don't have the spark that makes people want to come to work. One CEO we worked with came up with a company vision of "a 300 percent increase in profits." His team finally convinced him that such a goal had no substance; it provided no idea of what might be done to achieve it nor of why it was important to the company.

In contrast, here are two excellent vision statements:

> Progressive Insurance will expand its efforts to enhance awareness of the useless cost and trauma of automobile accidents, and to be creative about helping to reduce the numbers and costs of automobile accidents. This effort will help our customers and our society, and respond to strong personal emotions too many have endured when a friend or relative has died prematurely by automobile accident.

> In this dental office, we are committed to being conscious of our values both individually and as a team:
>
> - To be healthy and promote health
> - To be honest with our patients and with one another
> - To be broad-minded, creative, and courageous enough to stretch our capabilities
> - To be recognized and compensated for our abilities, achievements, and advancements
> - And to enjoy our freedom

How do we achieve a vision? Once again, we must recognize that visioning is not a one-time process that a group engages in; it is ongoing and constant. As we will see, visioning includes a number of stages.

Preceding Planning

A vision doesn't substitute for strategic and tactical plans; it precedes the plans. In fact, clarifying the mission and creating a vision are key to the strategic planning process. Planning often fails to catalyze results because it tends not to create the excitement and energy that an image of excellence does. Creating an image of excellence—a vision—starts with a bigger, more inspirational view and then works backward, identifying the steps that need to be taken to create such a future. It lays the foundation for breakthrough improvement by allowing the mind to break free of its current assumptions about how things are done and looking differently at what could be done. Creating an image of excellence requires the individual or the group to expand its thinking; only then should it narrow in and focus on how to accomplish the vision.

Given the emphasis on creating vision in business in the past decade, many people have attempted to create vision statements, but without learning to experience vision. Some managers think that a vision is a dream, a flight from reality, or naive idealism; in other words, they believe it is not central to the business of business. Some have even experienced the creation of a vision as manipulation, of being coerced into a process that was not to their liking. This can come about when a vision creates too wide a gap between where people are and where they want to be. Since a vision is a picture of a preferred future state, no one can be given a vision; it is a commitment and must be made personal.

Inspiring visions are not about specific outcomes (such as market share, stockholder value, earnings per share, or return on investment). Instead, they focus on developing aspects of the individual, group, and organization that have more meaning and that nourish creative potential. Visions gather momentum when they focus on how people will interact with each other and serve their customers or society in unique ways.

A vision has several specific qualities:

1.   It motivates and inspires.

2.   It is a "stretch," it pushes people toward greatness.

3.   It is clear and concrete.

4.   It is achievable.

5.   It reflects the company's highest values.

6.   It is simple, clear, and easy to communicate.

Creating a Vision: The Process

People experience vision in a number of different ways: Some see mental images of them, some experience them as sensations, others just have an unspoken sense of what they are. When people, teams, or organizations generate a vision, they most commonly refer to it as a powerful mental image of what they want to create in the future.

There are many methods for evoking vision. These processes start with inviting people to get back in touch with their hopes for the future. The techniques of using images, stories, metaphors, and symbols can help the people in a team or an organization accomplish visioning.

Imagery is the mental process of creating sights, sounds, smells, tastes, and sensations in the absence of actual external stimuli. It is a means of improving communication between the conscious and unconscious levels of the mind. With it, one can span time; one can use one's mind to travel to a time in the future when the vision has been accomplished. Imagery is less susceptible to personal censorship and can sometimes be more revealing than verbal expression. Imagery is an especially useful tool in the face of tasks that are complex, uncertain, and innovative.

Imagery is enhanced by a relaxed state of mind. To begin the visioning process, people must sit in a comfortable position. They allow some time to dream, to let the mind wander and "remember" the future. There is no "right" way to do this; the focus is to get a clear experience of what the future will be like. One allows the mind to move from focusing on business details to a time in the future. Another way to imagine the future is to select one of the company's or group's key values and allow oneself to imagine how he or she personally embodies this value, from the moment of entering the office until returning home in the evening.

Aristotle said: "The soul never thinks without a picture." Symbols are pictures or images that represent the vision. These are not artistic, carefully crafted pictures, but representations that mirror an image of the future. Each person can draw what they think the vision would look like. In a large group, one person may take all the images and pull them together into an integrated symbol. That person can use crayons, large sheets of paper, colored pens, tape, scissors, and other supplies to create a group image from the individual ones.

The technique of metaphor encourages people to compare their vision to something else. For example, a team can talk about itself as if it were a tree: The roots are the values; the trunk, the mission; the fruit, the outcomes of all the hard work. Sometimes describing the vision as a metaphor allows people to distance themselves from reality enough to produce a dream of the future.

In order to begin to craft a vision, for yourself, your group, or your organization:

1. Allow yourself to be in a relaxed state, where there is no pressure.

2. Avoid focusing on today's problems and what isn't working.

3. Focus on what really matters to you.

4. Focus on what you want to create, not how to make it happen.

5. Focus on imagining the future as if it were right now.

6. Express visions in the present tense (for example, "we are. . ."). Expressing the future in the present tense helps force out the answer to how one gets there.

7. Avoid such competitive phrases as being first, number one, or the best. Such statements can leave the group without a next step and reduce learning and innovation.

The process of creating a vision takes place best in a retreat, where groups of people who represent the whole company can take the time to reflect. This process can be jump-started with individual work, but there is no substitute for time spent working together on the vision. It is often helpful to have more time than you may think necessary to ensure that the vision is deepened by discussion, symbols, metaphors, and imagery. A common mistake is to devote two to three hours to "vision" and then stop with whatever is produced in that time. In our experience, it takes a group a while to clear out current business concerns and to enter a visionary state.

Involving the Organization

In many cases creating the vision has been the purview of the executive team. We have witnessed many instances where this team goes off site, creates a vision, and then returns to "roll it out in the organization"—often to massive resistance. This is often done because of the belief that it will save time and that upper-level managers have access to all the information needed to inform their visions.

But we have found that a process involving all levels of the organization's stakeholders (customers, suppliers, employees, stockholders, and community members) produces the most long-lasting results. In the words of a master at large group visioning, Mike Doyle, "You have to go slow to go fast." Design teams need to be made up of all these different people and need time and resources to accomplish their task.

If an organization spends time in planning the vision, the buy-in will be substantially stronger and the implementation phase will be a simple continuation of the process, rather than an unconnected castoff from the "planners" to the "doers." People involved in the process should be aware not only of their individual perspectives of the company but of the big picture. The first part of the visioning process is therefore to gather information about what the company does well, how it is doing, and what is happening in its environment.

The visioning retreat can create a new spirit by opening up a dialogue about the core identity of the company. Recently, a defense contractor held a series of visioning retreats. People nominated by their groups were sent to redefine how the company could use its vast expertise in a peacetime economy. They selected a series of strong competitive advantages and core competencies of the organization, and then projected into the future how these advantages could be the source of revitalization in the new environment. They envisioned new cities and new modes of transportation where they could help people work and live together. After creating this vision, they designated teams in each area to explore product and service opportunities. This process gave a new spirit to a company that was facing massive layoffs and a very uncertain future. The employees who gave input to it felt that they were able to make a difference in the company's future and did not have to wait helplessly to see what the economy, or management, would come up with.

Their vision, like all powerful visions, achieves the following:

- Explains where the organization wants to go
- Describes a preferred and meaningful future state
- Captures the desired spirit of the organization
- Is easy to read and understand
- Is compact
- Gets people's attention
- Guides decision making
- Gives people a better understanding of how their individual purpose may be realized in the group or organization
- Is felt and experienced, enlivens people when they hear it
- Is dynamically incomplete, so people can fill in the pieces
- Provides motivating forces, even in hard times

■   Is challenging and compelling, stretching beyond what is comfortable

■   Is perceived as achievable

As the design team engages in the visioning process it is important to keep the larger organization appraised of what it is doing. In effective visioning processes, there are several points at which the team communicates throughout the organization what it is doing and receives feedback. Communication of the overall plan through newsletters, all-hands meetings, and other methods is crucial. Everyone in the organization must feel that they have input into the process.

If people create the vision, they will "own" it, and implementation will happen more quickly. Thus, the process of developing the vision is as important as its outcome. It is important to note that there is a difference between a vision and the visioning process. The latter includes a review of values, mission, and vision. Top management must recognize the amount of time necessary for the visioning process for an entire organization. Subsequently, they must also devote the time and energy necessary to visibly establish the finalized vision as a tenant of the organization.

The following steps outline the overall visioning process:

1.   A representative design team for the organization is created; it will guide the visioning process.

2.   The design team scans environment and drafts a statement that summarizes the organization's purpose, its businesses, its products and services, its customers, and the value it brings to them.

3.   The design team compares this statement to existing mission statements.

4.   The design team generates questions it thinks the vision statement should answer.

5.   Various personal visioning tools get other people thinking

creatively about the vision questions. Individuals and teams generate their own visions.

6.   The design team drafts a vision statement. If it has not done so, this team, in consultation with top management and leadership, drafts or works from a mission statement.

7.   Draft statements are circulated to key decision makers and members of the organization. Feedback from these people is incorporated.

8.   The mission and vision are communicated to the organization, to external groups, and to customers.

9.   Team and individual mission and vision statements are developed.

After the vision has been clarified, it is important to take what the group has come up with to people in the next level in the organization and get feedback on what the vision represents to them. After this feedback is gathered, the vision often needs to be reworked; then the plan for its implementation begins to take place.

Implementing the Vision

Communicating the vision to other groups is a very important step in the development of an aligned organization. It is important for the people who were not directly involved in the visioning process to have an opportunity to discuss the vision, clarify the meaning of the words used, and find ways to understand how the vision will affect them. It is a time to focus on listening and clarifying, not defending the vision. Visioning often unleashes conflicting emotions. People feel hope and fear and anxiety about making the changes. It is important to understand that if this process is not experienced emotionally then the buy-in and commitment of people throughout the organization is more difficult to obtain.

Also, there is a tendency for groups to become upset and dissatisfied with the current state of functioning after they have visioned the alternative. If a group moves too slowly toward the vision, it becomes impatient and frustrated. This impatience can be tempered by helping people understand that this tension is normal and predictable.

Many visioning projects fall flat because they call into question basic assumptions of the organization and fundamental structural relationships, and the organization draws back from their implications. Often organizations want a "vision" but don't learn or respond to what they discover in the process; it is at this point that some efforts stall. To ensure that people do not become disillusioned, it is important to think the process all the way through and make sure there is support at important leadership levels for proceeding with implementation.

There is a long and dusty road between the vision and its implementation.[9] It is important to expect and prepare for some inconsistencies, to admit them, and to show that living the vision is a process, not a declaration. The learning is in the humble application and reapplication of the vision to daily action. Many leaders err in thinking that as long as they have the big picture, the details don't matter. But visions are lived in the details, the everyday choices. One should spend time getting one's own house in order so that one's behavior doesn't look off-kilter when people compare it with the vision. Trust is built from repeated behavior that people observe over and over again. If people are to trust in the vision they need to see it informing organizational choices, policies, and actions.

A vision should focus on creating an inspired environment inside the organization first and serving the customer second. Research has shown that how employees are treated inside the organization is reflected in how they treat customers.

Further, effective visions prepare for the future while honoring the past. No one likes to think of his or her past actions as having been done in the "wrong" way. People who are ashamed about their pasts tend not to stretch far into the future. But people who can accept their previous actions and see how they were stepping stones to the current reality can change more easily. Change occurs in creating a continuity from the past to the future. Honoring the past provides a springboard into the future.

Finally, the process of visioning often leads to a process of change in the organization. When an organization or team begins to see a greater sense of possibilities, it experiences the dissonance of the gap between where it is and where it wants to be. If this tension can be seen to be a rubber band, pulling the potential of the group upward, then the tension can be managed. However, if the tension between where the group is and where it wants to be is too great, it demotivates people; burnout occurs and energy is sapped. Each group and individual needs to determine how much tension can be tolerated. This may differ at different times in the life cycle of the organization and the individual. Growth seems to be a process of increasing the tension and then resolving it. Thus, the visioning process is not an easy one but the results can be dramatic.

Outcomes of Visioning

The following outcomes have been reported by individuals, groups, and organizations that have completed a visioning process.

Commitment.   Groups or individuals who have guided themselves through the visioning process notice that their vision often replaces rules. The vision guides decisions and focuses attention. Supervision then comes from within; people work not from compliance but from commitment.

Alignment.   People and groups that go through the visioning process have an increased sense of purpose and an overall congruence with the organization's goals. There is an increased sense of energy and excitement. Work in such groups has a deeper meaning.

Empowerment.   Visioning increases the sense of personal mastery, group empowerment, and organizational vigor. The experience of taking direct responsibility for outcomes they have crafted increases people's ability to act.

Respect.   Personal visioning provides a framework for appreciating strengths and putting action in perspective. Visioning provides a ground for shared participation and contributions are all treated equally in a team process. For a team or organization a shared vision is an image, like a recipe, to which everyone can contribute ingredients.

Interdependence.   Group visioning is a format for groups to experience ways in which they are connected with other groups in the organization. It provides a bigger picture in which to frame individual efforts. Visioning highlights the paradox between the larger effort and the individual choice.

Innovation.   Groups and individuals that have worked through a visioning process have increased their ability to generate divergent ideas of the future. They have stretched their ability to think beyond short-term goals and imagine alternative futures. This ability to generate visions and move toward them is a primary determinant of success.

The process of clarifying values, mission, and vision is both a personal and an organizational task. The process takes place at every level—the personal, the team or group, and the organizational level. Because the process starts with an individual's personal statement of mission, values, and vision, you don't have to wait for the leadership of your company to begin the process. You might start by answering the following questions for yourself:

- What do I want to be?
- What are my capabilities for achieving this?
- What do I want to be known for?

This process guides you in creating organizational or personal change.

In the next chapter we look at the chaos that comes when a person is actually in the middle of change, especially if that person wasn't the one who initiated the change. We look at the emotional phases of transition and how you can help yourself and your team or organization through the process.

7
From Denial to Commitment: Helping Yourself and Others Make the Transition

It should be borne in mind that there is nothing more difficult to arrange, more doubtful of success, and more dangerous to carry through than initiating changes. The innovator makes enemies of all those who prospered under the old order, and only lukewarm support is forthcoming from those who would prosper under the new. Their support is lukewarm partly from fear of their adversaries, who have the existing laws on their side, and partly because men are generally incredulous, never really trusting new things unless they have tested them by experience.

Niccolo Machiavelli, *The Prince*

When asked to name the most important skill they need to succeed in the future, managers and employees almost universally put "managing change" at the top of their lists. They know that their teams and organizations must shift from the traditional forms to the new organization, and they understand that to do so requires transformational change. And that stops them. They wonder, How do I get myself and how do I get others to change? What if they don't want to change? What about overcoming my own difficulty with change?

No one changes by wishful thinking. Facing the denial and the emotional resistance that arise in giving up old ways is a key that unlocks the ability to move into new ways. In this chapter we look at ways for people to move themselves and the rest of their organizations through transitions.

Giving up old responses and taking on new ways can be an emotional, uncomfortable experience. The process is similar for individuals, teams, and organizations. Understanding and guiding the human side of change, revealing resistance, and managing the emotional process of saying good-bye is part of the ability to lead change. Emotionally significant healing activities are needed to move the group toward transforming itself in response to the new environment.

We hold onto old ways for good reasons. The lag between the possible and actual, between our image of a preferred future and today's reality, can seem like a chasm, terrifying or impossible to bridge. Here, we hope to help you learn to live with the tension of living in the gap after you've envisioned what you want—and to help others do the same.

What is it like to live through change and come out on top? What will it take for you to work with people through the change and transformation process? This may be in part about personal transformation, for once you've decided that the same old things won't work, you need something new. Changing the organization and changing others have to do with how much you are willing to change yourself. It has to do with learning to understand the emotional reality of people who are going through the process of deep change.

MOVING TOWARD THE FUTURE

The tensions of working within any organization today are deep. In addition to finding out what the organization wants of them, which is continually changing, people must also strive to keep their soul and deal with their own needs and position. There are bound to be differences between one's inner view of what is needed or the way one knows things should be and the way they are. Seeing the gaps between the current reality and the vision is part of progress toward the future. As individuals and as change leaders, we must learn to live meaningfully in this in-between space. To see how to invest time and energy during this time, let us first define more clearly what we mean by the "gaps."

In a stable organization and predictable world, few gaps exist. The organization is coherent, and the perception of reality on one level is close to that of the other levels. The future looks somewhat like the present. When change speeds up, and uncertainty becomes the environmental context, gaps begin to appear—to those who are willing to see them. Adherents to the new paradigm look upon these anomalies and those who hold onto the traditional ways deny them.

There are two primary types of gaps:

1. There are *evolutionary gaps*, between the vision of and the present. For example, there is a gap between the values people want and those they live by, or between the skills they want or need and the ones they have. Managing the evolutionary gap involves designing a group or organization that holds onto its ideal vision, while spending energy moving toward it.

2. There are *stakeholder gaps*, between groups whose different work contexts lead them to different interpretations of values or of what needs to be done. For example, the reality of top management is different from that of people who are doing various work processes, and who are in daily contact with customers. Managing the stakeholder gaps means bringing groups together, building communication, and enlarging the vision of the different groups.

Living in the Gaps

Whether in the face of an evolutionary or a stakeholder gap, management is about attaining harmony and balance, rather than denying, avoiding, or overpowering conflict and differences. This view of seeing gaps and moving into them directly is different from the old way of seeing gaps as something to be avoided.

As people become more inner-directed and demand more meaning from their work, they begin to redefine their values. They can then perceive more clearly the gap between their values and those of the organization, and between sets of values and others' actual behavior. They look for congruence, for behavior reflecting values. The gap between vision and reality is to be expected, because the behavior of any organization, like that of any person, develops from the successful solutions to problems of the past.

Indeed, gaps are often motivators. If a company has succeeded by developing a new product every two years, or by offering successful customer service and modest price, those processes become part of the culture, institutionalized through the vehicle of mission and vision statements. Questioning what has been demonstrated to be successful on the basis of changes that are only perceived as important by some parts of the organization is difficult for any person, group, or organization. This is the dilemma of change: finding motivation for the difficult task of creating a new path and covering the cost of the shift. Effective change leaders learn how to respond to the emotional realities of change in themselves and in others, and to lead through denial and resistance to exploration and commitment.

The Emotional Roller Coaster of Change

To master organizational change, people must deal with its emotional and its action components. The emotional component is the personal response as people struggle to deal with new realities when they begin to move toward new ways. The action component involves moving into relationships and ways of doing things that are different in every way.

There are predictable roadblocks to change, some of which we explore in this chapter. Individuals, teams, and whole organizations go through phases of denial and resistance before they can explore new ways and recommit. Managing transformational change therefore means navigating through these phases, not wishing they didn't exist.

Emotional Literacy

Organizations that succeed at transformational change are technically competent, flexible, and *emotionally literate*. This ability to create relationships that encourage and support communication about change is a new challenge in organizations in which emotions were often shunned. An emotionally illiterate organization might, for example, plan to move people from Denver to Oakland over the weekend and expect them to do their work as usual on Monday. Individuals and organizations are now realizing that emotional literacy—a new level of communication—is required to accomplish change.

Emotional literacy starts with the individual and moves to others. If you aren't emotionally literate with yourself, you can't expect to be emotionally literate with others. How can a person do this, become the change leader, the one who helps others understand the changes and emotions that come up through the process?

As we learned when we started our work with AT&T during its divestiture and massive layoff, people feel worse when they begin to change. They become aware of all of the feelings and desires that kept them connected to the old way of working. Morale surveys reflect this, as individuals and groups begin to feel the emotional dimension of change. In those days, there weren't many inspirational change models. We had to learn how to revitalize the spirit of the people who stayed and how to deal with the issues of change in the organization that was left. We found that after this devastating organizational change, employees were simply expected to come into work immediately and perform.

The most healing thing we could do was to bring people together and let them talk. Most individuals did not give their feelings validity; they either denied feeling anything and went numb, or they felt they were crazy or disloyal to be upset. When they were together, they discovered they were not crazy or alone. Many people began to get better just by virtue of allowing that to happen.

One branch in Lawton, Oklahoma seemed to do better than others. What was the difference? This group had found ways to allow individuals to go through a mourning process and to tell the story in ways that helped them all move into the future. First, some of the people in the branch realized that it was during their annual Christmas party that they usually recognized people for what they had done and celebrated the achievements of the year. This year, with all the change and layoffs, the Christmas party would be missing a lot of people. So, they decided to hold their party on the day before the August 1 layoffs. They got a tree, gave gifts, and gave the people who were leaving a loving send-off. Surprisingly, those who remained were much less traumatized by the departures and the people who left were able to recover much more quickly.

This was not all they did that made a difference. The walls of their branch were covered with lively stories about people and handmade posters. Displays on one large wall told the history of the two branches that had been amalgamated in the change process. A large pathway was drawn leading from each into the center, where there was a big question mark. The question mark represented the new place they were creating. They spent time together telling stories about the old places and began to look at what they wanted to bring into the new team.

Other AT&T branches had other kinds of reactions to the divestiture. A branch in Texas took the threat of layoffs very seriously. Instead of leaving one by one, they took control of the change and decided they would auction themselves off as a whole team to the highest bidder. Instead of feeling like victims, they found a way to make meaning and find some sense of healing and control. Although a bit extreme, this kind of response to the imposition of change is representative of individuals and groups who do well during change. Those who find a way to take some control and make change work for them are the ones who do well.

We are interested in organizational renewal and revitalization. Change doesn't mean wiping out the old "bad" culture and bringing in the new "good" culture. That is not realistic—and it doesn't work for people. What we have tried to do is provide models and environments where people can work through their fears and revitalize their commitment by developing critical tools for success and core competencies for change.

Fear and Complacency

People fear change. It means disruption, loss of comfort, and often extra effort and risk. Identifying, acknowledging, and managing fear help create a sense of challenge during change. Two kinds of fear are experienced during change: enabling and disabling. Enabling fear can be a powerful motivator because it moves us toward a challenge. Disabling fear can paralyze us and cause us to feel helpless. It is important to understand that the amount of fear that is enabling to one person can be disabling to another. Action is the result when there is enough enabling fear and a reduction of disabling fear. Figure 7.1 illustrates this concept.

Too little fear can lead to complacency and lack of an edge, whereas too much is overwhelming. Research on anxiety suggests that the best level is in the middle, although just what the middle is differs for every person.[1] Consider the factors that inhibit and that support change:

Figure 7.1.   Enabling and Disabling Fear.

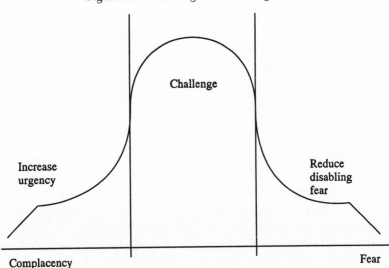

Factors Inhibiting Change	*Factors Supporting Change*
Comfort	Crisis
Fear of the new	Excitement about new possibilities
No investment in change, especially start-up costs	Investment in learning, process, innovation, and skills

To create change, an organization has to overcome the inhibiting factors and tendencies to accept the status quo. A frequent exercise for facilitating change is to look at the various factors that fit into each of the categories. The factors of crisis and disconfirmation need to be stronger than the comfort with the present and the fear of change. This often presents a real barrier to change because the comfort people feel with the familiar world offsets whatever difficulties they experience with the current system. New ways represent a threat to this comfortable world and there is little incentive to face the fear. Excitement about the possibilities needs to prevail. The investment has to be enough to cover the start-up costs of change, including the costs of teaching new skills.

Adopting new ways is scary for everyone, even for leaders. Even those who have been successful in incremental change may not be prepared for breakthrough change. Anxiety and pressure lower performance, making people more rigid and less flexible. They retreat, regressing into old patterns. Leaders who create a climate of fear and rigidity thus extinguish the motivation to change. In consequence, many organizations find that just as the need is greatest, the ability of the organization is diminished. Effective change leaders are able to push people out of their comfortable places by sounding the alarm or by weaving a spell about a possible future that captivates people.

A crisis is often needed to force people out of their comfort zones. Crisis is usually the first step in initiating change. It may be a sudden drop in income, a loss of a job, or a hot new competitive product. A good leader can help others see that there is a crisis on the horizon and mobilize them before it hits. A key to effective change is spotting the crisis as early as possible.

To become a change leader one must consider the individual as well as the organization. One effective change program began by asking managers three questions.

1.   Why do we need to change?
2.   What if we don't change?
3.   What's in it for me?

The change leaders built a new context for the managers' view of the organization by helping them to see that change had to happen, from both a personal and an organizational level. Only then did they commit to change. Unexpectedly, by exploring these questions, managers initiated a process, in which the entire organization participated, that led to a major redesign of the way they did their work. This process raised productivity, and managers also reported they began to enjoy coming to work.

THE FOUR PHASES
OF RESPONSE TO CHANGE

We have found that individuals and organizations go through four phases in their response to change. The stages are almost inevitable, and they signal a process of renewal, a passage from the old to the new. Most organizations either don't recognize these phases or wish they could avoid them. However, when an organization accepts and acknowledges the process, helping individuals and work groups through each phase in turn, it is then prepared to face the challenge of the future with more resilience.

Our model of change comes from our experience as psychologists working with people recovering from personal crisis and major unexpected illness. Psychiatrist Elisabeth Kubler-Ross identified five stages in a patient's experience of impending death.[2] These stages are the same in any crisis and change, for they represent a metaphorical death of the old, comfortable way.

Indeed, a heart attack can be seen as signaling the end of the era where the body can be taken for granted and demanding new self-care and self-awareness. People who made extraordinary recoveries from critical illnesses report that they experienced major personal transformations, created a new identity and sense of themselves, and sought out other people for support during the crisis.[3] The crisis of organizational change can be just as major and it demands similar deep shifts in one's sense of who one is and how one fits in.

The four response phases are represented in Figure 7.2. The transition curve moves ahead from attachment to the past to attention on the future, and from focusing on the exterior (the environment) to attending to the self, the personal effect of change.

Denial: Pretending It's Not Happening

The first stage is *denial*, refusing to believe that something needs to happen or feeling very frustrated when it doesn't happen instantly. Denial is probably the most problematical and prevalent organizational response to change and it is the greatest obstacle to real organizational change. It is a psychological defense against change that takes the form of either ignoring or not responding

Figure 7.2. The Transition Curve.

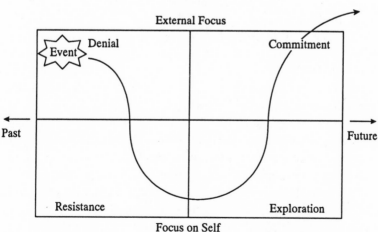

to information that shows a demand for change. Organizational denial can be seen when people are discouraged from bringing up problems, when a downturn or slowdown is dismissed as just a slight anomaly, when people say they don't have time to think of new things because they are too busy, or when a company fails to notice major shifts or problems, internal or external. Denial is an attempt to hold onto the safety and comfort of the past by ignoring signs that it is over.

Denial is by definition a disease that you don't know you have. The symptom is you think you are fine. You make yourself feel fine by ignoring the enormity of the problem. The change leader has to wake people up from denial. If they don't awaken with the first wake-up call but keep pushing the snooze button, the change leader must make another wake-up call, and yet another. The change leader needs to help people realize the reasons for the change, why they have to change, and why there can be no turning back or ignoring it.

In most organizations there is a reluctance at all levels to face up to problems. One of the most common responses to a crisis is for top management to closet themselves away from the rest of the company and plan a response. This is denial because they are removing themselves from the organization, in effect sealing themselves off from the evidence that things may be even more difficult than they think. By excluding middle and lower levels of the organization from the process, they make it more likely that their plans will be rejected. There is also the danger that they will become progressively more isolated not just from the problem itself but also from the response to the problem at lower levels.

Managers especially deny both their own need to change and the requirement for resources and long-term commitment. Top management's denial because of vested interests, arrogance, isolation, or blind spots can be one of the greatest obstacles to organizational transformation. Almost all leaders today acknowledge that their companies must change, however, far fewer will go on record as acknowledging that they themselves must change. They want change without questioning their inner beliefs, without disturbing their authority, and without changing the way they operate. Yet they can't have it both ways. They need to confront the truth and embrace the long-term need for guiding organizational change. Someone must challenge the established view of reality.

Managers also frequently want change to happen overnight. We call this the "Tarzan swing": People imagine they can swing from "We don't have any problems" to "It's all taken care of now." This idea allows the organization or the person to avoid all the doubt, anxiety, and chaos that are inherent in a true change process. Another version of the same problem is when some leaders, groups, and companies convince themselves that they have already mastered change; theirs is the deepest form of denial, for they haven't even started. Here we see Tarzan swinging across the chasm and disappearing; the people who try to follow fall into the pit. The words and action don't match.

We conducted an assessment of the personal style of some of the top managers of an innovative, Baldrige quality award-winning corporation. One aspect of their style was that, often for the first time in their careers, the managers received survey feedback from the people below them. We were amazed at the size of the gap between the executives and those below them, in terms of their perceptions. Top management represented a world where people had grown and succeeded and they did not welcome information that their style was not effective. They felt that the newer people were devaluing their old ways; they were angry and more than a little afraid. The people below them were trying to innovate and finding many of their new ideas blocked from above. The different levels of the organization lived on either side of this gap between the old and the new ways, with the old ways having more power at the top, and the new ways being represented by the creativity of the other people.

When top managers avoid or deny key information it has two immediate dysfunctional effects on the whole company. These effects are similar to the effects on a family when one member is an alcoholic, severely impaired, or incompetent but remains in a position of authority. The other people find themselves in what is called a double bind: They are afraid and even forbidden to discuss doing anything about the situation, and if they do succeed in pointing it out, they will be told the problem doesn't exist. Such denial comes from human failings. What is surprising is that the human failings are stronger than the needs of the organization. We saw a whole bank fall into unethical practices and eventually fall apart because no one wanted to confront the top officer, who was abusive and alcoholic.

The effect of this first perception gap in top management is what we call the Denial Conspiracy. Once they realize that top management doesn't want to know, the people below focus on helping them maintain their denial. Facts get doctored, negative information is explained away, and nobody looks where they know they will find difficulties. The goal is to keep the top managers from getting upset in the hope of keeping everybody from getting upset. Eventually, employees even stop perceiving negative information. A vast silence engulfs the organization until the disconfirming information can't be held back any longer. For a while, everyone in the organization feels less anxiety, but the cost is overwhelming. Sears, General Motors, and IBM all fell prey to various forms of the Denial Conspiracy.

Another dangerous dynamic results when there is pressure for change but management refuses to face reality. A division of a computer software manufacturer was in trouble and in need of refocusing and increased productivity. A new leader, who had a reputation for being results-oriented was appointed. He came in with a staff from a previous post and proceeded to demand results from the new division. The problems this division was facing were far different from those of his previous one, but he had been a winner in the past so he began to apply what he knew were winning techniques. He expected "world class" results, and fast. Some of the division chiefs came in with plans for modest goals, and he always sent them back telling them that they weren't reaching high enough. Finally it dawned on his team: Their leader didn't want realistic goals, he wanted absurd goals. They came in with unachievable plans and were told, "Now you're really breaking through to high performance." Nobody expected to achieve these incredible results, and the leader didn't get involved in working on their plans. The gap between where the organization was supposed to function and where it was actually functioning grew wider. Fantasy reigned.

The already-low level of candor between levels began to erode, as the whole division responded to its crisis with increasing unreality. In the end this division manager went on to his next post, certain that he had finally turned the division around. His replacement tried to institute what he called an "amnesty" period, where managers could come and tell him the truth. Although many managers wanted to begin to talk openly, enough of them were afraid that telling the truth would hurt them by reflecting on their ability, so they were discouraged from speaking out.

The effect of this second perception gap is what we call "the death of responsibility." If the goal is to keep information from getting in, then the goal of every employee is not to do anything that will bring real information into the company. The goal is to avoid responsibility; if there is a problem, find someone else to blame. When a problem comes up and someone is blamed and fired, the assumption is that that will bring things back to success. The work of the organization becomes finding people to blame, not solving problems.

The irony is that these processes arise at just the time when the organization is under attack, and they limit the organization's ability to defend and renew itself.

Resistance: The Death of the Old Ways

When people wake up from denial, they are still far from ready to change. Awakening from denial is traumatic. After the shock wears off, people need to go through a process of letting go of the past. They emerge from denial into the stage of resistance, which includes anger, depression, and bargaining. They ask "Why me?" and rail against the unfairness of it all. In resistance, people try to preserve their sense of meaning and identity, by retaining familiar ways of doing things. Each person has to mourn the death of the old ways before he or she is ready to step onto a new path. The resistance phase is about loss: loss of control, familiar attachments, community, and structures. Because of such loss, it is natural that people become more self-absorbed. They are trying to find out where they fit into the change and are less interested in the organization's needs. During resistance, people feel worse, stress is higher, and performance is at lower levels.

Many organizations become frustrated and angry about resistance, or they don't make allowance for it in their planning. We assisted in a merger of two hospitals, neither of which wanted to listen to two different cultures that were coming together until there was a huge strike. They didn't anticipate or manage the resistance. The top leadership was unable to manage the staff's resistance.

If managers push resistance under the table and say, "We don't resist. We are professionals. We don't do that here," the resistance goes underground and diminishes energy for the new initiatives. Resistance is normal: People need to go through the experience of hating the change. They can't be talked out of their feelings; they have to go through the grieving process. Resistance is normal, natural, and inevitable. There are many natural reasons to resist change. First, the old ways may be difficult, but they are comfortable and predictable; we know where we stand and have developed our niche. We have status and meaning. We have the skills to succeed. In contrast, we don't know whether we will be able to be as successful in the new regime, and we don't know where we will fit. We may not fit at all in this age of organizational uncertainty. No wonder we resist change. If resistance is not accepted by top management, disaster can result. If the staff's needs are not respected, it can turn on the organization (by subversion, lawsuits, and stress claims), on themselves (with such feelings as "survivor guilt" or "I must be crazy to feel upset"). They may withdraw, become self-absorbed, disoriented, immobilized, and unable to attend to the environment.

When top management is involved in a Tarzan swing they often discount the experience of resistance, even looking down on managers and employees who are experiencing the anger and loss involved in this stage. Or top managers push the team to plan together before they have overcome their denial and resistance. To insist on commitment to the new direction before people have let go of the old ways is to start the journey before people have released energy to focus on planning the future.

People in resistance have lots of excuses for not changing. These excuses reflect two kinds of resistance. One kind is expressed this way, "I hate this, but I'll get through it." The other kind is expressed this way, "This is wrong. This is bad. You need to rethink." It takes time and careful listening and consideration to distinguish the two types of resistance. At one company, a team in resistance said, "What if we know the new policy, or product, is really wrong?" In this company, the top management had to enter into a dialogue with the people who were being reorganized about why they were being reorganized. A revised direction of the change and, more important, the commitment of middle management to support it, came out of the dialogue. So concerns that are voiced must be listened to. Sometimes resistance reveals important information.

People resisting often are angry. After John Akers, former CEO of IBM, sent the company a memo saying they would have to change, people gathered in groups and shared their anger. His memo burst apart the corporate denial that was masking their fear and allowed them to vent their feelings, which came out like an avalanche. They needed to move from their anger to confront their fear and to ask questions about the future for themselves and the company. Eventually, this turned into a healthy process.

To manage resistance in a way that helps people work through it, the organization needs to understand first that people need time to express their feelings and understand where they stand in the change. They need to be respected as people, not punished for having a negative attitude. They need information that is clear, timely, and available. It may take some repetition before people actually hear the messages. People need to participate in making decisions that affect them. They need to share their ideas and feelings. And finally, people need training in the new skills and new behaviors that are expected of them. If they are going to work together differently, they need time to learn and practice the new ways. Each person will then experience what Kubler-Ross called acceptance; the shift toward seeing the positive side of the changes will begin. In our change model (see again Figure 7.2), this is the bottom point, where people cross the line toward commitment to the new way and become involved once again with the organization.

Exploration and Commitment: Change as Opportunity

At some point in the transition process, people stop feeling bad about what they have lost, or helpless to make it through; all of a sudden, they have time and energy to think about how they will accomplish the tasks ahead. At this point, they accept the change and begin to look for ways to meet the challenge. It is unlikely to be an instantaneous event, because we all tend to zigzag between resistance and exploration a few times before we begin to climb back up on the transition curve.

Resistance is followed by the renewal of exploration. We shift from holding onto the past to looking ahead at how we will fit into the future. An organization or a team that allows people to go through resistance is rewarded by a group of people who are committed and ready to help find new ways to meet the challenge. Now, people finally get on board. In the exploration phase, people experience open space, new possibility, chaotic action, exuberant inquiry, and fast learning. It is a time to try new behaviors, to experiment, to take risks. The person or group becomes the architect of change rather than the victim of it.

The exploration phase is positive and exciting. A team leader or supervisor must not direct but focus and encourage the process. There must be relevant markers, punctuation points, and results in order to make sure that the changes made are the right ones.

Commitment is the last phase in the response-to-change process, when the team has made a decision about how they will work together, learned the new ways, and settled into a new pattern. It is a time to celebrate achievement. They will need to use everything they have learned to continue to cope because the need to respond to change will soon emerge again. The transition curve begins again, and again, and again. What we have described is just a snapshot of a continuous process.

MANAGING OTHERS THROUGH CHANGE

This four-phase transition process offers predictability for individuals, teams, and organizations, even those that *want* to change. Even those who embrace change may be a bit naive about how long the process is going to take and how painful it may be. How can the cycle be minimized and shortened? There are several tactics:

- Respect the emotional struggle in yourself and others.
- Stick to a clear vision about where the organization or team is going.
- Involve people in designing the change; this dramatically reduces resistance and speeds up the change process.

In addition, sometimes the people who see the need for change must increase the urgency and decrease the fear to get those in the organization to move toward the change. A leader can help people move more quickly and more completely from one phase to the next. But no one should believe that he or his group can skip the difficult phases of resistance and exploration, and move directly to commitment.

It is our experience that some leaders' styles are more suited to leading through the danger (denial and resistance) phases, others to leading through the opportunity (exploration and commitment) phases. Leading through the danger phases requires the ability to wake people up, address difficult, complex issues, and then deal with the emotional outpouring as people go through resistance. Some leaders do not like the straight-out confrontation that is often involved in overcoming denial and are better prepared for the emotional barrage that is aimed at them during resistance. They are able to see that people are not upset with them personally but are experiencing grief and loss. Some leaders are best when it comes to acknowledging achievements and then setting another vision forward.

The challenge for a change leader is to be competent at all stages, not just one or two. We have found some core principles that help leaders at each stage of the process. Offer people validation (respect), information (about the change, why it is happening, and what is going on in the company), and participation (in figuring out how to respond to the change); think of them as VIPs. At its best, change leadership is a group process. People in a group facing change need to work together. First, they should be informed in person, as soon as possible, and preferably through direct contact with the people in the organization who are initiating change. Too frequently, managers or leaders, because of their own fear or denial, try to keep back information rather than share it. As one example, a bank did not share its plans to move out of town, even though the rumor mill was full of stories. The CEO said that he hadn't spread the word because he didn't want to upset people. Because of such fears, the news goes into memos, is sent out on Friday nights, or is shared behind closed doors. This informs but does not help people move through transition. It breeds distrust, anger, and fear and slows down the progression through transition.

Employees are not children; they can understand and deal with difficult news. People prefer to know, even if the final decision isn't yet made, than to speculate about what might happen. They also need to be invited into the process of making the changes work. Change plans are always incomplete, in that they usually have only the sketchiest notions of how the new teams, or the new initiatives, will be operated. When a change happens, a group immediately has to cope with how it will manage the change, what it will mean for them. When people have begun to grapple with the question of "What will happen to me?" they begin to free energy to work on what will happen to the whole group and the company. They move closer toward commitment.

The change leader helps people navigate through denial and resistance. We worked with one manager who was just a natural. He began by being successful his first try. He was transferred to a team that had spent the previous eight months going through denial and resistance. They were now ready to try new things and were filled with energy. His job was to focus the team and help them achieve results. He was celebrated as a successful, visionary leader, although his team had done half the work before he got there. The company then took him to a new site because it was believed that he was just the leader for a major change effort. But this time he found people in massive denial. To help break through the denial he began to have sessions in which people talked about "undiscussables" such as executive actions that did not match the vision—those issues that everyone was aware of but no one wanted to bring up. As the group was able to talk about issues that the past leadership had preferred to keep silent, the site began to move toward resistance and then exploration.

Communication that allows people to be a part of the process of change reduces resistance. People want to hear the truth, even if it is hard. In the process of closing a semiconductor fabrication plant, the design team for the closure asked the employees how they wanted to get the information about their staggered layoff dates. The employees wanted to hear all at once, all together; this was exactly opposite of the design team's original plan for each person to be told individually, in private.

Resistance is also reduced when people are involved in creating the vision of the future state. People have less resistance if they know where they are going and are given a hand in planning the vision's accomplishment.

For people to complete a change it is necessary for them to say a "good" goodbye to whatever they are losing. This may be seen as an additional phase, one of "ritual." A ritual is a special event that symbolically celebrates a passage, transition, or important value for the organization. Parties, ceremonies, or events that mark the passing of the way things used to be and the beginning of another phase can be useful. It is important for the people directly affected to decide how they want to do this. With the semiconductor plant closure just discussed, the employees decided that they wanted to have a "class book" with pictures, events, and awards for the people who worked in the plant.

Occasionally, all phases of the response-to-change process can be addressed in a single meeting. When a manager announced that the work of the group would be automated, she was met with blank stares and nods of compliance (denial). After she spent a few minutes more explaining the timing and logistics of the change, individuals began to ask questions about how it related to them, in other words, they asked if they would lose their jobs (resistance). After learning that everyone would remain employed, albeit in different groups, people began to make plans for a group disbanding party (ritual) and to ask questions about how they could look for jobs in other parts of the company (exploration) and they began to have ideas about how the work would be done when this was all over (commitment).

Going through all phases in one or two meetings requires the careful attention of the leader. The leader should not move too fast if only one or two people have moved forward. People move through different phases at different speeds. Teams do not finish each phase neatly, all at once. The challenge for the leader is to be responsible to all and not give so much attention to the stragglers (those in denial) that others (those in exploration and commitment) become frustrated.

One of the challenges that the team that is leading a major change effort faces is the disconnection that often occurs between it and the rest of the organization. The leadership team needs to be visioning several changes ahead so it often gets frustrated that the organization has not kept pace. They often fail to understand that they have had more time to prepare for the change, because they have been planning it and feel more control and ownership of it. They often see resistance in the organization as a sign of noncommitment rather than as a predictable stage on the path to commitment.

In the following section, we will see how a hospital provided support and resources to help its staff move through denial and resistance after some very consequential changes.[4]

TRANSFORMING A HOSPITAL: FROM CRISIS TO CULTURE CHANGE

Seton Medical Center, near San Francisco, faced a scenario familiar to many hospitals. Top management had to face up to a major crisis. A new administration had been appointed to carry out deep and painful cost cutting and a reduction in employees, along with some strategic and management shifts. The new direction, a renewed commitment to excellence, was clear, but the pain of this, the first major change in years, made it difficult to get employees on board for the second phase. In the process of making the changes, the administration felt as if it were encountering a stone wall in the form of employee and supervisor miscomprehension, resistance, or inability to make the necessary changes. The change effort threatened to dissolve into an adversarial standoff, with bitterness from the top toward the other employees, while they felt confused, resentful, and betrayed by the administration. The change effort faltered because the executives' strategy of implementation was faulty or nonexistent. The well-intentioned and desperately needed changes were stalled.

Stalemates such as this are the reality today in many companies. Top management struggles to find new directions amid the shifting seas of change and has difficulty making the changes "take" in the culture of the organization. Employees neither understand nor trust the nature or direction of change. How can partnership and a shared sense of commitment be established?

Seton's was a story of reframing the organization in order to move a new vision from the top into the "bloodstream" of the whole hospital. It began with a crisis and new management team, and evolved into a total redefinition of many activities in the hospital. The key to its success was that top management worked to bring the whole hospital into the changes. This process added time, energy, and resources, but the payoffs were solid and tangible.

The overall guiding philosophy for carrying out the changes at Seton was empowerment, which CEO Anna Mullins defines as "everyone being willing to take risks, be decisive, and feel they are involved in and part of what's happening." For health care professionals, Mullins says, "This means challenging some old ways of doing things, developing partnerships among physicians, among staff, and with the community, and between all these constituencies working together."

The ultimate goal was to get everybody on board and working as teams to make the hospital successful in today's environment, where resources are squeezed and pressures are growing. The challenge was to transmit the excitement, commitment, willingness to experiment, and openness to change from the top level down through the whole hospital. As the staff took hold of the vision, it became more clearly defined and developed in the process. The third year in a long-term redesign effort represented the turning point. Further success could only arise from the staff discovering new ways to add value to their work while continuing to cut costs. For the staff to feel ownership of the future, they had to take initiative to create change in each unit. The process of renewing the hospital could not be limited to the few people at the top. Everyone had to be involved so that new initiatives could come from anyone.

Stage I: The Campaign for Mission and Margin

Change at Seton proceeded through several stages in the first two years. Mullins called the first stage the "Campaign of Mission and Margin," because without a margin there could be no mission. Like many nonprofit community hospitals, Seton had been in financial crisis. When Mullins had come to the hospital as CEO in June, 1989, she inherited a desperate situation: a deep deficit and a hospital whose future was in doubt. It was a time to make hard choices to keep the hospital afloat. Mullins acted decisively to stem the hemorrhage, cutting costs and staff, reducing the number of top managers, flattening the hierarchy, bringing in a new leadership team. The new team was clear about what needed to be done and how they wanted to do it. But the rest of the organization was not. The employees in many cases hadn't been made aware of the financial data or the problems. Many employees didn't even know some of the new administrators. There was a lot of distrust, some of it a result of the previous administration's behavior. The changes were communicated to the staff in monthly Town Hall-like meetings, open forums that any staff member could attend to question Mullins and other administrators. These were difficult but necessary meetings.

At the end of the year the hospital was leaner. The top management level had been pared from twenty people to four, all new. The people who were left were in shock, scared, and wondering what would happen next. But there was also relief that someone had stepped in, made hard decisions, and kept the hospital open. By the end of the second year, the hospital was breaking even.

The new management team had quickly found that if there was to be real change in the hospital, the entire organization would have to operate differently. The process of discovery and learning experienced by the top management team had to be carried to every level of the organization. The top team formulated a general strategy, an overall outline and vision of the future, but it was up to each work team to define what this vision meant in their own working relationships.

During a series of retreats, the top management analyzed themselves on three levels:

1.   The **individual** level: They discussed their individual attitudes toward health and hospitals and their professional skills.

2.   The **team** level: They looked at their working relationships and behavior as a team.

3.   The **organizational** level: They reviewed the structures, policies, incentives, norms, and values that made up the hospital's culture.

The top team realized that change had to occur at all of these levels. Yet many change efforts operate at only one level. For example, even if they offered training in individual skills, the people might then go back to teams where supervisors operated by the old norms. Or if they rebuilt teams, they might never teach people the new skills and mindsets necessary to see the environment through the lens of empowerment. Or if they modified both team relationships and individual mindsets, the compensation system, or the promotion process, might still reflect opposite values. Yet if the change was not congruent at all levels, change would be stalled or limited. Thus they faced the dilemma of moving the change process through the entire organization.

The major difficulty in implementing change in an organization is getting all the employees committed to the shift. This means not just a shift in behavior but, in the case of implementing a service quality program and changes in the structure and organization of individual medical services, a paradigm shift in the way everyone works together. After drastic downsizing, as at Seton, employees are often afraid, confused, and angry. Too often, their gradual withdrawal becomes the expected behavior, leading to a decline in service quality and inability to implement change.

Part of the difficulty in creating new behavior among health professionals comes from traditional role definitions and expectations. Professional behavior and the ways of working in the hospital are highly ritualized. People feel that their procedures and staffing patterns are synonymous with quality patient care, so attempts to change them may be perceived as attempts to tamper with patient care to satisfy financial demands. In addition, the traditional ways are so familiar and ingrained that staff find it nearly impossible to imagine that the goals of the service could be achieved in a different way. Further, staff feel that doing things the "proper" way protects them against mistakes and liability claims, and they fear the responsibility inherent in innovation and experimentation.

Often the people who find it most difficult to change are the first-line supervisors, the nursing heads and department chiefs, who have been very successful with the old methods. An injunction to change from management will encounter resistance for some very real reasons, which must be addressed in the implementation strategy. The traditional roles were designed for an environment where there was little change, and people did what their functions prescribed, more focused on technical requirements than on service needs. But now the hospital needed employees who could be proactive in meeting patient needs and in solving problems.

This is where many organizational change efforts end, but at Seton it was only the beginning. Mullins recognized that the whole institution had been traumatized and needed a period of healing and reconciliation. Successful healing had to take place before innovation and new direction could begin. This is the stage of emotional transition that many organizations forget.

Stage II: Healing and Renewal

The second stage of the change process was aimed at restoring healing properties to the organization and building partnership. The phase began with a two-day retreat for the management team, where it was to create a vision of the next steps and renew its commitment to moving ahead. The format of the retreat included exploration of the phases of transition, changes in the health care environment around them, the key skills for individual performance during change, and how to lead change in the organization. To bring such understanding and the appropriate skills to the managers, a one-day managing change seminar was offered to all managers.

Many organizations tend to move directly from drastic organizational change in structure to training and management-development efforts and the implementation of specific innovations (such as team building, effective meetings training, conflict management). In working with mergers, reorganizations, and culture shifts in many industries, we find that leaving out the healing process results in excessive resistance and damage to the "human capital" of the organization. It has been our experience that to implement successfully large-scale change, the emotional process must be managed.

The managing change seminar was then offered to a cross section of employees at all levels of the organization. This process sowed the seeds of a dialogue about the new directions, and of individuals' feelings, perceptions, misperceptions, and ideas. One member of the management team attended each session. They became forums where staff could see that change was possible, that management was serious about change, and that all could be part of it. Many employees let go of their negativity. The key activities of the seminar were as follows:

Understanding the Changing Health Care Environment. The participants looked at recent changes in technology, patient expectations, reimbursement, competition, new services, and society and how they affected Seton. This was done not by lecture or presentation. The participants divided into groups to look at each area and generated lists of their own experiences. Each group then shared their findings, and a large map of key changes affecting Seton was generated by the whole group. The exercise gave some perspective on why the cuts had to be so sudden and drastic. People who believed that change would end soon, saw that changing would continue, but the map helped them see the direction in which it would go.

Seeking New Possibilities. In analyzing the nature of organizational change, the participants began to understand not only why things at Seton were changing but also what opportunities were expected in the future. In each group, the discussion was animated and excited as people began to look forward to new possibilities.

The Difficulty of Change. In this section, people looked at how they, and their teams, were experiencing the four response phases. They talked about letting go of the old ways, and about how difficult some staff members were finding it. They expressed fear, anger, confusion, and even bitterness as they talked of all the reasons for their resistance.

Talking with Executive Team Members. A representative of the executive team talked about the vision of Seton for the future and answered all questions. Misperceptions were cleared and people had a chance to air their frustration and confusion. People saw that the administrators were willing to listen. There was also some feedback about problems with supervisors or teams in the implementation of change; misunderstandings about the changes, feelings of unfairness, and concerns about low staffing. Each group gave feedback that was collected to go to the administration.

Experiencing Personal Empowerment During Change. This part of the seminar offered a chance to practice the key self-management skills for empowering oneself through change. The participants practiced in small groups. Each person looked at his or her own reaction to change and how to create a vision of the future, develop a positive attitude about the future, develop a clear focus and priorities, and raise difficult issues with others. They discovered that everyone had similar difficulties with change and saw how they could be more effective. Each person ended up with an action plan for managing change.

Creating a Vision for the Future of Seton. Small groups worked together to generate an image of the best possible future for Seton. Each group defined the key elements of their vision and came up with a chart of all the key elements. Everyone had a chance to say how they wanted a hospital to be. They produced very moving portraits, because instead of feeling like victims, they began to see that they could help shape the future. This exercise was especially powerful and significant.

The result of the seminars was that staff began to see that despite the difficulty of the change, there were positive possibilities for the future. People realized that every staff person could be a change leader and many positive suggestions were offered.

Stage III: From Survival to "Thrival"

The next phase was to move the behaviors of change into every process and relationship at Seton. Through the mobilization of team involvement in the redesign process, the practices of the organization became more focused on patient satisfaction. This is the core element in the process of teaching an organization to think and act differently. The design team shepherds the process of identifying projects related to key customer service or business issues, championing a team leader, and mobilizing the resources and support to make it happen.

If this were the end of the process, there would be a risk of the staff retreating into cynicism, feeling that the interventions were just a token gesture to get people to feel better, rather than a signal that more communication and collaboration would continue into the future. The goal of the third phase of change—which is still going on at the hospital—is to build collaboration into every corner. The vision has been labeled the "value-driven quality initiative," meaning that every new project will seek to increase the value of hospital services by adding quality, service, and caring to activities. By creating ad hoc groups and task forces, people from several different groups and levels work together on solving problems. The implementation team and the guidance team focus the work of many smaller teams. They identify promising projects and generate groups to develop and implement them.

The goals of this phase are the following:

1.   Build shared equity in the organization so that every staff member feels some responsibility toward improving Seton.

2.   Challenge the traditional structures, ideas, and relationships at the hospital.

3.   Develop and implement innovative solutions to recurring problems.

The implementation team has also designed a follow-up workshop that will teach the key skills that they have identified as most important for the staff to learn. These skills are conducting effective meetings, problem solving and conflict resolution, and brainstorming. Aping the medical terminology, these skills have been called "cultural dilators" because they help open up and expand the hospital culture. The goal is for every staff member to learn these three skills. Then they can be applied at all team meetings and in working relationships and will become part of the new values and structure of the hospital.

Seton seems to have built a solid foundation on which to create a new kind of hospital for the future, although it is too soon to evaluate fully the success of the reorganization. Success will not consist of one or two highly visible changes, but rather a culture of empowerment and commitment where every unit and every person explores new ways to become more effective. The lessons of this initiative are that the process of cultural change is much more complex than most leaders would like to believe. The process takes time and each change has to filter down to every level. Care in navigating the shock of initial change can pave the way for commitment to the subsequent, more far-reaching changes to come.

By looking at the extent of Seton's program, and the time and resources it demands, it can be seen how challenging it is to help a whole organization move through the change curve. A change leader needs to be aware of the emotional dynamics of change and utilize the skills of listening, offering information, and allowing people to participate in the plans for the change if everyone is to navigate the transition.

In the next chapter we look at how to build empowering relationships, by exploring ways to shift from work relationships based on authority and position to relationships based on collaboration and partnership.

Part Three

BUILDING COMMITMENT TOGETHER

8
Be a Partner: Fostering Collaboration, Mutuality, and Respect

Never doubt that a small group of thoughtful, committed citizens can change the world; indeed, it's the only thing that ever does.

—Margaret Mead

Anthropologist Riane Eisler[1] writes about two types of societies: the dominator society, in which relationships are based on control and fear, and the partnership society, in which relationships are based on mutual respect and self-expression. Her thesis is that the second model (which has, until recently, been somewhat ignored) is more appropriate for our current societal dilemmas. We need to learn more about this second model for our personal, work, and community relationships.

Indeed, the workplace is shifting from one that supported relationships based on obedience and domination to one in which relationships are based on cooperation, mutual respect, and shared responsibility. The new empowered workplace, and the new organizational paradigm, seems to be rediscovering the benefits of the partnership society. This represents a vast transformation in the nature of organizations. New bonds between people break down the organizational hierarchy, build bridges between groups working on key problems, and open up boundaries to customers, other companies, and the community. These changes are particularly practical because the challenges that we face in the workplace today cross traditional boundaries.

In the relationships of the new workplace, people recognize mutual interests and possibilities and share a stake in a vision or goal, while maintaining their personal interests and identities. Seen in this way, a partnership is an empowered relationship: Each partner empowers the other, visions are joined, and individual goals merge into shared, group goals. We are seeing that competitiveness and success in today's turbulent environment demand a full and willing partnership among all citizens of the organization. Slowly, but with impressive results, people in one group start their planning and visioning by talking to people in other groups. Walls break down and people feel free to talk to each other. The flow of information and of work tasks shifts up and down and in every direction across the organization. It gets much more complicated, but it also has the possibility of finding exciting new ways to achieve results. Partnership opens up the concept of the team, the open system, where members link with nearby groups and share goals and tasks.

Workplaces today are networks of collaborative relationships. People are important according to how they contribute to others, not in their inherent power. Such is the relationship-focused partnership.

Positive recognition is one of the activities that builds partnership. Each time one person notices and comments on the positive things another person does, an invisible web is drawn between the two and a channel opens up. When we are recognized or complimented, our self-esteem rises, we feel good about ourselves and the person who gave the compliment—and we want to do more. Recognition is one of the most powerful tools for sustaining commitment to the new workplace yet it is all too rare in organizations.

A study of the effect of recognition in the workplace yielded some astounding results.[2] Employees who are recognized, whose contribution is personally affirmed, are twice as likely to have the following attributes:

- Feel satisfied with the company
- Look forward to their work
- Feel that their supervisor inspires their performance
- Feel that their supervisor requires quality work
- Feel that their supervisor encourages improvement
- Feel that departments cooperate

Having a collaborative or partnership relationship with one's company, or within one's work group, gives a new sense of security that is different from that of the dependent child who is being taken care of. The new sense of security comes when people who are honest, fair, and candid make a commitment to do their best for each other. There is also lowered anxiety and greater trust, enabling all parties to focus on performance rather than watchfulness.

This is a positive and welcome change from the feelings of competitiveness or distrust that limit the traditional workplace when it is under pressure. In this chapter, we explore the shift from dominator to partnership relationships, which is one of the roots of change in the workplace as it moves toward the future.

PARTNERSHIP AS THE MODEL FOR BUSINESS

Successful businesses have been built on a foundation of partnerships: with suppliers, with allies, with customers. To speed up product development, every company is finding strategic partners with whom they can share new ideas, risks, and financing. Finding the right partners to develop and exploit a new technology is the key to success. New companies see that they do not need to manufacture, market, and sell their products all by themselves; some of the largest companies seek partners to help in marketing and sales, and they outsource their manufacturing and have a network of suppliers. These collaborations are increasingly close as the large customer needs to work with suppliers on quality, inventory control, and new-parts needs. Companies have found that developing a long-term partnership with a supplier, rather than bidding out every job competitively, enables the supplier to learn their needs and respond to them. Motorola, for example, shares its quality technology with its suppliers so that they can develop products at the speed and to the quality standards it needs. It also makes long-term commitments to its suppliers. These relationships are based on trust, fairness, and reciprocity. When problems come up, Motorola and its suppliers solve them together.

A similar partnership has grown up between employees and customers. Stores such as Nordstrom, Home Depot, and Wal-Mart focus on helping the customer. The employees respond to customer problems in every encounter and feel free enough of red tape to do what is needed, with prudence and responsibility. Nordstrom, for example, points out that even if it has made a mistake, it has a second chance to retain a customer. By responding helpfully, offering instant refunds with no time limit, fixing damaged goods, and going beyond the call of duty (for example, personally delivering the right package after the company has made a mistake), it can demonstrate its commitment to the customer. Each of these companies has found that helpful, informed salespeople, and systems designed for the customer's, not the staff's, convenience are keys to their success.

Providing value to the customer involves creating a relationship where one can understand and respond to the customer's needs. Even selling, which traditionally was a game of controlling the customer, is now shifting to a collaboration where the salesperson provides a "solution" to a customer need rather than pushing goods. Often the sale comes from showing the customer how to make use of the product or by coming up with a response to an external challenge experienced by the customer.

In the new workplace one reaches out rather than in. Instead of focusing on pleasing one's boss, one now focuses on the outside world. The individual, the group, and the team are each part of an open system. Moving to partnership thus involves a shift in perception, in focus of attention. Partnerships place us in a chain of service relationships. Work is not seen in terms of tasks done by individuals, but in terms of relationships where services are exchanged and concerns are addressed. Service implies mutuality. The concern is with understanding the customers, whether they are internal customers (people in other parts of the company) or external customers.

Looking Outward: Moving Toward Cooperation

British economist Tom Lloyd proposes a detailed theory of why companies need to, and will, evolve in the direction of altruism, cooperation, and taking responsibility for the long-term consequences of their behavior.[3] In studying hostile and cooperative mergers, Lloyd found that companies that practiced cooperative mergers far outperformed those that conducted hostile ones. Then he categorized British companies as "nice" or "nasty," depending on whether they had engaged in any hostile takeovers. The fifty-seven "nice" companies outperformed the thirty-four "nasty" ones by 86 percent, according to a variety of measures of financial success. Lloyd concludes that cooperation is the strongest corporate strategy for the organization. Cooperation between employees and management, with shareholders, and in the marketplace is also important. He reports on other studies that indicate similar financial advantages for socially responsible companies. One study reports that between 1974 and 1980 the "nice" firms grew faster (14 percent compared with 9 percent), were more profitable (7 percent compared with 5 percent margins), and received a higher return on equity (15 percent compared with 10 percent) than those that he categorized as "nasty."

When two groups that have lived separately from each other—or were even antagonists or competitors—begin to learn about each other, they shift into a partnership-style interaction. The two groups or individuals may be geographically close in an organization, but light-years away in terms of understanding each other's work. For example, the sales and installation teams in a branch office of AT&T each felt the other made its life hard: The salespeople would promise anything for a sale, and the installation people took their time getting equipment installed. The solution involved having the two groups move their offices together, and spend some time seeing how the other team worked. There was some cross-training. The upshot was that the two groups merged, and salespeople began to learn to do rudimentary installation while installers took on some sales functions and even began to look for opportunities for more work. As partners, they were far more efficient than as disconnected units.

In some ways, partnership is a recognition of the new reality that actually exists within and between organizations. Partnerships are becoming the essence of relationships between company and customer, between supplier and customer, between work teams, and between company and employee. We see customers and suppliers being invited to company meetings to share their perspectives and help design a response. The closed pyramid organization has begun to open.

But what if this is not the case in your company? Partnership need not be initiated as company policy or by top management in order for an individual to begin.[4] One person can begin to treat other people as partners rather than as bosses or subordinates. In fact, one may need to do this to get one's job done or to feel empowered in his or her work. For example, on his own initiative, Daniel Pagano, as the chief archaeologist for the city of New York, convened a conference of the people who made up what he defined as the "archaeological community" of New York.[5] He invited people from different interest groups together for a gathering and to form various task forces to explore the future of historic sites in the city. This was an opening up of the boundaries of his agency, which had traditionally done its work alone with a somewhat beleaguered attitude. Consensus was now created among many people about values, priorities, and a future vision to balance preservation with development.

Just like this archaeological community, the activities of many organizations involve not just their own people, but active commitment from customers, suppliers, clients or end users, and all members of the communities that are affected by the work of the company. Sometimes, this involves a community effort.

Responsibility to the Community

The partnership workplace feels a special connection to the surrounding community. It sees itself as having a responsibility and seeks to work with various constituencies of the community. That is not to say that the community becomes a full decision maker but that it joins in partnership with the company, and its rights and needs are respected in company actions.

The company owes the community a debt that is hidden by the nature of most accounting systems. The value that the community gives the organization is not ordinarily returned to it nor understood for its true value. Many free or below-cost services and goods provided to the company have traditionally not been shown on the books. These include costs of community services and subsidized goods like energy, waste removal, environmental cleanup, and use of natural resources. Without calculating these as costs to the organization, many companies have been able to show tremendous profits.

Environmentalist Garret Hardin proposed what has been called the "tragedy of the commons" to describe the effect of the long-term neglect of these costs.[6] In this parable, every individual in a small village pursues self-interest by grazing as many sheep as possible on the common land. Over time, as more and more sheep graze the commons, the soil becomes exhausted and the grass does not replenish itself. Ultimately, everyone's livelihood suffers because the sheep all die. The parable suggests that pursuing personal self-interest alone can have disastrous long-term consequences if the public and community resources are not considered and if attention is not paid by everyone to their renewal. The new organization, faced with nonrenewable and finite resources, must begin to calculate these costs and see itself in partnership with the community, not isolated from it. The new organization must not neglect its responsibility in this area. As the interconnectedness between organization and community is recognized, corporate management must seek common ground with community citizenry.

Many empowerment mechanisms also contain models for organization/community partnership, shared visioning, mutual responsibility, and shared learning. For example, consider what happened when Oregon wanted to make major changes in its health care system. Everybody wanted change, but how could they get the population to agree to radical change? They had to deal with how much could be invested in high-cost technology and how much in community care. The administration wanted to resolve this issue and began a process of convening community forums. They took lists of medical procedures and asked a cross section of community members which ones they believed were most important in preserving everyone's health. The resulting list of the fifty health procedures that the community members chose form the guidelines for the community-endorsed health insurance coverage. For example, prenatal and infant preventive health measures are considered more important to the overall well-being of the community than some high-risk organ transplants for older citizens.

The process shifted the focus from technology to community needs for the long term. Also, by bringing the community into the discussion, there was a democratic involvement process that created commitment to the ultimate results and helped them be "sold" in the legislature. This is community democracy in action.

When an organization faces a dilemma, such as a crisis within the community or a need for new products or ideas, it might consult groups of its stakeholders, using focus groups and community forums much as the state of Oregon did, rather than hiring outside experts for advice. The resulting commitment to the ultimate decision, because people are partners in it, more than makes up for the drawbacks of their lack of expertise. Companies that have gone to their communities for help with issues such as plant closings have usually ended up with a more humane and effective decision than those who tried to hide such distasteful actions—and ended up fending off lawsuits, stress claims, and bad press.

PARTNERSHIP AS
EMPOWERED TEAMWORK

The traditional labor–management belief that the two are opponents, with each trying to get more from the other, has built companies where distrust and manipulation are so endemic that neither group believes in or cares about the needs of the other. Customers do not want to buy goods made by employees at war with the company, who just want to get paid for as little work as possible, who do not care about the quality of the goods. Now, such companies and employees are under threat of extinction by competition from companies who achieve the highest standards of quality, at lower costs, while maintaining more benefits for the reduced number of employees. As a result, partnership is growing in every relationship in the workplace. Indeed, the new labor–management contract is one of partners bent on improving the system, whether through employee participation programs or increased teamwork.

Employee Participation Programs

Unions and management are initiating many experiments in which employees help define how work is done. The scope of these efforts vary. Some address only solving problems in the work team, with very firm limits on involvement in broader issues. Other efforts have grown over time to deal with more complex issues. The evolution is from a program where employees are asked to participate or share in decision making to a process where every employee is involved in a form of representative democracy, a sort of shared governance between labor and management.[7]

In a decade-long study of employee participation at a plant owned by Xerox Corporation, it was determined that the first employee involvement groups focused on somewhat minor issues. As the groups showed that participation could work, they began to tackle tougher problems. A crisis came when the company wanted to outsource the manufacture of a particular part, thus eliminating many in-house jobs. When the plant workers and their representatives questioned the decision, they were allowed to bid on the manufacture of the parts. Their willingness and newly discovered ability to reduce costs and increase quality won them the contract. This test of the ability to be partners made the relationships between labor and management stronger and has moved the participation program toward shared governance.[8]

Participation agreements rest on a perception of fairness and reasonableness in the two parties to the agreement. People need to feel that they are getting all the information and that decisions not made jointly are at least made openly and fairly. The two parties can even agree to share the pain and difficult times. For example, at New United Motor Manufacturing Inc. (NUMMI), the auto plant that is a partnership between United Auto Workers, General Motors, and Toyota, an employee notes that it is okay for the company to cut back, as long as employees have all the information and know that it is being done fairly and as long as the pain is shared. During a recent economic slowdown, NUMMI invested in training rather than lay-offs. When sales bounced back, productivity and quality were even higher than before, a clear return on their investment in people.[9]

Evidence indicates that everyone—workers and management—feels much better and more productive in participative workplaces.[10] A recent study of forty-three companies with such programs found that participation has a measurable effect on productivity and never has a negative effect.[11] It found that shared commitment to a common goal was premised on a sense of fairness and mutual trust. The most effective workplaces had the following attributes:

- Profit or gain sharing
- Smaller pay and status differences than in traditional firms
- Long-term employment guarantees
- Just-cause dismissal policies

Partnership does not just develop when a company declares it. It needs to be premised on give and take and mutual benefits. Employees have to have clear avenues to influence the organization and the results of their input have to be clear. In return, employees have to learn to be effective participants. They need to learn new skills and practice them. They have to show the benefits to the organization of their increased involvement.

Team Partnerships: Dialogue, Equality, Shared Equity

A team is a group of people who share a common task. Everyone may have a different function in the creation of the shared outcome or everyone may do similar things. The traditional team was a collection of individuals doing individual tasks; they presumably meshed automatically into a whole. The supervisor or manager was responsible for the integration, the control and the setting of tasks, and the mediation of conflicts. The only person on the team who needed to be informed was the manager; this person told the team what to do and how to do it. But if the team's work is continually changing, the pressure on the manager increases enormously. The more the manager controls, the more the voices of the team members are silenced. In such circumstances, the team members are not seen to be capable of engaging issues on the same level the manager is.

Traditional teams were not designed for environments where change happens so fast that the team must continually redefine what it does. Contrast that with the high-performance team, where everyone has a distinct role and is connected by a common mission, vision, and values. These team members feel free to take action and are responsible to the rest of the group for their results. The team members share information freely, quickly, and spontaneously. They know each other well and enjoy achieving success together. Such teamwork is in keeping with the new values of workers who want work that is meaningful and engages all of their talents and who want to be involved in deciding how things are done. It is also in keeping with a workplace that has similar needs.

Partnership helps connect people to the broader task of the whole organization and helps overcome the burn out of high-stress work. We worked with a law firm where the young associates, working more than sixty hours a week, were voicing great dissatisfaction and quitting. Talking to the senior partners, we found that they had created a policy of case management where young associates worked for long periods on pieces of a case, knowing little about the overall purpose. After gathering suggestions from the associates on how to reengineer the work in a more satisfying way, we proposed setting up regular meetings of everyone working on a case to share information and review progress. The senior partners would help the team see how they connected to the larger project. The initial response from the law firm was, "Do you know how much that meeting would cost us in billable hours?" However, the firm eventually found that such meetings saved them more in terms of increased output and positive feelings than they lost in billing time.

This was but one step in encouraging teamwork; the greatest shift in the new team requires still more. Ideally, the team can become a group where members feel free to say what they have on their minds, without worrying that their input is not wanted. They will share what they know only if they feel that other people are also sharing. They will offer their skills only if they feel that their skills are valued. They will invest themselves in making the group successful only if they feel they will be equitably rewarded. This is partnership, where everyone helps in the steering process.

High-performance teams tend to have little or no hierarchy. Members talk to each other directly and know each other's jobs. A study of cockpit crews[12] found that while the trios flying a plane have very different roles and skills, when they really become competent, they move from being specialists to being generalists. As they gain experience, they learn the jobs of the others. During the flight, they continually give each other feedback. If the pilot makes an error, the navigator may question the action. Each member becomes better able to see the whole context, as well as his or her individual task. Studies of crew errors have found that they arise when dialogue breaks down, and when the crew reverts to a traditional hierarchy. Indeed, in tapes made prior to crashes, the mistakes were usually evident but the team members weren't listening to each other. Dialogue had broken down.

Bill Moyers has noted that a democratic society is one in

which people have the information and the appropriate means to talk together about issues.[13] They feel they don't have to say what the person in authority wants them to say but what they want to say. Yet their opinions are tempered because they have access to information upon which to reflect. In the dialogue process, democracy is applied to the workplace. The individual work teams, and cross-functional and ad hoc teams that crisscross the company, engage in discussion, debate, and policy making. Out of the dialogue comes vision, values, strategy, and practices. While this is not necessarily pure democracy—some people have more power, and everybody is not necessarily part of every decision—the fundamental realization of the dialogue process is that the most important questions a group faces must be discussed and decided upon by the members of that group in a relatively egalitarian context.

There are several basic elements of the dialogue process:

Truth: Information is available to all.
Trust: Every person's input is valued.
Care: People listen to each other, learn, recognize, and support each other.
Fairness: Equity and rewards are shared; the dialogue is two-sided.
Reflection: The group does not just take action but also asks basic questions to break old assumptions and continually improves in its work.

We set up a dialogue process in a team of a company that was trying to rebuild commitment from its employees after many rounds of talking about the difficulties and need for layoffs. We talked about the key qualities of a dialogue, focusing especially on the sense that it involves being open to yourself and to other people. We asked people to make sure that everyone had a chance to ask questions of each other rather than assume they knew what the other meant. The group was very surprised by what happened. The quality of the group discussion was like nothing they had ever experienced. They felt a sense of ease and of caring, and they were able to explore the issue deeply and creatively. Previously, they had avoided the issue because of the painful and often angry feelings that some team members had. Now they found that feelings softened as they tried to discover the best way to respond to the company's difficult situation. They were able to utilize the principles learned in this dialogue in some of their other team work as well.

Facilitating the Team

Creating partnership makes special demands on the manager or team leader. Traditionally the role of the team leader has been one of deciding what to do and how to do it. In a partnership environment the role of the leader is to create a climate where the team discovers what to do or where individuals are free to take action.

One manager of a new product design group took it upon herself to initiate a team method of invention. She did not ask her own manager for permission to do this, she just did it. She got all the people on her team together to work on new product features. She included the younger interns and engineers, seeing this as one way to value their experience and help them learn. The new teams began to operate through dialogue and free exchange. Young people were close to their customers and needed to build confidence in their own opinions, rather than defer to the more experienced members of the team. Instead of bringing ideas to the manager alone, everyone thrashed out ideas and worked out decisions about products. By the end of the round of gatherings, consisting of twenty to thirty people, instead of feeling they were competing to get their ideas included, everyone felt a shared ownership of the whole outcome.

The key to shifting from traditional teamwork to partnership rests in a new form of leadership, as this manager demonstrated. The leader, following the principles of change we outlined previously, exercises power not by making the decisions but by setting the context in which the team can dialogue and move into an open, nonhierarchical exchange. Any person can initiate the new context by suggesting that the team change its style of working. This represents a second-order, transformational change.

After the many years that pyramid organizations have been dominant, people are conditioned to expect a leader to set direction and take control. But as organizations increasingly form ad hoc teams that cross functions, it becomes harder to know where to look for direction. Every team needs a person to facilitate it. The facilitator helps keep the team on track and watches its progress to make sure that it is doing what it wants to. A facilitator can be any member of a team who has the skills to do it, an outside person brought in to perform that function, or the formal leader. (It is important to note, however, that the formal leader can be an effective facilitator only if he or she understands the difference between traditional leadership and facilitation, and makes it clear to the team what role he or she is taking.) The facilitator can use process tools to create a climate of dialogue and an environment where the team operates without a formal leader.[14]

Using Process Tools

One function of a facilitator is to help the team understand clearly its purpose. Many people wander into meetings with no clear understanding of whether they are advising, gathering information, or making decisions. One technique is to place a purpose statement on the wall so that people can focus on it while they deliberate.

The facilitator tries to create a climate where everyone can participate, where the group remains open to options rather than forces people into premature or incomplete decisions. The facilitator looks for ways to help the team do its work. Sometimes the work is to help the group surface the information that individual members have inside them, or to help everyone try out new ideas. This is brainstorming. Team members are helped to tune into their inner ideas and share the information they have. At other times, the facilitator focuses on organization, on moving toward a decision, or on planning a process.

The team needs help simultaneously to see where it has

been, where it is, and where it is going. One of the most important technological breakthroughs for helping a team to move
into partnership is the development of graphic methods of recording to help a team remember what it has said and focus,
design, and move toward decisions.[15] When surfacing ideas or
gathering data it is very helpful to keep lists of information as
ideas emerge. Recording ideas on a flip chart, keeping a list of
decisions made, and, especially, creating graphic charts of organizational processes or visions helps keep the ideas before everyone
as they work. When the history is visually in front of the group it
helps the group keep what it has done in mind.

Once a team member records the group's process on paper
and tacks it on the walls, a group begins to create an ongoing
record of its process. The use of recording technology is one way
to shift the group's mindset toward process. People can build on
ideas as they move toward a decision. Putting notes up on the
wall rather than on individual notepads ensures that everyone
has the same record. It also keeps the focus outward. New software technologies allow this to be done on a projected computer
screen and even allow every team member to write on the screen.
At the end of the meeting, everybody can get a printout,
instantly.

Although there are many psychological shifts that people
have to make to move from a dominator to a partnership teamwork style, the use of facilitation and process tools can help people make them more easily. These tools change the environment
where the team works, and the new environment then guides
behavior. Environmental change is sometimes the gentlest way
to transform the work of a group. The new manager—the change
leader—can draw upon the skills of facilitation and the technology of process tools in order to help the team members become
partners.

THE MANAGER AS A PARTNER

New partnership relations mean letting go of traditional forms of
control and embracing an uncertain outcome, both of which are

hard for the traditional manager. In fact, many organizational transformations get stuck when they do not have an effective process to move the first- and second-line managers from control to partnership.

Managerial control is often the last vestige of the dominator style in an organization. Managers feel (often rightly) that if they let go of control there will be nothing left of their role and they will be expendable. Indeed, the ranks of middle management are thinning everywhere. But managers need to realize that they are expendable whether they change or not. More than any other members of the pyramid organization, they need to learn to work in a new way.

Managers have been greatly rewarded for what they do and their fear of the future is well-grounded. Their entire identity has been based on the outcome of managing others, and they have no sense of the role of self-management or personal empowerment in their work. What are the benefits of letting go of control? If managers give away control over who to hire, standards and schedules, performance, evaluating, and deciding how work is to be done, what will they do? How can they let go if they are still held accountable for their team's results but are not sure that their team will come through? Or what if the members of the team come through on their own and show the managers up? These feel like good reasons for managers to resist. They cannot change until they have learned a new role and begin to feel comfortable with it.

Collaboration: The New Managerial Role

The new managerial role is somewhat analogous to that of the coach: responsible for the team's results but able to let go after helping the team members learn what to do. As managers give up and let go of their old tasks and activities, they will have to take on some very new kinds of coordinating and teaching activities. In Chapter Three we described some of the new leadership functions of the person who becomes a change leader. These are all available to the new manager. More specifically, the manager can adapt a new role by shifting from control to partnership, from directing to facilitating, and adopting some of the following skills:

- They can teach. They can help scared, confused, and un-skilled employees face the challenge of the evolving organization. They can help them "get out of the river" in a different place, by learning new attitudes, skills, and responses. They can help their people learn the new skills of empowerment.

- They can learn to feel a new type of power. They can feel competency in themselves, with more options and greater flexi-bility. They can add to their own repertoire of skills by becoming generalists in team management and learning new relationship skills that are needed by the organization.

- They can become resource people. They can offer techni-cal skills not as outside experts but as partners, bringing their expertise while learning from the team members how to make their knowledge fit into the team's specific environment.

- They can offer their people maps. Maps help explain the complexity of change, and managers can help people navigate the four phases of response to change, from denial and resistance to exploration and commitment.

- They can rock the boat. Managers can become advocates for change in the organization, the change leaders.

- They can become vision keepers. They can help the group grow, developing its vision of the future. They can inspire the team in tough times.

- They can become facilitative, servant leaders. They can help teach skills for teams to evolve into the circle style of operation.

At a recent conference of safety managers, we heard the participants define their new role, which is evolving away from being safety experts. They note that work environments are now so complex and change so fast that they simply don't know what is safe. Only the people who work on the job know. The safety managers see themselves as moving from experts to consultants and collaborators who help the employees plan and work with teams as expert to expert. They need to learn how to become consultants, people who bring information and skills and advise and help the team do its work.

Learning the Partnership Style

How do managers learn their new role as partners if they have been rewarded for many years in a dominator environment? Many are having a great deal of difficulty learning the new ways, and many may not be able to learn. In a doctoral dissertation that looks at how controlling managers learn the new facilitator style, Al Pozos[16] cites several important factors:

- A crisis or event that disconfirms the traditional style or tells them it isn't working

- Willingness to consider letting go (as opposed to retreating or denying)

- Social support from peers, managers, friends and family

- Company support of learning, encouragement to make changes, and rewards for doing so. Only a minority of work settings can meet all of these conditions, making change rarer than we need it to be.

The managers learning new roles need not only to discover how they can be helpful to their team but also to be joined by the team members in acting differently. Since manager and team member roles are complementary, each one must change. The process is like learning a new dance step. Change programs that focus on one group—employees or managers—frequently get undone when the group that has been trained comes back to face the old behavior of the other group.

For example, in partnership with the United Auto Workers union, Ford undertook one of the most extensive and far-reaching worker participation programs in the eighties. Teams with control over decisions and work rules began to proliferate in plants. But success soon ran into confusion or resistance from managers, who felt their power eroding. Ford discovered that its employee involvement (EI) initiates had to be joined by managers' education in participative management (PM). Now, EI/PM is Ford's definition of organizational redesign.

Macy's recently began an experiment to get the store associates to become more empowered. The concern was that associates either wouldn't be responsible or wouldn't perform at the levels needed. So the concept of "license for success" was born. This is a shared agreement between associate and manager for each to change roles. The associates agree to take on new responsibilities and the managers agree to grant more authority in return. The mutual nature of the change is underscored. The stores using this model have higher ratings of customer satisfaction, and more important, higher sales per square foot, than do counterpart stores.

The change contract is in effect a bill of rights and responsibilities by managers and employee team members about change. Drafting one is an especially powerful and meaningful activity. The process of developing empowerment contracts between the manager and the team recognizes that each party has to make difficult changes in order to move toward a new style of work. The manager and the employee each need to give up or stop doing some things and begin to do others.

We go about creating these new contracts by having the manager and the rest of the team work separately. Both create their own lists of what they will give up or do and what they want from the other party in return. Then we compare the lists. To everyone's amazement, the two lists are usually very similar. When we compare the two, it is usually very easy for the two groups to develop a consensus set of changes for each to make.

As the contract process demonstrates, in order to change, people and groups need feedback about their effect on others. We have seen that the managers who got difficult feedback on behaviors that they were not aware of and who were able to listen to it, were the lucky ones who were progressed through an ultimately rewarding change process. New information, especially that you don't want to know or don't know you need to know, is essential to the process of learning new roles. Managers may, of course, ask for caring feedback from their team. It is also possible, if a little risky, for the team or one individual, to begin to ask the manager for new behavior. Feedback is not a special exchange that you need permission to engage in and that happens only once or twice a year. It is an ongoing part of doing business in the partnership model of work.

The manager needs to learn a new role and new skills to

lead a group. When the manager and the team members both begin to practice new behavior, then the team can become a partnership, even if the traditional structure of manager and employees remains in place.

PARTNERSHIPS TO GOVERN ORGANIZATIONS

In more and more companies and business units, the core entity in charge of the whole is not an individual but a team. The partnership organization has substituted a circle of leaders for individual authority. This is the essence of the shift from the pyramid to the circle, from the passive to the empowered workforce.

In the business world, large companies like General Electric, Banc One, and Royal Dutch Shell are run more by a management team than by individuals. In each of these giant companies, which have been successful in growing and managing change, the center of the organization is a form of council, where the heads of each business unit come together to make policy. The delicate balance is between individuals and the strategy and goals of the company.

At General Electric and Johnson & Johnson, each business unit can run itself as it wishes, but it must adhere to certain corporate values, financial targets, and policies. But they are all part of a team that meets regularly and shares not just financial information and success but also ideas and new opportunities. While both companies have strong CEOs, the locus of internal energy and the power and autonomy to take action rest with the units, not with the CEO. The organization chart is more like a confederation of states than a monarchy where individuals report to the chief. The center of gravity, the center of identity, and the locus of control of the new partnership organization shifts from the top to the council. The core is a process, not a person.

Banc One, which has grown into one of the largest regional bank systems, grew in the 1980s through acquisitions. Each acquired bank kept its autonomy but became part of the corporate council. The council has a center for sharing new ideas and opportunities, and solving problems. But the members are relatively free to decide to draw on a new idea or not.

The council model is carried out through the individual companies, duplicating the form of top management. Individual businesses and smaller units work in teams, rather than through single leaders. Council management diminishes "level consciousness," where employees automatically give power and authority to the highest person in a group, allowing teams to feel empowered. The new partnership organization does not lose the ability to take action, although some actions may take longer to focus or initiate. The scope of responsibility is drawn very precisely. Responsibility is not diffused, but held by everyone. In some councils, the individual members are responsible for taking action. Decisions must achieve consensus, not by everybody agreeing fully, but by everyone agreeing to try it and then assess the results. The old committee, where nobody took any responsibility, was a product of the pyramid organization; responsibility was lost on the way up to the authority figures.

Ben & Jerry's ice cream company has gained fame not just for its phenomenal growth in an industry dominated by giant food companies but also for its partnership-based management philosophy. When the company was going to build a new distribution center, rather than have it designed by outside experts management named a team of eight people, representing different levels and skills, to do the design.[17] "The passion you get by doing things in-house overcomes the expertise you can buy on the outside," company president Chuck Lacy said. The team was so successful that another team was named to design a new factory. The teams were amazingly quick in picking up the necessary expertise, and the new design represented the kind of balance of interests that the company most valued. After these successes, the company has named what it calls the "Big Nine" process teams to work on the key challenges facing the company. Each one is a team of employees that meets regularly, with implementation responsibility, to deal with issues such as new products, training, safety, customer feedback, and internal conflicts.

Such examples show how a whole team can act as a leader.

For people who have never experienced team-based leadership, it is hard to visualize such a process. They say, "How can you get anything done with nobody in charge?" But, in fact, everybody is in charge. As people learn to work in a council, the tendency for individuals to want to discuss every decision diminishes, as people delegate all but the most consequential areas to the individual who is responsible and most knowledgeable. The team members find they can informally approach the person with input or to talk about their ideas. As councils grow, the result is that individuals feel free to work, and the council acts as integrator and vision/planning forum.

Councils as Navigators to the Future

Country Cupboard, a small resort in central Pennsylvania consisting of a restaurant, a store, and an inn, has seen strong growth in earnings and profit in a difficult economy. It is owned and managed by founder Dan Baylor's son Gary and daughter Carole Hamm and their spouses. After managing the company as a team of four for a decade, they began to wonder about the future. Each one had other pursuits and interests, and they wondered how they could begin to move beyond the business.

The idea that emerged was to begin turning the management of the business over to the employees. Until that time, the company had been very paternalistic. Most decisions came from the owners, with very little information-sharing. The five department managers and staff saw work at Country Cupboard as a long-term commitment. The solution was to develop a leadership council, which would develop the skills needed to steer the company on its own.

At first, the council consisted of the five department heads, the Baylors, and the Hamms. But that was simply a continuation of the traditional pyramid and not really much of a change. How could they get a sense of partnership, shared ownership, and innovation throughout the company? The solution was to add an elected person from each group to the council. This was done with some trepidation by the owners, who were not sure what would happen and had never conceived of giving up that much control. But the elected members joined the council, and this led to every employee feeling more connection to the whole company. Each team had its representative, and because the jobs were rotated every year, anyone could look forward to future service on the council.

The council has grown as a steering unit. Information about the business that would not have been previously shared, including financial information, is given to the council. As a member of the kitchen staff observed, before the council, he would prepare the food but had very little idea of what happened afterwards. Now, with the council, information is shared. The council's first project was planning a new wing for the inn. Previously, Bob Hamm would have done this pretty much on his own. Now he became a teacher to some of the employees, who took over much of the planning, income projections, getting contractors, supervision of the work, and many of the decisions that had to be made.

Membership in the council and sharing information, authority, decision making, and control have triggered the desire to learn and grow among employees. With their new responsibilities and potential for leadership, several have begun taking courses in business, finance, and management on their own time. The desire to learn has come from the invitation into leadership. Employees have changed their relationship with the owners as well. Instead of looking to the Baylors and the Hamms for direction and coi.'rol, employees look to them as teachers and mentors as they have begun to teach what they know, with the goal of giving up leadership and control. Eventually, the Baylors and Hamms themselves will take turns being on the council, leaving only one representative of their group at a time.

At Country Cupboard, the council process does not end at the top. Minicouncils meet in each of the departments. What the council knows and decides is shared with each department council, and there is sometimes debate and problem-solving in the individual councils. From a traditional top down organization, during the course of a year a transformation was made to a team-based organization. Also, the income of Country Cupboard rose 30 percent in 1992 as it celebrated its twentieth anniversary.

The existence and effectiveness of the council has led to a transformational breakthrough in the partnership and empowerment level of the company. Country Cupboard has begun to evolve into a cluster organization.

Employee Ownership

The most consequential way for the company to become a partner with its employees is through employee stock ownership plans (ESOPs), which are becoming increasingly common. When Weirton Steel, a division of National Steel, faced a plant shutdown, an ESOP allowed its plant to remain open. Its new employee owners have brought it back to profitability and saved their jobs. But ESOPs are not primarily about rescuing companies that nobody wants. Recently, companies as large as Avis and United Airlines have been sold to ESOPs. Employee ownership allows companies to buy out older shareholders, who want to cash out their investments, and keeps a company from being acquired. The ESOP is different from a management buyout, where a few key managers raise money to buy the company; it keeps ownership with a majority of its employees, and it keeps the company in the community.

Two of the biggest problems for today's companies are raising funds and maintaining employee commitment. ESOPs, mandated by Congress in 1974 as an employee benefit, seem to deal with both. If a company's founder has no heir or wants to move on, the ESOP may be a solution. Similarly, if a company wants to reward and keep a large staff of employees who feel a special connection to the company, the ESOP may be a solution. While the ESOP has tax advantages for everyone involved, from the bank offering the loan to the buyers and sellers, what seems most exciting is how ESOPs have the potential to heal one of the most pressing organizational dilemmas of business today.

As companies get bought and sold, or are forced to produce short-term profits at the expense of long-term development, employees are caught in a squeeze. They feel the company has no loyalty to them, and respond by withdrawing energy and dedication to their work. The company suffers, and its value declines. When employees are partners in owning a company, their concerns align more closely with those of the company. Over time, an employee-owned company becomes more participative. The ESOP becomes one additional competitive edge for a company, leading to the kind of involvement, productivity and excellence that turned around Weirton Steel. It is a form of incentive compensation that helps a company motivate, maintain, and attract good people.

The concept of "ownership" is used frequently in discussions of empowerment. It is said that empowering employees gives them a greater feeling of ownership in the company. They feel ownership through their involvement and power over policies, working conditions, and corporate decisions. But sometimes it is hard to feel ownership if somebody else takes all the profits home. Even if they don't become full owners, employees can't feel full commitment to the goals of the company unless they share in the benefits financially. The ESOP, like other formalized forms of profit sharing, institutionalizes for the employees the key benefit of ownership—sharing in the profits.

To give a sense of the way that employee ownership affects commitment and empowerment in a company, here is a history of one of the oldest employee-owned companies in the country. The Bureau of National Affairs (BNA) publishes a series of financial and professional publications. Its employees are members of the Newspaper Guild, a union. In 1948, BNA became the first completely employee-owned organization in the United States.[18] Everyone in the company can buy stock. Eighty percent of its 1,700 employees own stock, and the stockholders elect the board. There are no special senior executive benefits or bonuses, and the CEO's salary is only ten times the lowest salary.

For more than twenty years, the company has been governed by a series of joint labor/management committees. While it has always had an informal and participative culture, the participation was not formalized, especially at the lower levels. Only recently has it pushed empowerment, so that control and participation is shared at all levels of the organization. The company has begun a series of shared governance initiatives. There has been a participatory process of strategic planning. After top management set goals and a vision at an off-site retreat, each unit and all employees have become involved, offering feedback on the plan and setting their own goals.

The publishing and data communication industry is developing fast, and BNA's technology is already outdated. The product audit committee is charged with looking at the future of all of BNA's products for the next decade or more. The group, composed of a cross section of employees, is the core of a reengineering process for the whole business. It must look at how its various work groups have become traditional, isolated product groups, determine how to integrate them, and begin to work across teams in information processes rather than in specific products. These changes will produce the greatest upheaval in the company's history. But because they are controlled and managed by the employees themselves, it is believed that the changes will be done fairly and effectively.

The BNA story illustrates the effect of ownership on employees. Ownership does not automatically build empowerment or commitment, but it can lead a company along a road that leads to a fully empowered workplace.

Partnerships for Corporate Transformation

The key to organizational transformation is the establishment of teams throughout the whole organization that work on partnership principles. In effect, these new teams become alternative structures, which Barry Stein and Rosabeth Kanter call a parallel organization.[19] A task force charged with authority to solve a problem and containing a cross-sectional, cross-level group of employees from throughout an organization is an example of such a group. Instead of doing away with the pyramid, the parallel team offers another pathway for information to flow, for people to work together, and for decisions to get made. If the parallel pathway is more effective and more satisfactory, then sooner or later it begins to become more important and more central in managing the company. As more and more of them form, they begin to minimize the negative effects of the pyramid structures. But they do this by showing results, and by growing, before the pyramid is dismantled.

One of the most powerful, complete, and revolutionary attempts to change a company from hierarchy to partnership has taken place within General Electric.[20] GE had done many things that began to shift from the pyramid to the circle. It had created small business units, made managers entrepreneurs, and designed a corporate executive council to communicate and make decisions across the vast company. But CEO Jack Welch grew increasingly concerned when people pointed out that managers were not "walking the talk," acting congruently with the organization's values. With a number of consultants he designed the process known as "workout." The purpose was to create a process that would redesign the relationships in the company from hierarchical to democratic. The workout is initiated when a work group or division faces a crisis or transition point.

At the workout session the group meets without its leader first and defines the issues and obstacles. Then the manager returns and holds a group dialogue, directly confronting the key issues. All the people involved in an issue are asked to attend, even if they come from other groups. What makes the workout session so powerful is that these are not advisory or information-sharing groups. The manager must make a decision on each issue right then and there, and justify it to the group. The process represents a drastic change in how the organization operates. Workouts have become a basic mechanism for unblocking issues and getting action. Although the confrontation may seem harsh, the reality is that it is refreshing. People feel more empowered and enabled than afraid of the process. With the workout session, the group is accountable for its results. The workout is an example of how a new system can be used to move the organization out of the pyramid, and create a new style in the company, just as the council, or the ESOP, can.

For another example of a team working to change a company from hierarchy to partnership, we look to Inland Steel. Here, individuals became empowered and then created a way to create change in the company. The Business Enterprise Trust, a foundation that honors acts of courage, integrity and social vision in business, gave one of its 1992 awards to Tyrone Banks, Vivian Cosey, Robert Hudson, Jr., and Scharlene Hurston of Inland Steel for working to make the company a place where minority employees could grow and develop their potential.[21] Their example represents how people with courage and persistence can create partnerships to change an organization. The four were concerned that Inland, although making some strides in hiring and promoting minorities, was not honoring its commitment to minorities, and that its white male managers did not seem to be aware of the problems. The four began to meet to discuss the issues. Although they all valued their jobs and their time at Inland, they also felt that something had to be done.

They chose a strategy of partnership to press their perspective, rather than confrontation. They selected a top manager they all respected, Steven Bowsher, and shared their concerns with him. At a dinner meeting, they pounded him with their feelings and concerns, leaving him, in his own words, thoroughly confused. He was not able to understand what they were talking about. Finally, without telling anyone, and on his own time and money, he attended a very powerful diversity workshop where the perspective of minorities working in companies was dramatized; and was profoundly affected. After that event, he was able to shift his perspective and meet with Banks, Cosey, Hudson, and Hurston not in a confrontational way, but with a shared concern for how Inland was using its talent and employees. They had moved into partnership. Bowsher realized that the issues of minority promotion and inclusion were not understood in his own team, and he recommended that they attend the same workshop. The workshop seemed to break through his team's comfort zone of not knowing how others were affected by the company, so that they were now aware enough to begin exploring how the company could use its minority talent more effectively. Many different actions (such as providing mentoring to minority team members, and being sensitive to how policies affected individuals) were taken to improve conditions, although an announcement of a new major corporate initiative was not made.

Bowsher had to approach the top managers of the company to get their support, and he made his case to them just as the four had to him. Thus, when Bowsher was sent to head a troubled division, he began by making respect for diversity one of his key strategic concerns. By building opportunities for growth and development for all employees, his division was able to engineer quickly a very strong turnaround.

This chapter has shown some of the ways that teams and organizations can move toward the partnership style of operation, which is one of the core elements of the empowered workplace. We have seen how managers need to change how they work, from doing things for their people to doing things with them. We have also examined some of the examples of partnership structures in organizations, including team leadership, employee ownership, and work systems. Partnership has a direct effect on commitment—people feel more committed to their partners than to someone who directs them. In the next chapter we look at another core aspect of the empowered workplace—the capacity for continual learning and growth.

9
Learn Together: Creating a Climate of Inquiry, Discovery, and Continual Improvement

Learning is the new form of labor. It's no longer a separate activity that occurs either before one enters the workplace or in remote classroom settings. . . . Learning is the heart of productive activity.

—Shoshana Zuboff

In order for people to grow and help the organization to evolve, they have to be good learners. The ability to learn continually means remaining open to experience, understanding instances when things do not work out as expected, spotting shifts in the environment, seeking new information, learning from customers and everyone else, challenging assumptions and beliefs, moving outside of the comfort zone, and tuning into inner creativity and wisdom in order to change behavior in response to external changes and to develop ever-greater capacity to achieve results. These are powerful and difficult skills to develop—for both individuals and organizations.

WHY ORGANIZATIONS HAVE TO LEARN TO LEARN

We think of learning as a people task, but the organization, and the work group, need to learn as well. Organizations cannot grow, change, or be renewed without learning. The ability to learn is as important to the future of organizations as personal learning is to individuals.

The following dilemma, experienced by one of our clients, could be that of any of a number of innovating corporations today. A visionary breakthrough in design led this company to the top of its industry, with an innovative product and execution of their strategy that made it world-renowned. For several years, it had unmatched growth and profitability. Then, over the course of three years, everything changed. First, the rate of growth slowed, as the company increased market penetration. Second, competitors paid the company the greatest compliment by copying its formula, and a slowdown resulted. The company faced two issues:

- How quickly would the company realize that this was not a cyclical downturn but a leveling-off of the growth curve?

- Would the visionary CEO and his associates be able to let go of some parts of their revolutionary ideas and come up with a major shift in design? At a time when the company was still successful, could it look into the future and learn to act in a new way?

These issues demanded individual and organizational learning, specifically, understanding the importance of new information quickly, letting go of old ways before a crisis hits, and creating new ways to work.

Learning is not about how many training dollars a company spends, nor how many classes employees attend. It is about the environment, the quality of the questioning, the work processes, the decision making, learning from mistakes, and incorporating what is learned into every employee's skills. The organization of the future needs to support learning throughout. The new organization will be based on learning rather than on protecting itself, maintaining a power base, or keeping things as they are.

The greatest obstacle to learning, both individual and organizational, is that it creates anxiety. Most people and organizations are like magnets, instantly pointing away from anxiety and distress. Yet learning comes from facing up to difficulties, and the unexpected, rather than denying them. As futurist Don Michael put it, learning is the ability to embrace error.[1] The learner is like a child who is so curious she comes too close to the edge of a precipice. The unpredicted and unexpected are, to the learner, a powerful source of new information. But to most people, the unexpected is something to avoid. Our client, for instance, was tempted to say that the slowdown was just the result of a temporary economic downturn, and thus not to question the current strategy. But learning organizations react more quickly and deeply to change, because they have mechanisms and individuals who are able to live with anxiety and face up to the unexpected.

Many of the dimensions of creating the new organization involve finding opportunities to learn. This chapter goes beyond individual learning to suggest how the organization can learn, and how you can help develop learning within your own work group or team and organization.

PERSONAL LEARNING WITHIN THE ORGANIZATION

Learning is a tool that enables us to master change and operate in an ambiguous and uncertain environment. The ability to learn increases personal control, satisfaction, and purpose. Learning is another framework for understanding the journey outside of the comfort zone and through the transition process, described in Chapter Seven.

As individuals, we learn by making ourselves aware of errors, new information, and challenges to our everyday world view. Learning requires listening to something that may challenge the status quo rather than ignoring it. The most powerful learning comes from other people and from events that come upon us. That is because some of what we know lies outside of our awareness.

Overcoming Blind Spots

The most important type of learning for both individuals and organizations lies in uncovering *blind spots*, areas where we think we know the score but really don't. Blind spots crop up all over— in the inability to see the downside of some of our most trusted associates, in the inability to see the difficulties emerging in our organizational strategy, or in the unwillingness to listen to someone outside of our inner circle or organization. Blind spots result when we stay within our comfort zone, denying that anything outside it exists, and are not open to learning. Very often our blind spots are absolutely obvious to those around us.

The dilemma of a blind spot is that unless a person is confronted with it, he or she may never learn it exists. Take, for instance, an encounter we observed between a supervisor and his director. The director told the supervisor that he was losing the trust of his subordinates; by micromanaging them, he left them feeling they could not act without his approval. The supervisor argued with this assessment, saying that his people didn't feel that way, that he was good at delegating and giving people lots of rope. Finally, we asked the supervisor, "If you are wrong, how would you know?" Indeed, how would he get information about distrust if the very issue was that his people did not feel comfortable telling him about his effect on them? He realized quickly that if he were losing their trust, he would probably never hear it unless he changed his behavior.

Learning about your blind spots can help you propel your company into a new direction of growth. One way to uncover blind spots is to foster an environment in which people can tell you everything, even things you may not want to hear.

Personal Learning and Feedback

In companies trying to institutionalize individual and organizational learning, feedback and performance appraisal systems are designed to allow every employee to say what they see. Performance is evaluated not just by the boss, but also by a selection of subordinates, peers, suppliers and customers, and co-workers from various projects. This feedback comes anonymously, at regular intervals. The intention is not to develop a continual state of anxiety about evaluation, but to create a climate where people continually learn how they are affecting others.

At first, everyone is uncomfortable with "360 degree" feedback, as it is called. But, as people become comfortable with regular information about how others see them they become more empowered, because they have access to information that they might normally avoid or deny. As one manager said, "Although it is painful to hear some of these things, in fact, most of what people hear is more positive than they expected, and they end their evaluations on a high note." Also, because a person can expect regular feedback, the likelihood of feeling frustrated, upset, or even angry because of repressed feelings is greatly diminished. In fact, working in such an open environment builds self-esteem and personal mastery.

Personal learning comes from respectful feedback. This consists of two crucial elements:

■ *Clear, direct, concrete information about specific incidents.* The information needs to be based on observable events and needs to be specific so that a person can understand what is upsetting others, what is the problem, and how things can be done differently. For example, a person is much more likely to learn when he or she is told something like "When you demand immediate results from everybody, I feel frustrated and even less motivated, and I avoid you instead of telling you the real problems I am facing," than he or she would from a blanket judgment such as, "You don't think about other people when you make demands."

■ *Demonstration that the person giving feedback values the person being reviewed and their relationship.* Unless the person providing the feedback is considered a partner, someone who wants the other to learn and grow, then the positive result of feedback will be somewhat undermined. That is why feedback needs to be offered in a constructive and positive framework.

People learn from disconfirmation of what they think they know and who they think they are. For managers who shifted from the controlling to the collaborative style, the initial step in learning was a significant disconfirmation in the form of feedback that they weren't doing as well as they thought or that they weren't as successful as they thought they should be.[2] That experience led the person to open up to learning new ways. Disconfirmation is only a first step in personal learning. Many people experience it and do not go on to learn because they remain stuck in denial. After disconfirmation, they need to make a personal commitment to learn new ways, and they need support of the new learning. They also need feedback when they really have become different.

Sometimes feedback involves teaching those we report to. For example, a new product manager met with his VP, who said he wanted the product in the traditional package on his desk immediately. The new product team had been working on other approaches to the issue and had several innovative ideas in the hopper but not yet fully developed. So the manager pushed them to get the traditional product solution ready at once. Upon reflection, he wondered if he should have asked the VP for a meeting during which he could have explained the options and asked for time for his group to finish work on their innovations, while still satisfying the needs of the VP and the customers. He realized that with this scenario, he might have taught the VP to go for an innovative solution, and avoided demoralizing his group.

Supporting Personal Learning

One way that a company can support individual learning as a corporate strategy is to value and support career development as a motivating factor in performance. If people know where they can aim within the organization and then set their learning plans in that direction, their motivation and ability in their work today will increase as well.

Several companies have begun to make career development their corporate policy. For example, a program at Tandem Computers was mandated by CEO Jim Treybig, who realized that the company was subject to a "brain drain," employees going to other high-tech companies. The career development discussion, which was part of a discussion held each year between every employee and his or her manager, was to set clear and specific goals about where people could go inside the organization and what they needed to do to achieve those goals. The company realized that unless people were able to learn continually, they would not give their best.

If, however, a company is not paying attention to one's personal development and learning, it is up to the person to do so. There are many ways that people can foster their own learning:

■ They can seek out people around them for open exchange about their jobs, and how their work connects. They can spend time finding out how other groups work, so that they can do their jobs more effectively. Companies have found that lending a person from one department to another department for a few weeks or months, or even for a two-day visit, can result in the learner having a broader sense of the meaning and context of his or her work.

■ They can visit other companies. People limit their learning when they stop looking outside themselves, at competitors, the marketplace, and other, even nonrelated companies. The "not invented here" (NIH) syndrome is a common defense against learning from others. A company may, for instance, believe that it is so special and unique that anything being done anywhere else is not state of the art. NIH keeps them from looking at what others are doing that could help them improve.

■ They can learn from their elders. Younger employees can attach themselves to older "mentors," who teach them and bring them along while they offer help in return. If one can receive internal mentoring by someone who is not one's supervisor, perhaps not even in the same work group or division, but who is a good teacher and an inspiration, one's commitment and learning will improve.

■ People can become mentors for others in the organization. Being a mentor is a learning experience because it requires reflecting on one's unconscious wisdom and putting into words how things are done in the organization. This can help people become more effective.

You can begin each of these activities yourself: seek new information across boundaries, visit other workplaces, find mentors, and connect to other learners. When you become a learner in this way, you increase your power and influence in the organization, by tapping into informal but readily available knowledge. Each of these forms of learning enables you to see the larger picture and gives you more possibilities for getting results and succeeding.

THE NATURE OF ORGANIZATIONAL LEARNING

A learning organization continually gets better and improves its basic processes. If learning is absent, a successful company can fall apart. Consider, for example, the toy company Worlds of Wonder. It developed two successful toy ideas—the talking doll Teddy Ruxpin and the game Laser Tag—yet two years later, it was bankrupt. It had not learned how to learn, to develop processes to continue to develop innovations within the highly competitive toy industry.

Organizational learning is not about "hiring geniuses and letting them loose," as one high-tech company defined its strategy. What is learned must be freely available to everyone, not hoarded by a few people at the top. Further, organizational learning gets translated into processes throughout the organization. Individual learning has to take quite a journey before it becomes organizational learning.

Organizational learning was less critical in other times. In a stable period, when the organization can control and predict its future accurately, there is little utility in learning. In the traditional organization, learning was only for the few people at the top. People in other levels needed to do, not to learn. In contrast, because organizations, teams, and individuals today are continually thrust into new and unexpected situations, facing futures that are more uncertain than predictable, the ability for everyone to learn becomes critical.

When the organization gets more complex, experts create systems for getting work done. When there is massive change, individuals need to be able to take independent action to do what is needed in their particular niches. But, as shown in Figure 9.1, when the work of the company is highly complex and there is continual change, there is a need for shared learning in order for a company to thrive.[3] Learning, adaptation, innovation, continual improvement are the pathways to success in such a complex environment.

Because an organization's core processes are made up of its solutions to past problems, in a changing environment its actions will always lag behind current demands. Therefore, the ability to spot errors, which are the early warnings of the need for change, and then adapt and respond, is what learning is all about.

From Individual Learning to Organizational Learning

What is the difference between individual and organizational learning? Many people in a company can learn from experience,

Figure 9.1.   Effective Organization Under
Different Environmental Conditions.

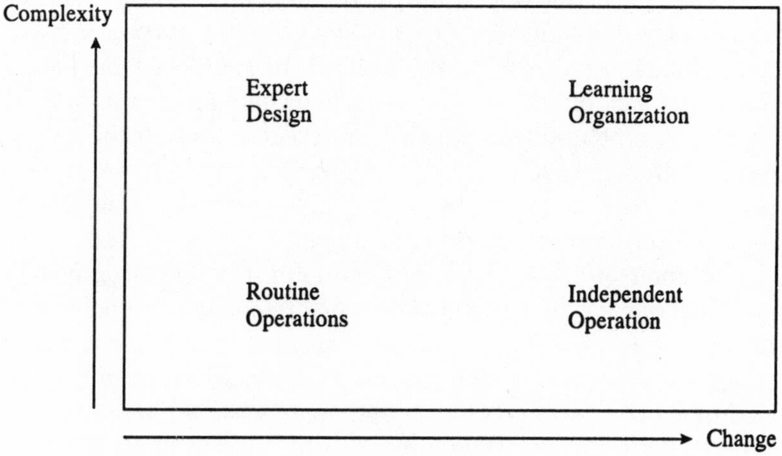

yet if they keep their learning to themselves or if they do not have mechanisms and processes where they can pass on what they know, there can be no organizational learning. Consider some of the following examples of individual learning:

- A wise and creative CEO has been responsible for the company's new product ideas, single-handedly.

- A crackerjack salesperson knows exactly how to customize the company's products to suit his customers.

- An employee has been with the company since it started and knows everything about how things get done and how the company has developed.

- An order-department clerk is the only person who knows how to prepare orders for a certain kind of company.

- The leader of the new product development team keeps the momentum going and morale high.

If these individuals leave the company, they take with them specialized knowledge. How can their learning become part of the company itself, so that it does not leave when they do? The company needs mechanisms to impart learning and wisdom from these stars to the rest of the company.

Often, when a person leaves, his or her learning is transferred to another individual. That is a very limited and precarious form of organizational learning. What if the knowledgeable person is out sick or traveling or more than one person needs to know? Learning results when a person teaches others. If the process of learning becomes part of the organization as a whole, and individual skills or capacities are available to many people, the organization can be said to have learned.

A more profound and important form of organizational learning concerns how well it is designed to change internally in response to external changes. Does it respond to changes, can it anticipate changes, is it one step ahead of the environment, including its competitors? Does it anticipate what will be needed by customers and the environment rather than wait to spot a trend that is under way and lose valuable time? And, can it do this only at the top, or in one part of the organization, or is this ability distributed throughout all levels, in all parts of the organization? Can a company *create* a trend by offering something valuable that consumers didn't even realize they needed? Do they have the capacity to keep all this up? The level of organizational learning depends on how well individual groups within the organization, and the whole culture, ask important questions, are open to new information, and explore and act in new ways. The highest form of organizational learning is the ability to keep on learning, innovating, and anticipating the future. We call this *learning how to learn*.

Transformational Learning

First- and second-order organizational learning reflect the ability to create first- and second-order changes, or incremental and transformational change, as we discussed them in Chapter Five. An example of first-order learning is transferring learning from one person to another. Second-order or generative learning transforms the system itself.

First-order learning is learning specific skills in response to one task. It allows people to get the product out, complete the task, or transfer a clearly defined skill. In contrast, second-order learning and change involves learning on an ongoing basis by creating structures and processes to repeat success and reach higher levels of performance. This transformational, or breakthrough, learning involves learning how to learn as a continual process.

Transformational organizational learning changes the capacity and nature of the system. The organization acts so that it can learn from its experience.

Learning may be the core competency of the high-performance, new paradigm organization. As CEO Ray Stata wrote, "I would argue that the rate at which individuals and organizations learn may become the only sustainable advantage, especially in knowledge-intensive industries."[4]

Learning from Others

One of the simplest and most common forms of organizational learning is for people on a team, or across several teams, to learn each others' jobs. For example, if every team member can do only one job, then the team cannot function if one person is absent. Or if people cannot move between teams and fill in for each other, the coverage of different tasks can be limited and downtime can result. Cross-training is the key to greater efficiency. Cross-training is potentially even more important than just having several people who can do two jobs. As people learn other jobs in other teams, they develop empathy and understanding of the perspective of that group. They can see the similarities between the two jobs and perhaps ways to streamline the two functions. Thus, in a group of service and salespeople, for example, the salesperson could remain with a customer to provide service and repair, and provide more continuous support to the customer. Everyone would be responsible for sales and service. Finally, cross-training becomes transformational when members of two groups are able to see beyond their individual teams to the big picture of how their work fits into the whole organization and even ways in which the whole company can become better.

We worked with the maintenance staff of a manufacturing company as they learned how to learn. Initially, the maintenance group was housed in a separate building, and they had thirteen different job descriptions. Each person was an expert on one type of equipment and did all the maintenance work on that machine. If a machine went down, nothing could happen until the appropriate person came and fixed it. Production workers knew nothing about maintenance and were not to touch a machine that was not working right. This was a very old-fashioned, costly, and ineffective way to organize work.

First-order learning required that the whole maintenance staff learn the skills to fix all types of machines. There was tremendous resistance to this. They had spent years learning how to be experts on one system; how could they possibly learn thirteen? But much to the workers' surprise, it took not years but months for each person to learn a second system. Then the learning curve took off exponentially: Within a few weeks each person learned a third machine and suddenly, it seemed, everybody knew them all. After the third round, the workers had begun to see patterns and understand the underlying principles of all the machines. All of them said that although at first they had thought the change was terrible and impossible (denial and resistance), after the learning began, the reinforcement of their success motivated them to continue; they were surprised and exhilarated by what they learned. The cost of maintenance went way down, and job satisfaction went way up! Learning had boosted the workers' commitment and their self-esteem. By the end of the process, when they had passed through exploration into commitment; they knew how to learn. This represented a second-order change but only for them as individuals. The organization had not yet reached that point.

After two years, a second innovation was proposed: Each maintenance person was to be assigned to a work team as a teacher and technical resource. Their jobs were no longer just to fix machines but to teach others how to do routine maintenance and more complex repairs. This would cut downtime because production workers could spot developing problems or even anticipate them. The people who had been technical experts found that their role was changing again. Now they were teachers. This was once again second-order learning, developing a new capacity within the organization. Machine downtime dropped rapidly as people made their own repairs; costs were cut and quality also improved.

The problem that might be anticipated is the following: After this task was completed, would jobs remain for the maintenance staff? Most of them were near retirement age and there was natural attrition. Some of the others became senior maintenance teachers, specializing in learning about and teaching new technology. And finally, some members of the group did find their areas obsolete, but the new teaching skills and the ability to learn about technical systems led them into new areas in the company. Several got into new product development and designing new technology, tasks that would have been unthinkable for them four years earlier, when they had been considered only skilled maintenance people.

This organizational learning had immediate effects on productivity, motivation, and the capacity of the organization to continue to improve. It is an example of how people can learn how to learn, after they resist initially, because of their fear of the future and doubts about their abilities. It is also a tale of how organizational learning allows technical and blue-collar employees to become generalists rather than experts in a narrow area.

A Shift of Perception

Organizational learning can be the result when the people involved in a conflict situation switch from blaming individuals to seeing the real problem that needs to be solved. In a classic example of such a shift in perception, when the Toledo public schools faced increasing performance demands, they saw the problem not as one of personnel but of organizational learning. In 1980, they began offering the twelve best teachers each year the opportunity to leave the classroom and to act as mentors to new teachers and to intervene with veterans who were having problems. Since its establishment, this program has been copied by many other communities. The school system had discovered that it had a resource in its veteran creative teachers and found ways to bring their wisdom through the system. Rather than blaming individuals, they solved problems. The teachers union president says that the program has gotten them away from damaging and pointless struggles about dismissing teachers to shared work to improve the system. The respect for people as teachers placed new value on learning and began questioning of the standard procedures. Teacher competence is no longer questioned by administrators, but 90 percent of the problems are now defined and solved by the teachers themselves. Teachers and administrators are partners, not opponents.[5]

In situation after situation, we have seen breakthrough change through system learning. In another example, Motorola has challenged the boundaries about the nature of learning. In designing an executive learning program for fast-track executives, the administration decided that the company would select a real business problem and ask the learning team to craft a solution and implement it. For the first two learning teams, they selected problems the solution of which would add great value to the company. The first was integrating the software for all of their important products, and the second was opening the new markets of Eastern Europe for their products. Each team could command resources and contract for skill-learning as they needed. By using real problems, the groups built a sense of teamwork that went beyond work team boundaries. They dealt with real problems by creating new networks and building learning in the organization as a whole.[6]

Such questions and resulting changes will lead to quantum leaps in the organization's effectiveness. But with breakthroughs come real difficulties. Although people may have a hunch that there is a better way, they can't prove it until they try it. This requires an investment in change without any evidence that it will be beneficial. Groups that operate through breakthrough or second-order learning have to be willing to invest in their hunches, if prudently. They also have to be willing to deal with the discomfort of the learning process. They should be aware that as they learn, they will find themselves going through cycle after cycle of the four phases of response to transition—denial, resistance, exploration, and commitment—as described in Chapter Seven.

PROCESSES FOR ORGANIZATIONAL LEARNING

Some of the key qualities of a group or organization that engages in continual learning are described below. We have already encountered many of them in the exploration of self-empowerment and individual learning. We include the descriptions here as a summary of the kind of action process a group should aim for in order to have true organizational learning.

Have a Systems Perspective.   People, groups, and the organization must move away from an individually focused cause-and-effect view of actions to look at the whole system and see what needs to be done for a desired result. This is a radical shift in thinking; perhaps the most difficult shift in the accomplishment of organizational learning.

The systems perspective is of the organization as a whole, operating in its environment.[7] Rather than seeing action as caused by individual intentions, the systems view looks first at the larger system as a whole and explores how the system is designed to produce a certain outcome. Then it looks at what must be changed to produce a different result. Looking at the larger picture is perhaps the most consequential shift of focus.

Offer a Free Flow of Information.   Information is immediately available, easily accessible, and relevant. For example, the new MIS-based PC networks make information that previously took months to develop and was then confined to the top level available to everyone. Information about policy decisions, new initiatives, and even what other parts of the company are doing is also shared. The greater the information flow, the more people can learn. Individuals decide what information to use and what to reject; the organization doesn't filter it for them.

Diffuse Intelligence.   The organization creates structures and processes that widely and quickly distribute intelligence throughout the organization. The glimmer of an idea in one person may give a boost to an intuition of someone else in a group far away, as long as their ideas can come together. Different kinds of structures are designed to bring learning from individuals to groups, from computer networks to learning councils.

Value All People as Learners.   Because great ideas and innovations can come from anyone in the organization, everyone in the organization is expected to be a learner. Everyone has to get information, be a part of activities, and have jobs structured so that everyone can learn and teach others.

Broaden Roles to Include Learning and Teaching. The change leader, who often was previously a traditional manager, now acts as a learner (empowering him- or herself) and a teacher (empowering others). This person's new role is not to get a task done directly but to create an environment where every person in a group can learn to get a job done. The role has broadened from doing a job to creating conditions for others to be able to get it done, to improving the ability of the system to do the job. It is especially important to challenge and educate the people above.

Undertake Process Learning. Work units and organizations continually explore work processes, hidden agendas, and the ways in which they are getting results, as well as the results themselves. This reflection on the quality of the process is characteristic of continual learning; it is also a characteristic of transformational learning, which, indeed, is constant in the organization that is continually learning.

Question Everything. As Hewlett-Packard notes in its corporate values statement, "The old ways won't work." Nothing is so sacred that it cannot be questioned, even the organization's values themselves. The more possibilities for people to ask questions and reflect on how well they are doing and how they might do better, the more possibility there is for both individual and organizational learning. Learning begins when one takes a new look at something old.

Take Risks. Organizations that are continually learning have empowered people taking personal risks and leaving their comfort zones. People are encouraged or at least allowed to share and test hunches and ideas about new processes or products.

Get Feedback. Feedback is of a different kind than in the traditional organization. It is quick, readily available, offered directly, and about specific things that can really be changed. It is not punitive or blaming. Everyone needs this kind of information so they can learn and improve. The quality of the learning is related to the quality of the feedback.

Conduct Inquiries to Learn from Mistakes and Successes.
Whenever an important event—whether a successful one or a
failure—takes place, the company or team gets together and asks
what can be learned from it. Then the appropriate changes are
made.

Discussing the "Undiscussable"

A great frustration in the organization has been expressed as follows: Why are groups of smart people sometimes so inept? Why
is it so hard for intelligent people to form intelligent organizations? Unfortunately, although an organization can be smarter
than its people, more often its actions seem to reflect a lower
intelligence level.

Organizations aren't as smart as they could be because people don't discuss the "undiscussables." Too often what is really
going on in a group is not what people are talking about. The
reality is the issue below the surface, an "undiscussable" issue.
The group may discuss how to approach a problem when the real
issue is that they do not trust their leader, or feel angry at some
policy, or have not been allowed to do something that they all
agree would be helpful or promising. Undiscussables include
people's feelings and concerns about organizational policy,
values, and culture. People fear that they will be punished if they
bring such things up, so they remain silent.

The Abilene paradox[8] describes a phenomenon where every person in a group feels a certain way but assumes that he or
she is the only one who feels that way and that his or her input
would not be appreciated. For example, every member of a group
may be frustrated by a task and feel ineffective, but no one
speaks up. They all feel that a group norm prohibits talking, and
so they keep silent. In such a group, perhaps a member does
present an idea, but is derided or punished for it; so everyone
continues to decide to keep silent. In this way, the traditional
organization institutionalizes a low ability of groups to change.
To counterbalance such an effect, a company we worked with
had what they called the "Pit Bull" award; this was given to the
employee whose idea was at first firmly resisted by the boss but

ultimately proven right. It rewards people who have the courage to tell others what they don't want to hear, going against all of our conditioning in the pyramid organization.

Similar to the Abilene paradox is the Groupthink phenomenon; this is a common process whereby group members shape their ideas to fit what they think the leader wants to hear. Groupthink is a defense against group anxiety; it is a way to preserve the pyramid structure of a team. It avoids and limits new information and the chance to explore alternatives rather than embrace them. It has led to some truly evil political decisions.[9]

Given these problems, is it any wonder that many of the smartest people have found ways to avoid or distance themselves from groups? Many smart professionals don't like groups. They find that other people interfere with their achievement. They feel this way about most organizations that evaluate the contributions of individuals only, not of groups. In the traditional system, people are given a set of performance goals or standards and are assessed on how well they achieve them. Feeling uncertain about their organization and their future in it, individuals keep their knowledge to themselves. They wonder why they should help others or the organization as long as they make their numbers. Because of the low level of trust in such relationships, they only give their organization or team a tiny bit of their capacity.

How do we know we are making progress toward organizational learning? Increased conflict is often a sign. Team members start to stand up for what they want and fight for it. They start telling each other about the things that they are noticing or about things that they are not noticing, but would like to. Change leaders push the group to learn by helping undiscussables to surface.

When groups start to discuss the undiscussables, energy is released. The group may be stuck on an issue that is impeding the work of the organization. For example, if people or a team are not initiating contact with horizontal groups, there may be hidden levels of norms, incentives, or values that contradict this desire. The norm may be, for example, for groups to compete with each other; this keeps the contact from happening. But once people reexamine the norm in terms of how it is affecting change, real learning and change become possible.

Helping a group or organization learn is often difficult because there is some confict between the primary tasks of the individual and the group. The organization is defined by its mission, vision, and values, to which the people who work there are supposed to adhere. Unfortunately, individuals have more powerful needs and drives that sometimes keep them from doing what the organization needs them to do.[10] That is why many people in power use their teams and organizations for their own purposes, rather than to get a job done, and why individuals may seem unwilling to face up to realities of change. Groups are often derailed to focus on individual agendas, which prevent them from feeling responsibility to the whole organization.

In addition, there is conflict between being willing to learn and saving face. Harvard researcher Chris Argyris outlines many mechanisms that individuals and groups adopt to preserve their illusions and defend against learning.[11] They prefer to avoid anxiety rather than get a job done. Before a team can achieve high performance, it must overcome such tendencies.

Thus the key to moving a team toward learning is to find ways to challenge the hidden undiscussables in the group that are hindering learning. The person who can help a group do this becomes one of the most valuable people.

Developing Process Awareness

Argyris designed a powerful method for revealing the hidden level. It may be summarized as follows: A team or pair have their discussion. A transcription provides the participants with feedback, yet they can see themselves in action at one step removed. In this way, people can observe and ask questions about their own behavior. The transcripts are written on the right side of a piece of paper. On the left side, individuals write down what they weren't saying but were feeling. This left-hand column represents the hidden dimension, which is then explored through conversation.

Because this reflection on a meeting looks at what isn't being said, it leads to a discussion not about what the group is doing, but about how it is doing it and how people are respond-ing within themselves. After repeating this exercise several times, people begin to develop an ability to look at their actions and the hidden dimensions of their conversations and question them. Anyone can try this exercise by taping a meeting or even simply recalling as clearly as possible what one said and what others said at a meeting.

Two types of comments can be made about a relationship or an event:

- A *content comment* is about the subject under discussion. For example, you might talk about the agenda, the deci-sions, the work that is being done. All content comments involve first-order learning.

- A *process comment* is about the system itself. One questions the way that the group, the personal relationship, or the process works.

When one redesigns a system, or explores alternative ac-tions, or questions a culture, one moves from the content to the process level. In order for there to be learning, an individual, pair, or group must come out of its ordinary content consciousness to a process consciousness. This is a shift to second-order question-ing. People inquire into how the system works and realize that the way they do things can be changed.

A process comment can be very simple; anyone in a group can make one. We can say, "Are we being effective at our task?" Or we can ask, "Are we clear about what our task is?" Or we may suggest, "We seem to be moving all over the map in our discus-sion. Perhaps we could get in focus more clearly if we spent a minute reflecting on the problem itself, and then have each per-son say what they think should be done."

When a process comment is offered, people are asked to think about and participate in deciding how they are going about a task rather than to keep their focus on the task itself.

In order for any group to learn, many people need to under-stand that the process level is as important as the content level. They must continually consider together: Are we doing what we are doing in the best possible way? Could it be done better? They become responsible for sharing their thoughts and ideas. A process comment is best on the spot, because it involves something that involves a different order than the current agenda. It is never out of order, although other people may want to table process questions.

The most powerful person in an organization is the person who steps out of his or her narrow specialization and sees the widest possible context. The suggestion based on this wide-angle view is most likely to be the most effective suggestion.

Yet the going may not be easy. If team members respond with denial and resistance, pioneering is more difficult. So, when a person begins to challenge the basic ways of doing things, he or she must prepare to be patient, to gather supporting data, and to manage the responses of others. He or she must be open to learning when an issue is raised. The objections of others often are based on important considerations.

There are many points at which a group can effectively look at its own process. They can do it when a large project or task is completed so they can apply what they learned to their next challenge. Or they can take time out when something is not going as planned, or when one person feels that things are not right. Listening to such hunches can help avoid some disastrous events. For example, an inquiry into the group process of the company that designed the Hubble telescope—which went into satellite orbit with a design flaw that made it almost useless—revealed that many individuals had had intuitions or seen information that needed to be questioned. Because few people raised questions, and few took seriously what questions were raised, the seeds of a disaster were sown.[12]

QUALITY, REDESIGN, AND LEARNING

Group learning is the cornerstone of continuous quality improvement. Quality is more than making good products; it is continually improving the processes by which the organization makes its products. Quality means moving the company to a higher stage of effectiveness and development by continuing improvement. And as with organizational learning, everyone in the organization, not just those at the top, is responsible for quality.

Making the shift to a focus on quality is more than a cosmetic or even a motivational modification. Quality involves setting one absolute standard of value for the entire system—perhaps fully satisfying the customer—and then reexamining all processes of the organizations in the light of that core value. Each group must see its activities in relation to that overall goal and judge itself by that standard. Doing this involves examination of the organization's output to see how the product is actually used. It involves communication across groups and being open to new data and information. When a company has a quality program, the organization must come together to talk about what it really values so that different groups are aligned. A quality program is also a request for learning; the company is expected to continue to question how it does things and continue to try to do them more effectively.

Quality Improvement as Organizational Learning

Quality is the design for organizational learning. People must understand how they accomplished their tasks so that their achievements can be repeated. Maintaining quality is very similar to maintaining organizational learning. It consists of the following similar elements:

- *Management by data.* There is continual feedback on how the organization is doing according to key measures.

- *Goal of satisfying the customer.* The company delivers the right product, on time, defect-free, and user-friendly.

- *Repeatable processes.* The goal is to get the job done and to develop repeatable processes so it can be done again.

- *Continual improvement.* A group keeps trying to improve its performance, no matter how well it is doing.

- *Process consciousness.* Everybody feels a connection to the process of continual improvement.

The journey toward quality involves not just incremental changes but periodic breakthrough change into drastically new ways of working.

At a recent talk to a network of organizations with quality programs, we asked how many were finding that their programs weren't having the desired effects. Almost every one of the two hundred quality managers in the room raised their hands. The consensus was that the difficulty came from the fact that the programs weren't really being followed. One company provided a good example: Its problem-solving groups came up with good ideas. However, the response to ideas was slow because the ideas had to be implemented according to the pyramid model. But when people see that their ideas are not explored, they soon give up and stop thinking.

A real quality program generates transformational change within the organization. The changes move out across groups and challenge the organization's methods. This can be threatening, because it often is not what management has in mind when they started a quality program. They talk about slowing down, about ideas being impractical (although they have no evidence), and then they reexert control, cutting off the energy that had begun to flow.

The Shift to Quality

Helix Corporation (a fictitious name for a real company) is a company that successfully developed a quality program. The company, formed in a merger of several software development companies, has experienced impressive growth and success as well as some major challenges.[13] There is continual pressure to improve and to keep pace with technological advances in the market by delivering ever more complex products. There are production, delivery, and quality problems. And finally, the pressures of growth have strained existing systems, and made obvious the lack of repeatable processes necessary to maintain reliability and quality. In response to these difficulties, the company president asked one of the most respected managers to initiate a corporate quality program.

Helix's future, like that of other high-tech start-up companies, lies in transforming its culture from one of an ad hoc entrepreneurial organization to one where data direct decisions, that is organized with repeatable processes, and that continually looks at how things are done and how they can be done better the next time.

Before a program could start, we needed to know how key managers understood "quality" and to help develop an awareness in all that quality was important. We interviewed a cross section of top managers at Helix. Some managers saw a clear need for a quality program; others were less clear about how any systematic effort could produce the desired changes. We uncovered several key themes, norms, and values that would hinder a quality program:

1. Rewards and status went to crisis managers.

2. There was a deadline orientation.

3. Procedures were ad hoc.

4. Personal autonomy was highly valued.

These themes are common in many entrepreneurial companies and seem at first to contribute to high performance: Highly autonomous people are dedicated to getting the job done any way they can. These organizations gain their competitive advantage through this individualistic orientation. A focus on quality would change such a culture. Less individualism and more teamwork would be needed. It would be just as important to know how the job was done as to get it done. And every process would be scrutinized to see how it fit with customer needs. How could the people be persuaded to make the necessary changes?

In our initial sessions as consultants to the company we asked a cross-sectional group to redesign their way of working. The people who did the work were asked to design and carry out the improvements. The sessions combined teaching quality and exploring the problem areas in the system's work processes.

Inclusion of key managers was an essential success factor. Top management, who were very results-oriented, questioned the value of adding quality as a criterion to every job; it seemed an unaffordable luxury. "What can it do for me now?" was the question most frequently asked. We began by taking a persistent problem in one part of the company and using the quality process to demonstrate real results. The effort could start quietly in this one area and become more widespread when something real had been achieved.

The slice of the company that included sales, order administration, manufacturing, and shipping was a highly visible sore point, causing frustration for customers and clearly affecting corporate performance. Three representatives from each of these divisions convened for a conference and formed the "Shipment Quality Task Force." Everyone was concerned and eager, but no one had prior familiarity with quality improvement.

During the first session we familiarized the group with concepts of quality and customer service, including the notion of internal customers. The meeting began with an invitation to banish the concept of blaming individuals for problems; we suggested instead that systems were the cause of most problems. Some of the internal resistance to quality comes from the belief that to admit a problem is to admit a mistake or to expose a colleague or oneself to blame.

The organization of the task force, and the interaction between its members and their constituent groups had to be addressed in early meetings. Follow-up and communication back and forth to work groups were essential to our success. It was necessary that the task force not become isolated from the rest of their teams.

During the first meeting there was considerable skepticism. Individuals had many ideas but felt that they had had little real impact on the organization in the past. But now they found that they could participate in defining key processes to change within the task force group and then move to their own groups and ask them to change. They felt in more control of the process. Even in an entrepreneurial firm, this was a new experience for some. The small quality discussions that each task force member initiated in his or her own team became a circle organization, parallel to the formal organization. In observing, measuring, and redefining the processes, their attitudes changed. Instead of seeing process as something separate from people that was outside their control, they realized that a process stems from human interaction and can be changed. The task force began to rebut their negative, and helpless feelings.

During the second meeting, the task force created a wall chart of the sales-to-delivery cycle. This focused on the process and showed how it could be streamlined to get the customers what they wanted from the first. During the third session, the group looked at the concept of measurement. After training in data generation and measurement, the members were asked to go back and ask their own groups to suggest the best available, objective measure to assess their own work. Each group was thus in charge of measuring itself; this minimized feelings of loss of control, pressure, and blame.

Subtask forces from the sales, order entry, and manufacturing and shipping teams were then formed. Each team's representative to the larger task force chaired the subgroup. Each group went over much the same ground as the larger group—they learned about quality and getting beyond blame, how to rethink processes and how to build an ideal model, and they suggested ways to measure results. The team members took time to observe their work and review processes. They generated baseline measures. After two months, each group had defined its baseline quality measures, was collecting its own data, and was using its meetings to suggest specific process improvements. Each team's work was integrated at the larger task force.

Creating a group history notebook, in which everything done by every group was recorded, was a critical success factor. With the notebook a group memory was created as well as an ongoing process that reinforced and underscored decisions, helped in follow-up and transfer of data from group to group, and measured and assessed the groups' progress. The fostering of such a collective memory is one of the key elements in organizational learning. The learning is taken out of individual minds and put into a collective consciousness so that new people, those outside the task force, and other groups, can refer to it. Such tools too often stay on the shelf; this one did not, however.

The quality process was hugely successful—leading to a decrease in costly mistakes and improved effectiveness and productivity in all parts of the company.

Quality, like learning, is self-reinforcing and self-motivating; it is its own reward. Helix's employees felt in greater control of their work and more responsible for the company's success. They also were more productive and their interactions less conflictual. Morale improved.

Measurement and Learning

Measurement is a form of feedback and it is critical to learning. People have to know where they stand in order to improve. Numbers and other data were traditionally kept by the top levels of an organization. With the advent of a total quality process, the data about a group go directly to the group itself. It then can orient itself not just according to narrow data like sales or financial returns (which are also important), but according to work process–related success criteria.

Quality entails *a shift in everyday activity from responses to difficulties based on direct sense experience or intuition of what is needed, to responses to information generated by systematic data collection.* Some problems cannot be seen directly; they only become explicit when data point them out. They may be counterintuitive or related to factors that are not seen. Also, without data collection, the results of experiments in new behavior cannot be fairly judged. Design processes in companies are so subtle and complex that direct-sense experience can't encompass them, so work groups need to develop new sources of experience, such as visits to other companies and new, more timely and accurate measurements of their processes.

The recent interest in benchmarking is an example of learning through measurement. In benchmarking, a company seeks to learn from the organizations that represent the best practices in their area and to get a measure of how well it is doing in comparison. Then the company aims at reaching or surpassing the benchmark organization.

Companies have begun to cooperate by sharing their own measurement processes. This form of cooperation achieves two learning goals. First, they show how something might be done differently and how to be successful. Second, they offer concrete measures for comparison.

At Helix, the different groups selected their own measurements. These measures of process success were developed in consultation with their internal and external customers and suppliers. The measures were therefore meaningful to the people who were involved in the process, and most important, they were under the people's control.

Indeed, what you measure is what you get. When people are attuned to numbers, they orient their behavior to make the numbers. In a phone company, operators are evaluated on the amount of time they spend on phones not on the relationships they build. Hence, they have very short and often frustrating encounters with customers. The numbers go up but quality goes down. One group began to ask whether it could measure both time and satisfaction in some way. Then the group could see how it was improving and what mix of changes was best. The point is that measures should not be an absolute value, but a means to see how well people are doing, and where they can improve. If the numbers are limited, the attention of a group will be also.

The world will not stand still while we and our organizations move toward our visions. We need to be learners in order to be alert to new possibilities and to incorporate continually new ideas gained from experience. If we try something and it doesn't work, we need to discover another way. If we want to achieve something, often we need to learn before we can reach our goals.

In this chapter, we have seen how organizational and group learning differs from individual learning. If you want to become a learner with your group or team, you will need to help the group talk about its "undiscussables," develop awareness of process, and institute a process-improvement program that includes measures of effectiveness.

The need for organizational learning is directly connected to the recent emphasis on quality and customer service, and the heightened ability of many in the marketplace to deliver ever-higher levels of both. A company that has to keep innovating and developing higher quality and service has to keep learning. So under the rubric of continuous quality improvement programs, we see teams and whole organizations beginning to initiate processes of organizational learning and partnership, that are a great departure from the way that business was done in the past. Some of these attempts to innovate are undone because they try to change without transformation. They want to get innovation and service without empowering or challenging how they do things.

In this final part we have outlined two major elements of a transforming workplace—partnership and learning. To accomplish each of these, groups must find ways to work together that challenge the conventional pyramid workplace. Very few of the practices of the traditional organization would survive the scrutiny of a continuous quality improvement program. If the company looks outside itself for its goal—to the customer and the changing environment—it has to ask itself if its methods will bring it success. Further, although partnership and learning are processes that start with the individual and the team, their effects branch out throughout the whole organization. And as individuals begin to challenge their teams to become partners and to learn the person who was withdrawn or only partly connected to the company often finds himself or herself pulled back into the organization, gaining a new sense of commitment and empowerment. This is the legacy of the change leader; this is the promise of empowerment.

EPILOGUE:

If You Don't Do It, Nobody Will: Pioneering the New Workplace

We believe that the foundation for renewed trust and commitment in our organizations and in ourselves is built by personal change and empowerment, by becoming a change leader and by forming empowered relationships. To these ends we have given you some concepts, tools, and techniques to use in rebuilding your own commitment to your organization—even if your trust in the organization has been eroded. We have presented a variety of ways for you to begin to rekindle your commitment, by changing yourself, your working relationships, and, ultimately, your organization.

Like millions of others, you may be upset or angry at the turn that life at work has taken of late. Instead of waiting and hoping that things will be different someday, we urge you to make the decision to take care of yourself, to build and enhance

251

your capacity in the new workplace. In this book, we have out-lined the new competencies, but the most important task is yours: You must make the choice to change how you manage your relationship to your work and your organization.

If you choose to take this step, you can modify the depth and pace of your change along the way. Indeed, we suggest that you work in one area at a time, expanding your personal sphere of power in stages. As you experiment, you will begin the process of learning, which itself will suggest new pathways.

Organizational change starts with one person seeing a pos-sibility and taking action on it. We must each look within our-selves for the wisdom, the vision, the ability, and the motivation to change our workplaces. Fortunately, what we must do for our-selves and what we must do to help organizations succeed are closely aligned today. As we empower ourselves, we become change leaders, taking care of ourselves and helping our organiza-tions to grow and thrive.

We can each grow and help our organizations grow by rec-ognizing that our actions affect the actions of the people we work with. The manager or the person in charge is not the only change leader in a work group. Anyone who begins to treat peo-ple differently, to look for the best in those around them, and to encourage others to shift the way they work can be a powerful and successful leader. Doing these things can help create a differ-ent context or environment in which the group can act. We have suggested many activities for you to undertake; for each one, a requirement is starting to learn yourself and helping your team to learn.

Many organizations today are making changes; CEOs and top leaders have begun to explore new organizational structures. Their stories make for inspiring reading; those we have included here may leave you longing to work in these special organiza-tions. But the reality is that every organization is beginning to change and that all organizations will change, the only question is when.

We don't mean to paint a one-sided picture. We don't wish to be accused of having too rosy a view of organizational renewal. We know well that the hurdles to substantive change are very large and very real. We have struggled with too many good companies that were not able to achieve all their goals to believe that change is easy. However, we believe that there is no choice. Change is difficult and some of the strategies we suggest may put you at risk. But ask yourself: "If I don't do this, who will?" and "If I don't do this, what is my alternative?"

People who decide to wait or to be political and see which way the winds will blow give up their own power and push themselves out of the organization. But empowered people are not politically naive. They learn to survive in their organizations—but not by hiding or by remaining silent. They take risks, they attempt to create the changes that are needed. They help create the workplace they want and need

When people create change in their workplace, they are rarely alone. Their commitment and action are matched by that of the other pioneers who have decided to help create the best possible place to work. We invite you to join the growing ranks of these risk-takers and to become a pioneer of the new workplace.

NOTES

PREFACE

1. A survey by the research firm Yankelovich Partners found that only 12 percent of the respondents trusted public statements made by corporations, while over 70 percent agreed with the statement, "I'm the one in charge of my life." See Stratford Sherman, "A Brave New Darwinian Workplace," *Fortune*, Jan. 25, 1993, p. 51

2. John Adams in his edited volumes *Transforming Work* and *Transforming Leadership* (Alexandria, VA: Miles River Press, 1984 and 1986); Michael Ray and Alan Rinzler in their edited volume *The New Paradigm in Business* (New York: Tarcher/Perigee, 1993); and Willis Harman and John Hormann, *Creative Work* (Indianapolis, IN: Knowledge Systems, 1990) are three important volumes making this point.

CHAPTER ONE

1. Reich, Robert B. *The Work of Nations*. New York: Knopf, 1991.

2. Johnson, H. Thomas. *Relevance Regained. From Top-Down Control to Bottom-Up Empowerment*. New York: Free Press, 1992.

3. Peters, Tom. *Liberation Management*. New York: Knopf, 1991.

4. Meyer, Christopher. *Fast Cycle Time*. New York: Free Press, 1993.

5. Cited in Fisher, Anne B. "The Morale Crisis." *Fortune*, Nov. 18, 1991, p. 71.

6. Marks, Mitchell, and Mirvis, Philip. *Managing the Merger: Making It Work*. New York: Prentice-Hall, 1992. Also see Fisher, Anne B. "The Morale Crisis." *Fortune*, Nov. 18, 1991, pp. 70–80.

7. Kim Buch, a study of 365 quality professionals, reported in *Training* magazine, May, 1992.

8. Kim Buch, a study of 365 quality professionals, reported in *Training* magazine, May, 1992.

9. Northwestern National Life Insurance Company. *Employee Burnout: America's Newest Epidemic*. Box 20, Minneapolis, MN 55440, 1991.

10. Golumbiewski, Robert T., Munzenrider, Robert F., and Stevenson, Jerry G. *Stress in Organizations*. New York: Prager, 1986.

11. Golumbiewski, Robert T., Munzenrider, Robert F., and Stevenson, Jerry G. *Stress in Organizations*. New York: Prager, 1986.

12. Maddi, Salvador, and Kobasa, Suzanne. *The Hardy Executive: Health Under Stress*. New York: Dow Jones Irwin, 1984.

13. Berkman, Lisa, and Syme, Leonard. "Social Networks, Host Resistance, and Mortality." *American Journal of Epidemiology*, 1979, *109*, 186–204.

14. Karasek, Robert, and Theorell, Tores. *Healthy Work*. New York: Basic Books, 1991.

CHAPTER TWO

1. Young, Dennis, "The Transfer of Ideas from Nonprofit to Business Management." Working paper, Mandel Center for Nonprofit Organizations, Case Western Reserve University, Cleveland, OH, 1993.
2. Deal, Terrence E., and Kennedy, Alan A. *Corporate Cultures*. Reading, MA: Addison-Wesley, 1982. Also Schein, Edward. *Corporate Culture and Leadership*. (2nd ed.) San Francisco: Jossey-Bass, 1992.
3. Vincze, Eva. Unpublished doctoral dissertation, Saybrook Institute, San Francisco, 1993.
4. Drucker, Peter. *Post-Capitalist Society*. New York: Harper-Collins, 1993.
5. Kotter, John, and Heskett, James. *Corporate Culture and Performance*. New York: Free Press, 1992.
6. Sashkin, Marshall, and Williams, Richard. "Does Fairness Make a Difference?" *Organizational Dynamics*, Fall 1990.
7. Alan Westin of Columbia University has given us the description of this process, based on his research of over a decade with Federal Express, in several presentations to the Research Council of Healthy Companies, a Washington, D.C. think tank.
8. From a presentation by Kermit Campbell at the 1993 Conference of Most Admired Companies, hosted by *Fortune* magazine.
9. Hertzberg, F., Mausner, B., and Snyderman, B. *The Motivation to Work*. (2nd ed.) New York: Wiley, 1959.
10. Kohut, Andrew, and DeStefano, Linda. "Today's Workers Want More from Jobs." *San Francisco Chronicle*, Sept. 4, 1989.
11. Maccoby, Michael. *Why Work?* New York: Simon & Schuster, 1988. See also Mitchell, Arnold. *The Nine American Lifestyles*. New York: Macmillan, 1983.
12. Yankelovich, Daniel. *New Rules*. New York: Random House, 1981.
13. Rokeach, M. A., and Ball-Rokeach, S. J. "The Stability of

American Values." *American Psychologist*, May 1989, pp. 775–84.

14. Bardwick, Judith. *Danger in the Comfort Zone*. New York: AMACOM, 1991.

15. Bluestone, Barry and Irving. *Negotiating the Future*. New York: Basic Books, 1992.

16. Lawrence, Paul, and Lorsch, Jay. *The Organization and Its Environment*. Cambridge, MA: Harvard University Press, 1967.

17. Kiechel, Walter. "How Important Is Morale, Really?" *Fortune*, Feb. 13, 1989, pp. 121–22.

18. Hankoff, Ronald. "Companies That Train Best." *Fortune*, Mar. 22, 1983.

19. Bray, D. G., Campbell, R. J., and Good, D. L. *Formative Years in Business: A Long-Term AT&T Study of Managers' Lives*. New York: Wiley, 1974.

20. Handy, Charles. *The Age of Unreason*. Cambridge, MA: Harvard University Press, 1991.

21. Quigley, Philip, Pacific Telesis, presentation at the Change Leadership Conference, Second quarter, 1992.

22. Hillman, James. *Healing Fiction*. Tarrytown, NY: Station Hill Press: 1983.

CHAPTER THREE

1. Fiedler, Leslie. *An End to Innocence*. Boston: Beacon Press, 1955.

2. Kidder, Tracy. *The Soul of the New Machine*. Boston: Little, Brown, 1981.

3. Kanter, Rosabeth. "Power Failures in Management Circuits." *Harvard Business Review*, July–Aug. 1979.

4. Zalesnick, Abraham. "Leaders and Managers: Are They Different?" In John Williamson (ed.), *The Leader-Manager*. New York: Wiley, 1983.

5. Howell, J. P., and others. "Substitutes for Leadership: Ef-

fective Alternatives to Ineffective Leadership." *Organizational Dynamics*, 1992, 19(1), pp. 21–38.

6. Hirschorn, Albert O. *Exit, Voice, and Loyalty: Responses to Decline in Firms, Organizations, and States*. Cambridge, MA: Harvard University Press, 1970.

CHAPTER FOUR

1. Hayward, Jeremy. *Shifting Worlds, Changing Minds*. Boston: Shambhala, 1987, p. 10.
2. In addition to our consulting work, this line of inquiry has been pursued by Dennis Jaffe in his study of new physicians, a study of people recovering from extreme trauma, and in an earlier work about members of the "counterculture" of the 1960s who became social activists. The model for change from a traditional paradigm to a visionary perspective is similar for all, although the contexts are quite different.
3. Ringer, Robert. *Looking Out for #1*. New York: Fawcett, 1981.
4. Kaplan, Robert. *Beyond Ambition*. San Francisco: Jossey-Bass, 1992.
5. Hemphill, Hellen. "The Upward Mobility Experiences of High-Level Women Executives." Unpublished doctoral dissertation, Saybrook Institute, San Francisco, 1991.
6. Brand, David. "Sticking Your Neck Out." *Time*, Aug. 8, 1988, p. 8.
7. Hornstein, Harvey. *Managerial Courage*. New York: Wiley, 1986.
8. Pinchot, Gifford IV. *Intrapreneuring*. New York: HarperCollins, 1985.
9. Peters, Thomas, and Waterman, Robert. *In Search of Excellence*. New York: Warner, 1982. This model is also detailed in Beer, Michael, Eisenstat, Russell A., and Spector, Bert. "Why Change Programs Don't Produce Change." *Harvard Business Review*, Nov.–Dec. 1990, pp. 158–66.

CHAPTER FIVE

1. Welsh, Tricia. "Best and Worst Corporate Reputations." *Fortune*, Feb. 7, 1994, pp. 58–69.

2. Mills, D. Quinn. *Rebirth of the Corporation*. New York: Wiley, 1991. Also Galagan, Patricia. "Beyond Hierarchy." *Training and Development*, Aug. 1992, pp. 21–25. And Ostroff, Frank, and Smith, Douglas. "The Horizontal Organization." *McKinsey Quarterly*, 1992, 11, pp. 148–68.

3. Levering, Robert. *A Great Place to Work*. New York: Random House, 1988. Also Levering, Robert, and Moskowitz, Milton. *The 100 Best Companies to Work for in America*. New York: Doubleday, 1993.

4. Watzlawick, Paul, Weakland, John, and Fisch, Richard. *Change*. New York: Norton, 1974.

5. Kuhn, Thomas S. *The Structure of Scientific Revolutions*. (2nd ed.) Chicago: University of Chicago Press, 1970.

6. Peterson, Donald. *A Better Idea*. New York: Houghton-Mifflin, 1991.

7. Land, George, and Jarman, Beth. *Breaktime and Beyond*. New York: HarperCollins, 1992.

8. Staying Power, presentation at the Ford/UAW Conference, Detroit, May 18–19, 1993.

9. McGregor, Douglas. *The Human Side of Enterprise*. New York: McGraw-Hill, 1960. Also Weisbord, Marvin. *Productive Workplaces*. San Francisco: Jossey-Bass, 1987.

10. Lawrence, Paul, and Lorsch, Jay. *The Organization and Its Environment*. Cambridge, MA: Harvard University Press, 1967.

11. Dimancescu, Dan. *The Seamless Organization*. New York: Harper Business, 1992, p. 7.

12. Harman, Willis, and Hormann, John. *Creative Work*. Indianapolis: Knowledge Systems, 1991. Also Ray, Michael, and Rinzler, Alan (eds.). *The New Paradigm in Business*. Los Angeles: Jeremy Tarcher Perigee, 1993.

13. Walton, Richard. From Control to Commitment in the Workplace." *Harvard Business Review*, 1985, 63(2), 76–84.

14. Barr, Morton, and Ketchum, William P. "Creating the Organization of the Future." *Human Resource Management Journal*, 1993, 32.

15. Komer, Roger, and Shafer, Gerald. "Employee Involvement Resources." Paper presented at Staying Power, a conference for companies with over a decade of experience in employee participation, Ford/UAW Joint Conference Center, Detroit, May 18–19, 1993.

16. Houghton, James R. "The Age of the Hierarchy Is Over." *New York Times*, Sept. 24, 1989.

17. Semler, Ricardo. "Managing Without Managers." *Harvard Business Review*, Sept.–Oct. 1989. Also *Maverick: The Success Story Behind the World's Most Unusual Workplace*. New York: Warner, 1993.

18. Senge, Peter. *The Fifth Discipline*. New York: Doubleday Currency, 1990. This is the most important book to make this point.

19. Banathy, Bela. "Organizational Design." Presentation at Saybrook Institute, San Francisco, Jan. 1993.

20. Weisbord, Marvin (ed.). *Discovering Common Ground*. San Francisco: Berrett-Koehler, 1992. Weisbord writes about gathering large groups for environmental scanning retreats and the effects of these interventions.

21. From Keith Merron.

22. Staying Power Conference held at Ford/UAW Joint Conference Center, Detroit, May 18–19, 1993.

23. Yoshida, Sidney. "Quality Improvement and TQC Management at Calsonic in Japan and Overseas." Paper presented at the Second International Quality Symposium, Mexico, 1989. Cited on p. 118 of Whitely, Richard. *The Customer-Driven Corporation*. Reading, MA: Addison-Wesley, 1991.

24. "Note." *Fortune*, Feb. 22, 1993, p. 72.

25. Hampden-Turner, Charles. *Charting the Organizational Mind*. New York: Free Press, 1990.

26. Petronius, 60 A.D.

27. Savoie, Ernie. "Recognition and Renewal." Paper published by the Employee Development Office, Ford Motor Company, Detroit.

CHAPTER SIX

1. George, William. "An Open Letter to Tom Peters on Spirituality and Motivation." *Minneapolis Star Tribune*, Apr. 19, 1993.
2. Schmidt, Warren H., and Posner, Barry Z. *Managerial Values in Perspective*. New York: American Management Association, 1983.
3. Howard, Robert. "An Interview with Robert Haas." *Harvard Business Review*, Sept.–Oct. 1990, p. 134.
4. Deal, Terrence E., and Kennedy, Allan A. *Corporate Cultures*. Reading, MA: Addison-Wesley, 1982.
5. Schmidt, Warren, and Posner, Barry. *Managerial Values in Perspective*. New York: American Management Association, 1983.
6. Tichy, Noel, and Sherman, Stratford. "Walking the Talk at GE." *Training & Development Journal*, June 1993, pp. 26–35.
7. Beckhard, R., and Pritchard, W. *Changing the Essence: The Art of Creating and Leading Fundamental Change in Organizations*. San Francisco: Jossey-Bass, 1992, p. 39.
8. Campbell, Andrew, and Nash, Laura. *A Sense of Mission: Defining Direction for the Large Company*. Reading, MA: Addison-Wesley, 1993.
9. An excellent case study of vision as an organizational design principle is found in Marjorie Parker, *Creating Shared Vision*, Dialogue International, Clarendon Hills, IL: 1990.

CHAPTER SEVEN

1. Janis, Irving. *Stress and Frustration*. New York: Harcourt Brace Jovanovich, 1971.
2. Kubler-Ross, Elisabeth. *On Death and Dying*. New York: Macmillan, 1969.
3. Jaffe, Dennis. "Self-Renewal: Personal Transformation Fol-

lowing Extreme Trauma." *Journal of Humanistic Psychology*, Fall 1985, 25: (4).

4.   Much of the section that follows was previously published as "From Crisis to Culture Change" by Cynthia Scott and Dennis Jaffe, *Healthcare Forum Journal*, May–June 1991, pp. 32–41.

CHAPTER EIGHT

1.   Eisler, Riane. *The Chalice and the Blade*. New York: Harper-Collins, 1988.

2.   Savoie, Ernest J. "Recognition and Revitalization: Fundamentals for Sustaining Change." Paper published by Ford Motor Company, 1993.

3.   Lloyd, Tom. *The "Nice" Company*. London: Bloomsbury, 1990

4.   Weisbord, Marvin (ed.). *Toward Common Ground*. San Francisco: Berrett-Koehler, 1993. In his book, Marvin Weisbord describes a model for partnership in which a large number of people, within and outside an organization, come together to form a community to look ahead at the future, and its meaning for the organization.

5.   Pagano, Daniel. "Design of a Collaborative Community to Manage New York City's Architectural Resources." Unpublished doctoral dissertation, Saybrook Institute, San Francisco, 1993. The future search conference described in the dissertation was done with the consultation of Anna Ewins.

6.   This dilemma is explored at length in Andrew Schmookler's *The Parable of the Tribes*, Berkeley: University of California Press, 1983.

7.   Verma, Anil, and Cutcher-Gershenfeld, Joel. "Joint Governance in the Workplace—Beyond Union-Management Cooperation." *IRRA Annual*, 1993.

8.   Cutcher-Gershenfeld, Joel. *Tracing a Transformation in Industrial Relations*. U.S. Department of Labor monograph BLMR 123, 1988.

9. Kauffman, Richard. "Working Partners." *Diablo Business*, Spring 1992, pp. 22–28. Also see case presentation on NUMMI by Bill Usery, consultant, former U.S. Secretary of Labor; Denis Cuneo, VP, Corporate Planning, NUMMI; and George Nano, Chairman, Local 2244, Bargaining Committee, United Auto Workers; at Staying Power conference on participation, Detroit, May 18–19, 1993.

10. Bluestone, Barry and Irving. *Negotiating the Future*. New York: Basic Books, 1992. Also Lawler, Edward E. III. *The Ultimate Advantage*. San Francisco: Jossey-Bass, 1992.

11. Levine, David, and Tyson, Laura D'Andrea. "Participation, Productivity, and the Firm's Environment." In Alan S. Blinder (ed.), *Paying for Productivity*. Washington, DC: Brookings Institute, 1990.

12. Hackman, J. Richard (ed.). *Groups That Work (and the Ones That Don't)*. San Francisco: Jossey-Bass, 1990.

13. Bill Moyers interview in *San Francisco Focus*, Feb. 1993.

14. Numerous manuals contain descriptions of process tools to help in group facilitation. See, for example, McWhinney, Will, and Eleanor McCulley, *Creating Paths of Change*, Venice, CA: Enthusion Inc., 1993, and Sibbett, David, Drexler, Alan, and the team at Graphic Guides Inc. *Graphic Guide to Best Team Practices*. San Francisco: Graphic Guides, 1992.

15. David Sibbett has been a pioneer in graphic facilitation and visioning techniques and tools through his organization, Grove Consulting.

16. Pozos, Al. "Executive Transformation." Unpublished doctoral dissertation, Saybrook Institute, San Francisco, 1994.

17. Sonenclar, Robert. "Ben & Jerry's: Management with a Human Flavor." *Hemisphere*, Mar. 1993.

18. This case account was delivered at the Staying Power participation conference, in Detroit on May 18–19, 1993, by Bureau of National Affairs (BNA) employees Jacqueline Blanchard, Director of Employee and Labor Relations, and Kenneth May, co-chair of the BNA unit of the Newspaper Guild and a legal editor.

19. Stein, Barry, and Kanter, Rosabeth Moss. "Building the Par-

allel Organization." *Journal of Applied Behavioral Science*, July 16, 1980, pp. 371–88.

20. Tichy, Noel, and Sherman, Stratford. *Control Your Destiny or Someone Else Will*. New York: Doubleday, 1993.

21. The Inland Steel Case study was prepared by the Business Enterprise Trust, Stanford, CA: 1992.

CHAPTER NINE

1. Michael, Donald. *On Learning to Plan—and Planning to Learn*. San Francisco: Jossey-Bass, 1973.

2. Pozos, Al. "Executive Transformation." Unpublished doctoral dissertation, Saybrook Institute, San Francisco, 1994.

3. Adopted from Lawrence, Paul, and Lorsch, Jay. *The Organization and Its Environment*. Boston: Harvard University Press, 1967.

4. Stata, Ray. "Organizational Learning: The Key to Management Innovation." *Sloan Management Review*, Spring 1989, pp. 63–74.

5. "Note." *Time*, Dec. 23, 1991, p. 64.

6. Wick, Calhoun W., and Leon, Stanton. *The Learning Edge*. New York: McGraw-Hill, 1993, pp. 208–22.

7. The most complete account of organizational systems theory can be found in Peter Senge's *The Fifth Discipline*, New York: Doubleday, 1990. His view of organizational learning puts systems thinking at the center.

8. Harvey, J. "The Abilene Paradox: The Management of Agreement." *Organizational Dynamics*, Summer 1974, pp. 17–34.

9. Janis, Irving, *Victims of Groupthink*. Boston: Houghton Mifflin, 1972.

10. This notion developed from the work of the theorists coming from the psychoanalytically oriented Tavistock Institute in London. They believe the primary role for groups of any type is to help the individual avoid anxiety. Only secondarily, and under more or less ideal conditions, is their role to achieve their work task. Their model posits why groups and

organizations often act so counterproductively in the face of the pressure for change. People are trying to avoid the fear and anxiety that comes from facing the realities, so they retreat into various forms of defensive behavior. A key work in this tradition is *The Workplace Within*, by Larry Hirschhorn, Cambridge, MA: MIT Press, 1988.

11.   Argyris, Chris. *Learning in Action*. San Francisco: Jossey-Bass, 1993. Also Senge, Peter. *The Fifth Discipline*, New York: Doubleday, 1990.

12.   Capers, Robert S., and Lipton, Eric. "Hubble Error: Time, Money, and Millionths of an Inch." *The Executive*, 1993, 7(3).

13.   This case was previously published as "Quality Consciousness as a Stage of Organizational Growth in an Emerging High Tech Company." *Vision/Action: Journal of the Bay Area Organizational Development Network*, Mar. 1991, 10(1). The assistance of Malcolm Macfarlane is gratefully acknowledged.

INDEX